New Religions and the New Europe

RENNER Studies on New Religions

General Editor
Armin W. Geertz, Department of the Study of Religion, University of Aarhus

Editorial Board
Johannes Aagaard, Department of Systematic Theology, Center for New Religious Studies, University of Aarhus
Steffen Johannessen, Department of Danish, Modern Languages and Religious Studies, The Royal Danish School of Educational Studies, Copenhagen
Helle Meldgaard, Department of Systematic Theology, Center for New Religious Studies, University of Aarhus
Ole Riis, Department of the Study of Religion, University of Aarhus
Mikael Rothstein, Institute of the History of Religions, Department of the History of Religions, University of Copenhagen
Margit Warburg, Institute of the History of Religions, Department of the Sociology of Religion, University of Copenhagen

RENNER Studies on New Religions is an initiative supported by the Danish Research Council for the Humanities. The series was established to publish books on new religions and alternative spiritual movements from a wide range of perspectives. It will include works of original theory, empirical research, and edited collections that address current topics, but will generally focus on the situation in Europe.

The books will appeal to an international readership of scholars, students, and professionals in the study of religion, theology, the arts, and the social sciences. And it is hoped that this series will provide a proper context for scientific exchange between these often competing disciplines.

NEW RELIGIONS AND THE NEW EUROPE

Edited by Robert Towler

AARHUS UNIVERSITY PRESS

Published with the financial support of the Danish Research Council for
the Humanities

AARHUS UNIVERSITY PRESS
University of Aarhus
DK-8000 Aarhus C
Fax (+ 45) 8619 8433

73 Lime Walk
Headington, Oxford OX3 7AD
Fax (+ 44) 1865 750 079

Box 511
Oakville, Conn. 06779
Fax (+ 1) 203 945 9468

ANSI/NISO
Z39.48-1992

Preface

The Danish Research Council for the Humanities, which is under the Ministry of Research and Technology, established a few years ago a series of research networks for the purpose of developing and consolidating research areas in need of concentrated national and international effort. One of the research areas which was given priority in a recent Council strategy plan was new religious movements. The Council invited bids for a network in which ethnographers, sociologists, historians of religions, lawyers, psychologists and theologians might contribute to a coordinated effort to document Danish and European new religiosity, to analyze the voluminous documentation already assembled in Denmark, to elucidate the social, political and normative changes which accompany conversion to alternative or new religions, and finally to elucidate how new religions comport themselves in relation to the rights and privileges of the freedom of religion in democratic societies.

The Council awarded a two-year network to a coordination committee based on two separate project groups, the one primarily humanistic in focus, from Copenhagen, and the other primarily theological in focus, from Aarhus. In Denmark, as elsewhere in the world, these two types of scholars have been entrenched in polemical discourse. With the establishment of RENNER, a two-year experiment was initiated during which the various academic positions could develop a scientific discourse with one another. RENNER is not meant to *integrate* humanistic and theological positions and strategies, but to *coordinate* the scientific activities of humanistic and theological scholars. Our hope that critical dialogue in mutual respect would enrich subsequent cooperation succeeded so well that the Council awarded RENNER a new two-year period.

RENNER is *not* an information centre. We do not maintain archives, data bases or libraries. We are not a hotline for distraught parents or persecuted representatives of new religions. We do not serve as consultants for local and national authorities nor do we take active part in the mass media. RENNER is a network intended to coordinate research being done on new religions and alternative spiritual movements. It is a corporate body with scientific goals ultimately answerable to the Ministry of Research and Technology, but it does not interfere with its members who *do* engage themselves in the proliferation of information to the general public, to the development of archives and data bases, to serving as consultants, and to debate in the media.

What we do, largely, is to bring scholars together, make it possible for them to establish information networks and engage in research projects, and to provide channels for the publication of their research results. Our goal is to encourage graduate students, young research fellows and established scholars to engage themselves in the study of new religions and spiritual movements. This is being done primarily through arranging seminars and workshops as well as through publication activities. We have initiated two monograph series, one in English and the other in Danish, and we have established a newsletter.

One of the most important activities RENNER was involved in during 1993 was participating in the international conference held at the London School of Economics during March 25-28, 1993 on 'New Religions and the New Europe'. The conference was hosted by the three major information centers of the world: INFORM, CESNUR and ISAR. During this well-organized and highly stimulating conference RENNER was given a warm-hearted welcome by the hosts and by other centres and networks. For this we are deeply grateful.

It is therefore with great pleasure that we launch the first volume of *RENNER Studies on New Religions* with this outstanding collection of papers presented at the London conference. It is a great honor for us to be involved in a cooperative venture of this sort, and I hope that the future of European studies on new religions and alternative spiritual movements will lead to further cooperative ventures.

Armin W. Geertz
Director of RENNER

Introduction and Acknowledgments

The papers in this volume represent a selection from nearly eighty contributions to an international conference which was held at the London School of Economics (in the United Kingdom) at the end of March 1993. The conference was held under the joint auspices of INFORM (Information Network Focus on Religious Movements) in London, who organized and hosted the gathering, CESNUR (Centre for Studies on New Religions) in Turin, and ISAR (Institute for the Study of American Religions) in Santa Barbara, California.

The selection was constrained by the availability of written papers, but from among those available only a small number could be included. The editor has not chosen only the best, and he has omitted many excellent contributions with deep regret; the fifteen papers presented here have been included because they form a coherent collection, organized around a few central themes within the broad topic of the conference's subject. Other themes could have been included had space permitted, and one which deserves special mention is new religious movements and the law, which might have constituted a further section of first-rate specialist contributions.

This book appears some two years after the papers were presented, and, inevitably, not every author has been able to revise his or her contribution, though some have done so. None of the contributions is dated or out-of-date in any matter of substance, but the reader is asked to bear in mind that certain factual details may be incomplete, and in some instances it has not been possible to make reference to books and articles which appeared since the conference was held. Some papers, however, have been re-written extensively by the authors, for which work the editor is sincerely grateful.

One paper — that by James Beckford — was not given at the conference, although it is on the same subject; the paper he gave has already appeared in print, and he has kindly provided a newer and fuller treatment which is included as chapter 6. 'Old Sects and

New Religions in Europe' by Bryan Wilson first appeared in *Handbook of Cults and Sects in America*, edited by David G. Bromley and Jeff K. Hadden, and published by JAI Press,and we are grateful to the publishers for permission to reprint it.

Editing this volume has been a stimulating and challenging task. All the papers were given in English. English was not the mother tongue of every author, however, and so the editor had to re-write extensively several of the contributions. He hopes that the changes he has made to the several contributions will have enhanced their quality and their accessibility, and not distorted or obscured the authors' intentions.

Robert Towler
INFORM, London
July 1995

Contents

CHAPTER 1

Old Sects and New Religions in Europe

Bryan Wilson

Minority religions are today objects of study for social scientists, but for a long time almost all scholarly comment about sects and cults came from historians and theologians. These comments were almost always evaluative and judgmental, and the words them-selves, 'sect' and, 'cult', acquired strong pejorative connotations, connotations which in public and journalistic usage they still retain. But if we are really to understand such movements — their origins, appeal, organization, development, and ideological orientation — we cannot afford to indulge in prejudices and preconceptions, nor to take the accounts of journalists without scrutiny. The sociological approach — ethically neutral and value-free — is an imperative prerequisite. It took some time for sociologists to liberate their concepts from the theological parti-pris with which these terms were invested, and even the early sociological work, in juxtaposing the sect — the 'dissident', 'deviant' sect — to the Church — the wholesome, normal, orthodox faith — by implication continued to stigmatize sectarianism as in some ways perverse, and possibly heretical. Today, serious study of minority religion has disavowed that evaluative inheritance, and I should make it clear at the outset that I shall use the terms 'sect', 'cult' and 'new religious movement' in the spirit of impartiality, objectivity and ethical neutrality. Given the plurality of religions in contemporary European society, given the decline in Church practice and belief, and given the declining relevance of the Church as a reference point for understanding minority religious persuasions, it should be increasingly easy for us all to adopt this position.

The new religions have captured much more of the public's attention than the old sects ever did, but we need to remind ourselves that some of those older sects continue to be a vigorous if less publicized presence in Europe. Some of them have hundreds of thousands of members, and in the case of the congeries of Pentecostal movements, even millions. These bodies are much bigger than any of the new religions, and those new movements which do command a large clientele generally have a much more segmentary hold on their following than do old sects, whilst those new movements which demand total and encompassing commitment — such as the Hare Krishna movement or the Unification Church — tend, in Europe at least, to be quite small. Further, those older sects, which once were mainly found in Protestant countries — Britain, Scandinavia, Switzerland, Holland and Germany — have in recent decades been of growing significance in southern Catholic Europe, where they have made deep and impressive inroads. By way of example, we may recall that Jehovah's Witnesses alone number about 120,00 in France, 88,000 in Spain, 37,000 in Portugal and 180,000 in Italy. For all these reasons, in considering the new religions in Europe, it is important to do so in the context of older manifestations of religious diversity. The older sects were, of course, almost all of Christian provenance, but we have to remember that, in the days of their beginnings, they, too, were new religious movements and it is worth recalling, under seven broad headings, what they and our contemporary new religions might have in common.

1. It is a plausible generalization to say that new religious bodies tend, at least initially, to be lay movements. Genuinely new spiritual impulses appear to arise typically among the laity. (Where they arise among clergy, either the Church channels them into approved courses, such as new religious orders, or they are disciplined and suppressed, as was the worker-priest movement in the Roman Catholic Church.) The lay leadership of a new movement usually remains unprofessional, rejecting the typical traditional claim of clergy to have a monopoly of access to spiritual power. They reject the idea that clergy alone are enabled to perform indispensable services for laymen. Laymen claim to be competent to fulfil such functions. Thus, in their day, Quakers dispensed with clergy; the Baptists, although evolving a ministry, rejected sacerdotalism; the

Methodists, inheriting a ministry through Wesley himself, author-
ised lay preachers; the Brethren, Witnesses and Christadelphians
assigned all authority to laymen; Pentecostalists and Adventists,
although acquiring a ministry from among their earliest pre-
sectarian converts, gave wider opportunities for participation to lay
people, and the spiritual inspirator of the Adventists, Mrs Ellen
White, was herself never ordained. The Mormons adopted a
different strategy: by making every adult male a priest, they
asserted the typical sectarian equality of commitment but in a
churchly guise. For contemporary new religions, the Christian
clergy are a less likely reference point, but they are almost all
profoundly lay in spirit; if professional leadership develops, leaders
tend to adopt a secular rather than a clerical model.

2. In similar spirit, new movements have usually offered a more
proximate salvation. No matter in what form salvation is conceived,
the new movement offers its votaries a shorter, swifter, surer route
to reassurance, whether it focuses on promises of post-mortem
prospects, the elimination of untoward experiences, the neutralizing
of the influence of witches or other evil agencies, the attainment
of a better present or reincarnated life, or simply the opportunity
of healing. Salvation is held to be available without the strictures,
conditions, or rituals of established orthodox religion. The new
movement suggests that a way has been discovered, at no cost, to
dispense with the pretensions of the clergy and the accumulated
cultural baggage which has accreted to the Church. The sect offers
to divest spiritual exercises of what have become arcane, traditional
elements in which the patina of antiquity has been confused with
the aura of sanctity.

3. New movements tend to be demotic movements. Even when they
embrace an abstruse biblical exegesis, sects have emphasised the
simplicity and accessibility of their teachings and practices. When
Shakers proclaimed their 'gift to be simple', or when Christian
Scientists declare their faith to be 'as logical as mathematics', they
make the same kind of claim, namely, that the truth is readily
available and straightforward, whether it is offered as a rejection
of intellectual pretensions or as the logic of common-sense. A new

movement makes an offer of salvation that is congruous with the life circumstances of the public that it addresses. In times past, that public might have been the peasant population of a particular region, as was the case with the Waldensians in northern Italy, or the class of artisans such as joined pre-Reformation millennial movements in the Low Countries and the Rheinland. Lower classes were the recruiting grounds for new sects such as the Christadelphians in nineteenth century Britain, whilst some better-to-do people in early twentieth century Britain and in mid-century Germany, were drawn to Christian Science. Contemporary new movements have often had a more specifically generational focus; thus the Hare Krishna movement and the Moonies have tended to recruit very young adults, whilst Transcendental Meditation and Scientology appear to attract a slightly older clientele of people in their mid-twenties and thirties. But, whatever the actual constituency, the new movement offers a conception of salvation that is relevant to the social experience of its particular clientele. There is a tendency, which arises both from the way networks operate and from the terms in which spiritual power is offered, for like to attract like, and for the composition of each new sect to acquire a distinct cast in relation to age, gender, education, status and other social attributes. Distinctive constituencies are related to the particular appeal of each sect, and in themselves they reflect the process of structural differentiation of the social experience of different segments of the public at large.

4. In challenging existing religious institutions and in offering alternative avenues to salvation, each new movement must claim a unique sources of legitimacy, or at least a new definitive understanding of whatever old sources it has occasion to invoke. Within the old context of Christian sectarianism, the obvious and almost invariably invoked source was, of course, the scriptures. Each sect necessarily claimed uniquely valid access and insight into these writings, evolving from them a body of teachings in greater or lesser measure at variance with, and in contradiction of, the received understandings of the established Churches. Such new interpretations were frequently augmented by subsidiary sources of legitimation, but, even without these, the received Protestant

inheritance of an open Bible and every man his own interpreter, was often sufficient for the proclamation of a significant re-reading of the old texts. As long as the framework of discourse remained Christian and emphatically biblical, newly emergent sects worked generally in that tradition.

4a. As toleration steadily extended from the time of the Reformation onwards, so alternative sources of inspiration were invoked. The obvious and easily assimilated legitimation for sect teachings was new revelation — a significant part of the platform on which some nineteenth century sects established themselves. In Mrs Ellen White, the Seventh-day Adventists acclaimed a prophetess who, in her trances, had visions on the basis of which for decades she counselled the ordained leaders of that church. Mrs White insisted that her revelations be accepted only as long as they were consonant with the Scriptures, and she disavowed any supernatural faculties of her own except as a vessel through whom revelations might come. Her Church generally heeded her, and her words have sometimes been taken by Adventists as fully the equivalent of the Scriptures themselves. Joseph Smith Jr made rather bolder claims to charismatic inspiration, and added new sacred literature to the Bible. Claims made by Mary Baker Eddy went perhaps further. Not only did she produce a key to the scriptures, but her followers hailed her as the woman clothed with the sun prophesied in the book of Revelation. If these were all serious departures from Christian orthodoxy, the claims of Sun Myung Moon, founder of the Unification Church, have gone still further, since last summer he proclaimed himself and his wife jointly to be the awaited Messiah.

4b. Charisma is a readily available resource for legitimation in religious movements more than in any other type of institution. Yet, as long as Christianity provided the framework within which new sects arose, the possibility of charismatic claims were circumscribed. For Orthodox Christians, the book of Revelation closed the era of prophecy, but beyond this lies the fact that any strong claim to charisma must in some sense derogate from the claims of Christ himself, as the supreme charismatic being. Thus, the stronger the claims of a sectarian leader to special charisma, the less acceptable to existing Christian Churches that movement becomes. This of course is not the sole ground on which orthodox Christians might withhold recognition of a sect, but it is a crucial test of the acceptability of a movement within the broad family of Christian bodies. Thus it is that whilst the Adventists operate at the fringes of Christian orthodoxy, Mormons are generally regarded by such inter-denominational organizations as being beyond the pale, and Christian Scientists are perhaps even further from acceptability, whilst the Moonies are manifestly rejected, and from them other Christians withhold that very name. These movements, in ascending order, test the bounds of Christian toleration: but outside these bounds, charisma could exercise freer rein, and in the new movements arising in the last three or four decades the charismatic leader has been able to make claims unbridled by considerations of Christian restraint.

4c. A source of legitimation also capable of some measure of accommodation to the Christian tradition has been the claim to a secret gnosis. Sometimes combined with charismatic claims (as in the case of Mrs Eddy), the idea that a secret, perhaps arcane, message was to be derived from scriptural or extra-scriptural sources has given rise to new movements, the leaders of which have claimed to possess the key to unlock secret mysteries. Such groups have tended to be small, since esoteric knowledge, even if supposedly accessible to all right-minded people, loses much of its appeal when it becomes too readily or too widely available. Whilst the gnosis has sometimes been a subterranean stream of quasi-Christian ideas, as among some movements in the early centuries of the Christian era, devotees of the occult have also incorporated alien elements alongside, or to replace, Christian features. Gurjieffism, Theosophy, the Wicca movement, neo-Paganism and contemporary New Age cults are legitimated by the claim to possess such special wisdom.

4d. This source of legitimation merges readily with another — the search for wisdom of ancient provenance. As Christian belief has waned, so the search for other more accommodative religious and spiritual philosophies has grown. Beginning with the appeal of Buddhism as the subject of fashionable, if initially perhaps rather shallow, intellectual discourse in late nineteenth century Europe, there has been a growing receptivity to beliefs and practices of oriental origin. In part, these ideas appear to have appealed because of the supposedly unsullied nature of the cultures from which they came; in part, because they are uncompromised by the centuries of Christian co-existence with western culture. These exotic patterns of belief and practice achieved most when emissaries from the orient visited the west to introduce their teachings, largely to the leisure classes of Europe and the West — the leisure class of middle-aged and elderly ladies as early twentieth century devotees of Vedanta and Theosophy, or the leisure class of students as the late twentieth century votaries of the Hare Krishna movement and the Divine Light Mission.

4e. Not least among other legitimations for belief is one that has at times co-existed with Christianity but which in its radical form must remain at odds with it — legitimation by reference to the inner self. The Quakers espoused an early form of this orientation, favouring it above the legitimation provided by scripture. The 'inner light', or the voice of conscience, was a highly subjective claim to religious legitimacy, and risked the possibility of condemnation from the Churches as a form of antinomianism. To know, solely from within, what is true and what shall be done, risks thwarting all the agencies of social control which for centuries had been reinforced by orthodox Christian teaching. The claim that man is potentially entirely self-sufficient has been strongly asserted by contemporary new movements, giving rise to the idea, the kernel of which is to be found in Mormonism, that man is prospectively god-like and can realise that 'god-within' if only the appropriate faith is summoned and the proper techniques applied. The idea underlies the Human Potential movements, from *est* to Exegesis; it is incipiently expressed in Christian Science and more audaciously in Scientology and its various derivatives; whilst in Soka Gakkai Buddhism, the possibility is held out for everyone to realise his Buddha nature. This mode of legitimation stands in sharp contradistinction to the claims of Christianity to an objective divinity and the need for frameworks of objective social order. It converges with the subjectivity of New Age movements and in general with the post-modernist current of contemporary society. In this sense, Quakers and some antinomian groups apart, it is least likely to be found among the long established sects of the preceding three or four centuries.

5. For traditional religion, new movements always appear to be both iconoclastic and desacralizing. New sects reject ancient prescripts for religious order, and their procedures depart from sanctioned and sanctified routines of the established faith. New movements have similar needs to those of the Churches, but they seek to satisfy them in radically new ways. Usually they find the need to raise money, to keep their members informed, to proselytize, and to organize regular occasions of coming together. But their methods of dealing with such matters differ from those that have become traditional for established Churches. Thus, to finance their activities, instead of long legitimised tithes, they depend on solicitation, sometimes, as in Seventh-day Adventist 'in-gathering' or Salvation Army 'self-denial' weeks, by begging from the general public. More shocking are the salesmanship techniques of Jehovah's Witnesses in selling the *Watchtower* and *Awake!* from door to door, but these sales have incurred less opprobrium than the fund-raising practices of the Moonies and the Hare Krishna people selling potted plants or candles at airports and on the streets.

These fund-raising techniques, however, are no more than the application of rational planning to religious causes. No less rational has been the use of mass circulation literature by the sects, ensuring that all members had before them the same reading matter at the same time, so that the whole movement might be catechized in the same lesson more or less simultaneously. The Christian Scientists hear the same printed sermons each week; the Seventh-day Adventists circulate the same discussion material for their weekly Sabbath schools; the Witnesses systematically produce question-and-answer articles for public instruction on a weekly basis; and of newer movements, a similar monthly distribution of doctrinal literature is undertaken in Soka Gakkai Buddhism. Yet all of these adoptions of rational organizational techniques lead to easy condemnation of minority movements because they depart from procedures recognized as distinctly 'religious'. In consequence, as new sects, they are condemned for being 'merely after your money' and 'not religious at all'. Other facets of rational organization attract similar strictures. Thus, Witnesses proselytize not casually or randomly, but systematically according to a well designed plan for each congregation's territory. All Christian Science churches purvey identical lesson sermons, and are designated as branch churches, much as a bank has branches. Similar rational organization characterizes the Human Potential movements, whilst L. Ron Hubbard claimed that whilst Jesus and Buddha had useful insights into soteriological possibilities, only Scientology specified the prospect of salvation as a rational, systematic, and comprehensive programme.

New movements have adopted rational organization because these techniques were available in the contemporary secular society in which they emerged, and were well adapted to its needs. It would have been curious for a new movement deliberately to disavow more efficient organization in favour of the imitation of what to them were the antiquated patterns of Church structures. For any religious body, the employment of rational methods must imply a measure of tension. At some point, spiritual orientations confound rationality, and all religious behaviour must ultimately justify itself in terms that defy the canons of strictly rational practice. While sects, since the mid-nineteenth century, have increasingly rationalized their operation, a Christian sect can scarcely afford to jeopardize the irreducible mystical content of faith. Lacking such restraints, the non-Christian movements of our time have been able to adopt both more radically rational techniques, and also to claim, more strongly than Christian movements, that they have access to a supra-rational sphere of understanding and operation. Thus Human Potential movements typically employ methods reminiscent of modern educational practice, but they also make bold claims to give their 'students' access to power that far transcends the empirically established capabilities of the human being.

6. A common characteristic of old sects and new religions is their need to set themselves in a historical context. Each movement

reinterprets the past with the specific point of claiming its own place in the longer-term scheme of things, regarding itself as the most important phenomenon ever, locating itself at the very pinnacle of history. All preceding events, all previous religions, have together constituted no more than a prelude to the emergence of this one organisation. Man's pilgrimage has been moving towards this point, the fulfilment of mankind's potential and destiny. Thus, the past is devalued, and with it the bulk of past culture and previous human achievement. The new sect encompasses all that is worthy of preservation, since society has no other worthwhile legacy but that which is encapsulated in the sect's own teaching and practice.

7. New religious bodies tend to proclaim their mission as one of extreme urgency. At some point beyond its immediate offer of therapy, benefit or salvation to the individual believer, the sect sees its ultimate destiny as being to save the world, or those in the world who are worthy of (and perhaps destined for) salvation. Whereas the Church claims to have a timeless mission, the sect claims to have a timely mission, in the sense that 'now is the accepted time'. Thus, Witnesses seek to bring together the last of those who are to be saved before the imminent apocalypse; the Maharishi seeks to persuade more people to practise Transcendental Meditation, certainly for personal benefit but also to effect a reduction in crime, addiction and other forms of social pathology in the community in which mediators live; Soka Gakkai aims to get one third of the population to chant to usher in an age of world-wide proclamation of its version of Buddhism; whilst the eventual goal of Scientology is 'to clear the planet' by inducing people to take courses to eliminate hindrances to rational thought. For all of them, the urgency of mission justifies intensity of belief.

All of the issues so far mentioned indicate continuities of orientation among minority religions, whether old sects or new movements, but besides such features in common there are also sharp differences. Many contemporary new religions do not merely deviate from Christian orthodoxy, but invoke traditions that are entirely alien to it. Even groups that claim a specifically Christian inheritance, such as the Unification Church and the Family of Love, depart much more radically from it than was general among sects flourishing up until the Second World War. The Unification Church embraces elements that are manifestly derived from Korean concern with ancestors, and a belief in spirit-beings which has not been part of the Christian repertoire since the apostolic age; whilst the Family of Love has espoused an antinomianism which inverts the normal prescriptions of Christian sexual morality. Some new movements draw directly from Hindu, Buddhist, Sikh or Muslim origins. Others recollect, or more probably reconstruct, what passes for paganism. At the opposite extreme the religious scene has also been affected by currents stemming from the modern endorsement of science in the emergence of numerous scientistic cults, therapies and philosophies of which Scientology, the Forums Network and other Human Potential movements are ready examples. The diversity of the sectarian scene has vastly expanded.

Many of these diverse quasi-Christian and non-Christian groups totally reject a premise that was at the heart of European spiritually. A central tenet of orthodox Christianity is that man is born a sinner, with no prospect of salvation without redemption through Christ. Man's inherent sinfulness has been at the core of Christian faith. A steady shift may be discerned, even among groups claiming to be Christian, as successive new movements came to re-formulate this proposition. We have noted the Mormon dictum, 'As man is, God once was; as God is, man might become', which might be seen as a theological precursor of what was more directly claimed by later Human Potential movements. Without absolutely abandoning the idea of the need for redemption, Christian Science declared that man's spiritual heritage was to triumph over sin as well as over sickness and death. Similar tendencies occurred in Universalism, and a still stronger rejection of this bed-rock element of Christian teaching has been evident among the proponents of positive thinking and Prosperity Theology.

The defection from this doctrine had been an accommodation to changing social conditions, but as long as Christian doctrine was respected at all, there was a limit beyond which this tendency could not go. The new movements were under no such constraint. They could espouse optimistic celebration of a man-centred religion and match this creed to the advancing secular ethos. This shift in ideological orientation, variously emphasized as man's capacity for 'empowerment', to attain buddhahood, or to live 'in present time', may be taken as the major distinction between the old (generally Christian) sects and the new movements.

Two divergent trends are evident in contemporary spirituality. On the one hand some seek to transcend quotidian common-sense explanations with promises of deeper access to esoteric mysteries, sometimes including the avowal of new magical powers embodied within their therapies such as are found in movements as diverse as Sukyo Mahikari, now a spreading cult on the continent, or in a Human Potential movement like Exegesis. On the other hand, there is also a powerful inclination in some movements to lay claim to scientific credibility, the cardinal example of which is Scientology. There may also be found a convergence of these two apparently divergent tendencies: ostensible scientific procedures give place to transcendent claims that go beyond all realistic prospect of empirical verification — a phenomenon evident in movements as different as Transcendental Meditation and Scientology. These diverse bodies have in common an emphasis on personal access to spiritual power rather than on a public cult of worship. They make little effort to function as a collective ideology for the wider community within which they operate. They exemplify privatized religion in which individual benefit rather than public good is the focus. The concept of religion as a duty, as an obligation to God and one's fellow men, is relinquished, and spiritual benefit is regarded as the right of those who practise as the faith requires.

Consonant with this disposition, these new spiritual bodies manifest patterns of association which bear little resemblance to those of older Christian sects. They are less congregational since the collectively of adherents is less disposed to identify itself as a discrete self-conscious entity; adherents are primarily identified as so many individual clients, practitioners or devotees. Often there is relatively little collective life. Some groups function primarily through courses of instruction; others by promoting discussion sessions to air personal problems and testify to spiritual progress; yet others promote demonstrations of therapy or training. Adherents may be linked in loose networks with only intermittent, loosely structured contact with one another. Movements derived from oriental religions often cultivate ritual activity, but even here — in Transcendental Meditation, various forms of yoga, in Soka Gakkai Buddhism — most of the prescribed ritual practices can be undertaken by individuals performing on their own. Whereas old sectarians were worshippers, the clientele of the new movements are more often participants in seminars, audiences for lectures, readers of publications, patients for therapists, mediators or chanters for the solution of personal problems, or clients for wonder-workers. Consonant with the nature of these activities, the models of association which characterize these groups are drawn from secular organizations rather than approximating to traditional religious forms.

The changes in the ideology and organization of minority religious bodies reflect the pattern of change occurring in the wider society over recent decades. Most obvious has been the breakdown of the broad religio-cultural consensus in the christianized societies of Europe. The crisis of confidence in the Churches is evident in the diversity of views on a variety of doctrinal and moral issues from the virgin birth, the resurrection and the status of biblical miracles, on the one hand, to the acceptability of birth control techniques, abortion and divorce, on the other. Christian influence over secular affairs has markedly diminished. Even the most authoritative cleric, the Pope, is unable to influence most of his flock with regard to some sexual practices, and this despite the evident hunger for the sort of charisma which is widely ascribed to him.

Paradoxically, secularization, the process of increasing dependence on purely secular techniques and regulation, opens the way for spiritual experimentation, but does so by shifting the goals of spiritual endeavour. By and large, people come increasingly to believe that their aim is not to do the will of God but to get the best out of life for themselves. Such is the advance of technology that the world is seen not so much as God-given but rather as man-made. Rational planning has replaced prayerful supplication as the primary resource in organizing society's affairs. At all points, there is increased reliance on technical devices rather than on traditional dependence on collective moral consciousness as informed by traditional faith. The shift is observable, to take one example, in the development of agencies of social control. The Church used to maintain social order by moral injunctions controlling not only men's minds but also their bodies, but these sexual mores are now widely disregarded. New technical devices, for example methods of birth control, displace dependence on the ancient Christian virtues of chastity, restraint and moral probity. New techniques for control, from traffic lights to credit ratings, from electronic eyes to tax liabilities, are now expected to ensure regulated patterns of social interaction. Nowhere is the point more obvious than in the case of AIDS. The old wisdom would counsel sexual restraint and declare promiscuity to be sinful and dire in its consequences. Modern governments balk at such 'old-fashioned' moral messages, and prefer to counsel the use of technologically devised appliances — condoms! Such is the shift from circumstances in which, for the orderly conduct of affairs, societies depended on the collective moral conscience, to circumstances in which reliance is placed on human contrivances specifically designed to achieve well-defined goals. Since the old messages and the old functions of religion are rendered otiose in this process of massive cultural change, religious movements canvassing new, privatized functions find easy access to people seeking personal spiritual solace or the enhancement of personal well-being.

The effect of secularization has been reinforced by the political demands (issuing from the Council of Europe and the United Nations) for toleration, to a point where European states have become more markedly neutral in religious matters, increasingly disposed to guarantee freedom of religious practice to all law-abiding groups. Laissez-faire philosophies which, no less in religious affairs than in secular matters, put consumer choice at a premium, have augmented this process. The effect is to induce a certain cultural relativism in religious affairs, promoting in many respects a parity of faiths, each entitled to increasingly equal rights. As orthodox Christianity has declined, so other spiritual bodies have enhanced their claims, enjoying increased tolerance from state and public alike. The development has been reinforced by the incursion of immigrants from non-Christian cultures, some of whom, finding it difficult to distinguish between orthodox and heterodox versions of the religion of their country or origin, have espoused some convenient version of their traditional faith which they found flourishing in the new host societies. The Krishna Consciousness movement, in particular, appears to gain from this pattern of response from Indian immigrants to the West.

The accelerated pace of technological change has had another important consequence in the dissolution of the old religious orthodoxy. Rapid change puts youth at a premium and age at a discount. In the technical sphere, in the first instance, the young acquire new knowledge, and the older generation, once respected for their experience, become 'have beens', trained in obsolete techniques. Long experience, once the passport to a better job, becomes a handicap. The work-order no longer wants the 'experienced man' but rather the man newly trained (or re-trained). Although this consequence of change is strictly relevant only in the sphere of technology, communications, and styles of man-management, the effect carries over, totally inappropriately, to the spiritual and moral realm. Thus, older people — and they are of course parents and grandparents — lose social and moral authority simply because they have lived longer and are therefore easily assumed to be 'out of date'. Loss of prestige in the arena of work leads to loss of esteem in matters spiritual and moral. To a growing segment of the young, traditional religion appears to be no longer relevant to their aspirations and ideas because that religion is the preserve of old or older people, who use old-fashioned language and rituals, and canvass old ideas no longer congruent with modern conditions, as the young perceive them. New movements capture the current emphasis on change, whether their newness is an ancient wisdom re-discovered or the result of purportedly scientific research. Whereas old sects sought to recruit whole families and were often inherited by one generation from its predecessor, new movements appeal more readily to single, mostly young, often socially or geographically mobile people. For these organizations with their frequent emphasis on quick therapeutic results, generational transmission is too long-term a concern: they function for individuals rather than for families. The older sects were conservative, even if what they sought to conserve differed from the traditional as cherished within the mainstream Churches. They resisted change, not only in their own ideology, but also in the wider society, whilst many of the new movements are the committed harbingers of new departures in both religion and morals.

There is one particular feature of change, characteristic of some, albeit not of all the religions. This is the shift from the traditional ascetic ethic of Christianity to the legitimation of a hedonistic orientation. The Christian ascetic ethic which counselled hard work, frugality, postponement of gratification, temperance, self-denial, forbearance and long-suffering was a teaching entirely consonant with a producer society. In conditions of scarcity, when every effort was to be made to limit consumption, to conserve energy, to avoid waste, to 'make do' and eschew self-indulgence, asceticism was a congenial teaching. It was the spiritual and moral parallel of prevailing economic endeavour. The ethic was espoused by virtually all the old Christian sects, transmitted from generation to generation among groups which earned a reputation for this particular constellation of values. But since the Second World War, European countries have been transformed from producer to consumer societies, regularly producing more than they need to consume, and creating vast surpluses of basic commodities.

In such societies, an ascetic ethic, were it widely canvassed and adopted, could only worsen prevailing economic and social problems. What such societies need, and what they do now in fact generate, is a hedonistic ethic, an ethic which licenses self-indulgence, immediate gratification, pleasure in every form, and not the postponement of these desiderata to some posited heavenly after-life. The demand for 'heaven now' implies the abandonment of inhibition and restraint, encourages enjoyment, and urges people to get all they can out of this life and to do what they like. The mood affects not only dispositions to consumption, waste, and work, but also personal habits. Sexual inhibition has been increasingly relaxed together with the relinquishment of time-honoured attitudes (now seen as time-worn attitudes) to other, economic, forms of consumption. The expanded development of the tertiary sector, and in particular of entertainment, advertising, and leisure industries, have promoted consumption and con-spicuous waste, and encouraged the values of consumer societies. The endorsement of self-indulgence, enjoyment and relaxation by those engaged in the advertising and entertainment industries (themselves in the old Marxist or Catholic sense 'unproductive' activities) has affected the new modes of spirituality burgeoning in Europe. Many new religions virtually legitimize the whole hedonistic ethic, a trend also evident in some variants of mainstream religion: positive thinking; Prosperity Theology, which is now burgeoning in Sweden; and much American televangelism, now widely available on European television screens. The new movements may not condone sexual promiscuity (although Rajneeshism and the Family of Love should not be forgotten), but they readily accept serial marriages (through divorce), abortion, homo- and bisexuality and, above all, birth control and prophylactic techniques that promote pleasure without the risk of untoward consequences. Indeed, even to mention these various ways in which self-restraint has been relegated, is to sound old-fashioned, so taken for granted have these elements of the hedonistic ethic become. The new religions are merely in line with much of the 'de-moralised' modern thinking in endorsing the current permissive ethic and in promising mankind's salvation *now* rather than as some — perhaps remote — post-mortem prospect.

The general conditions of accelerated social change have been a powerful factor in stimulating new orientations in religion and in prompting the organization of new cults which specialize in offering benefits consonant with the emergent value-orientations of contemporary society, and equally appropriate religious legitimation for them. A change in social climate encourages the growth of new species, which perhaps could not have developed in earlier circumstances. Nor were those earlier conditions propitious for the recent wider proliferation and enhanced diversity of styles, orientations and ideologies. New developments in secular knowledge, in scientific findings, and in technology, have induced new types of impulsions in spirituality. Scientology was partly derivative from psycho-analysis and science fiction; the Human Potential groups acquired ideas from earlier sensitivity training; Rajneeshism depended on cheap and speedy international travel; whilst other groups acquired ideas from space exploration. Just as the new movements present a different social image from that of the older Christian sectarianism, so the social and the sociological problems which they engender are no less distinctive.

The old sects often sought, and sometimes won, exemption from involvement in various civic responsibilities — military service, compulsory trades union membership, jury service, obligatory medical treatment (inoculations in schools or in military units, or blood transfusions in the case of Jehovah's Witnesses), attendance at school assemblies, Sabbath-day work, or official pressure to salute national flags or to join in the singing of national anthems — among other things. The new movements rarely take exception to such civic obligations. Generally, a few new religions excepted, they leave their members free to take whatever place they choose in the wider society. The old sects often acquired a high reputation for conscientiousness, integrity, their work ethic, sobriety, and the low incidence, indeed the virtual absence, of delinquency among their membership. Thus far, the new religions have to make their mark in these regards. Their conflicts with the law and the civic authorities usually turn on other matters, conspicuously in the matter of recruitment of the young and the persuasive techniques sometimes employed.

The sociological questions which the new religions pose also differ from those of the older forms of sectarianism. There is less concern with what might be called the career structure of the movement — new religions are unlikely candidates for the process of denominationalization, in the form in which it occurred among some, particularly Pentecostal, sects. Nor is the perhaps now rather old-fashioned concern with the relationship between sectarianism and social stratification a particularly relevant issue for an understanding of the new movements. Social class has not been a significant variable in their appeal. The emphasis has shifted to generational differentials — to such an extent that in Germany new movements have been lumped together as *Jugendreligionen*. The educational and occupational correlates of membership in new movements remain a subject of importance, particularly since the better educated sections of younger generations appear to have been disproportionately attracted. Those in the tertiary sector of the economy appear to have been conspicuously drawn to the Human Potential movements, whilst Soka Gakkai Buddhism has an unusually high proportion of people who are self-employed and who work in the graphic and performing arts and in the caring professions.

Conversion and recruitment have attracted the attention of sociologists of both the older and new movements, but these issues have become socially more pressing and sociologically more absorbing because the new movements have so deliberately directed their propaganda at the young. The charge of brainwashing, by that or any other name, was not an issue in the study of older sects, in which many young people adopted the faith of their parents, or when proselytizing groups attracted converts either at revival meetings or by doorstep evangelism. The charge has come largely from the media, and cumulative media sensationalism has made the study of so-called 'cult' phenomena a livelier part of contemporary sociology than ever was the case with earlier sectarianism, even though, as Eileen Barker has shown, the high turnover of clientele for example among the Moonies, illustrates a serious intellectual weakness in the allegation of brain-washing. That there has been a high incidence of defection among members of new religions is also doubtless related to the fact that those recruited were so often young, single, and sometimes isolated individuals. The closed character of the older sects, and the likelihood that whole families were in membership, generally prevented defections from being so common, or at least so visible.

In reaction to the processes of structural differentiation occurring in the wider society, a few new movements have sought, in a way not uncommon among older sects, to re-create their own encapsulated social world untainted by external influences. They have sometimes espoused the principles of communitarianism, such as have prevailed among the Hutterites. But, lacking expertise in rural living or finding urban communitarianism insufficiently insulated from the wider society, various groups among the so-called Jesus movements discovered such principles difficult to apply. Other new movements have experimented with communal living — the Unification Church in some measure, the Family of Love, and Krishna devotees — but they are exceptions. They differ radically from those more numerous bodies which seek only a segmentary commitment from (most of) their adherents, and which settle for large numbers who maintain a less encompassing and less exclusivist allegiance. These nominally much larger organizations (the various Human Potential movements, Scientology, and Transcendental Meditation, for example) do not seek to embrace the entire life activities of their members, but only to infuse their distinctive therapeutic orientations at crucial points in the client's mental and relational experience.

In these mental therapeutic movements, the all-pervasive vision and no less all-embracing demands that characterize sect allegiance are missing. Spiritual orientations, which in old sects were assumed to suffuse the thought and pervade the entire way of life of the believer, in these movements have relevance only in certain discrete areas of his experience. Just as structural differentiation comes to characterize modern society, so, in this particular type of new movement, what is conceived as spiritual may be reduced to particular concerns that were once no more than component parts of a more holistic orientation. In some instances, the spiritual becomes almost exclusively the therapeutic; in others, it is pre-dominated by preoccupation with the arcane and esoteric. In some contexts, spirituality is interpreted as something largely recreational; in yet others, it serves as a substitute educational function. Move-ments adopting one or a mixture of these surrogates are responding to the course of structural segmentation of the social system. In all such areas, these organizations seek to augment, and perhaps to supplant, secular provision, as one sees in the claims of Human Potential seminars to motivate people and to 'enable' or 'empower' them, or in the endeavours of Scientology to supplant psychiatry, or in the claims of Transcendental Meditation to reinforce society's agencies in the control of deviancy.

An occasion of the sort in which we are now participating, prompts one further reflection about the relationship of new re-ligions to old sects. The sects were conservative, generally secretive bodies, committed ideologically to restraint on conduct, to circum-spection, to seriousness of demeanour, and to the cultivation of a self-sufficient inner piety. They were less concerned than the new movements to establish themselves socially, less interested in selling themselves to the world. The newer bodies have readily exposed themselves to public view, have courted publicity by advertising, street displays, and canvassing, distinctive dress, and what, to most Europeans, are often bizarre ritual procedures. Not least, some have been aggressively litigious, which has contributed to their becoming the targets of sociological (as well as of journalistic) enquiry. Even journalistic sensationalism has not always been unwelcome to them. In keeping with these public orientations, some of them have been far more willing than were the old-style sectaries to open at least some of their cupboards to inspection. Their literature may be less informative, but in keeping with modern mores, they are quite willing to be interviewed and to fill up questionnaires. Certainly, one could not have envisaged a conference of this kind convening to discuss diverse old sects, and certainly one would not have found their representatives willing to make presentations to such a gathering of detached, unconverted, perhaps unconvertible, interested outside persons.

CHAPTER 2

The Secular Anti-Cult and the Religious Counter-Cult Movement: Strange Bedfellows or Future Enemies?

Massimo Introvigne

A large body of sociological literature exists concerning the so-called 'anti-cult movement', both in the United States and internationally. Most students of the anti-cult movement, however, fail to realise that this movement consists of two separate and increasingly conflicting sub-movements, one secular and the other sectarian. The distinction between a secular *anti*-cult movement and a religious *counter*-cult movement was introduced by J. Gordon Melton and by the present author.[1] The terminology distinguishing between 'anti-cult' and 'counter-cult' organizations has now been adopted by specialized *counter*-cult publications such as the *Christian Research Journal*[2] and surfaced recently even in the pages of *Christianity Today*.[3] On the other hand the distinction is normally not used by the *anti*-cult newsletters and journals. At least an official document of the Roman Catholic Church — the pastoral letter *New Religiosity and New Evangelization* by Monsignor Guiseppe Casale, Archbishop of Foggia — mentioned the distinction between the anti-cult and the counter-cult movements, elaborating on the main differences (and criticizing both movements from a Roman Catholic standpoint).[4] In this paper I will comment further on the differences between the anti-cult and the counter-cult movements, and assess how these differences are relevant in the social interaction involving the movements against the 'cults', the new religious movements themselves and the scholars. In the last part I will offer some final comments on the 'question of truth' that seems to be a main point of contention involving the anti-cult movements, the counter-cult movements, the Churches and the scholars.

1. A typology of the movements against the cults

In this first section of my paper I will list the main areas of difference and dissent between anti-cult and counter-cult movements and introduce two further sub-typologies, one doctrinal and one sociological.

1a. We could distinguish between *subjective* and *objective* differences between the anti-cult and the counter-cult movements. From a subjective point of view, the counter-cult movements are composed almost invariably and totally of Christian pastors and laymen concerned with the growing rate of defection from Churches to 'cults' and other religious movements perceived as being outside of the Christian fold. Although Catholic counter-cult movements (such as G.R.I.S. in Italy) do exist, the large majority of the counter-cult movements are Protestant, and the large majority of the Protestants involved are Evangelical. The anti-cult movements have a secular origin, and a significant number of their members and leaders are non-religious secular humanists or secular members of the mental health and legal professions. The subjective criteria, however, are neither absolute nor sufficient in order to distinguish between the two movements. Clergymen — Protestant and occasionally Catholic — are involved in the *anti*-cult movements; in this case, they tend to adopt its language and style (a case in point in the United States is Father Kent Burtner, a Roman Catholic priest). Additionally, although a few representatives of the Jewish community have a distinctive counter-cult attitude, a surprising number of Jews, both secular and deeply religious, are involved in the *anti*-cult movements. Of course the reason is sociological and connected with the fact that the Jewish community has been particularly affected by defection to the 'cults'; this explains the hard line taken by a number of prominent Jewish leaders and their cooperation with the anti-cult movements. However, some anti-cult leaders with a Jewish background have themselves offered an alternative explanation. Judaism is not a missionary religion, and

— its Orthodox branch, at least — has always regarded conversion with some suspicion.[5] Judaism traditionally does not seek conversions and, although the attitude of Reform and Conservative Judaism is somewhat different, Orthodox Judaism regards a 'genuine' conversion as something quite rare. As some Jewish leaders of the anti-cult movements have suggested, it is possible that even the most secularized Jews maintain a suspicious attitude towards religious conversion in general — the more so against 'sudden' conversions — and are accordingly inclined to join the anti-cult movements, which are equally suspicious of the conversion dynamics.[6]

Accordingly, the subjective elements are not crucial to identify the differences between the anti-cult and the counter-cult movements. The objective features are more relevant. The key feature, and the standard slogan, of the secular anti-cult movement is that it only discusses deeds, not creeds. It is not interested in whether any particular religious persuasion is true or false; it claims to be interested only in *behaviour* which it regards as harmful to individuals, to families or to society at large. The secular anti-cult movement wants to free people from 'cults'; it does not presume to tell them what religious or philosophical ideas they should espouse once they have left the 'cult'. A fraction of the mental health profession has added fuel to the fire of the secular anti-cult movement by advancing the controversial theory of 'brainwashing'. Pop psychology has contributed the still more dubious theory that 'subliminal messages' are hidden everywhere from rock music to apparently innocent books.

The counter-cult movement disagrees with almost every priority espoused by its secular counterpart. Its proponents maintain that the borders between belief and behaviour are less clearly marked than the anti-cult movement would prefer to believe. Counter-cultists insist that false belief — a heresy — breaks the law of God and that this is at least as dangerous as any behaviour contrary to the laws of men. A 'cult', from this point of view, is not primarily a money-making enterprise, but a heresy. One problem with this perspective, of course, is that each religious persuasion has its own definition of heresy and hence of 'cult', and counter-cult movements of Protestant and Catholic origin are surely different in many respects. Another difference between the counter-cult movement and the secular anti-cult movement is that counter-cultists are obviously not happy when someone simply leaves the 'cult', unless he or she is converted to the 'true' faith.

1b. A sub-typology may be introduced distinguishing between a *rationalist* and a *post-rationalist* brand of both anti-cult and counter-cult movements. Why do 'cults' continue to grow? Explanations may be quite different. In the 'rationalist' groups, the main explanation is that human beings are indeed gullible, and it is a fact of life that they will become victims of clever frauds, particularly in religion. Anti-cultists will emphasize the secular features of the fraud (e.g. 'bogus' miracles) and the counter-cultists its religious elements (e.g. 'manipulating' the scriptures), but the fraud explanation remains prominent. The post-rationalist explanations of why 'cults' succeed, on the other hand, invest 'cult' leaders with almost superhuman powers and abilities. For the religious post-rationalist counter-cultists, 'cult' leaders are in contact with Satan or the occult. For their secular counterparts of the anti-cult movements, 'cultists' have the more-than-human power of 'brainwashing' their victims; but, as it has been noted, 'brainwashing' in some anti-cult theories appears as something magical, the modern version of the evil eye.[7] The post-rationalist phase of the sectarian counter-cult movement has been reinforced by the 'spiritual warfare' theories. The 'spiritual warfare' movement, born in the 1970s and 1980s in Californian Evangelical and Pentecostal circles, gained international prominence in 1986 when the best-selling novel, *This Present Darkness* by Frank Peretti,[8] was published. By 1991, one and a half million copies of the novel had been sold.[9]

Peretti's novel is about a battle fought through exorcisms and prayer, by both humans and angels, against devils and against human beings who become 'demonized' and promote a wide range of 'cultic' ideas and behaviours, including Eastern 'cults' and the New Age. After Peretti's success, the idea that 'cults' are spread through 'demonized' individuals has become common in Evangelical circles, and also in some Catholic circles heavily influenced by Evangelical and Pentecostal 'demonization' theories.

Different possible attitudes about 'cults' according to the model are represented in Figure 1.

Figure 1. Four possible visions of the 'cults'

	ANTI-CULT	COUNTER-CULT
RATIONALIST	Religious opportunist	'Heretic' as fraud
POST RATIONALIST	Brainwashing	Demonization: 'spiritual warfare'

The first model is the *rationalist anti-cult movement*. The basic paradigm of this movement is fraud, perpetrated by religious opportunists in order to make money at the expense of the gullible. The most typical rationalist anti-cult movements are those of the 'professional sceptics' whose aim is to 'debunk' the claims made for religious miracles and psychic phenomena. Although the existence of professional sceptics is at least as old as psychical research and spiritualism (stage magicians, for example, took pleasure early in the nineteenth century in showing that they were able to replicate the phenomena of the spiritualist mediums), currently the most influential group of sceptics in the international anti-cult scene is the US-based Committee for the Scientific Investigation of the Claims of the Paranormal (CSICOP), publisher of the widely read magazine *Skeptical Inquirer*.[10] In Europe, an organization very similar has been established in Italy under the name of CICAP (Comitato Italiano di Controllo delle Affermazioni sul Paranormale, Italian Committee to Control the Claims of the Paranormal). Although administratively independent, CICAP emphasizes its connection with CSICOP. The main spokesman for CICAP is television journalist Piero Angela, who has for years written books and produced television shows against the paranormal and the 'cults'. He has been successful in enlisting the aid of popular writers such as the comic novelist (and amateur philosophy historian) Luciano De Crescenzo, and of famous scientists such as Italian Nobel prize laureates Carlo Rubbia and Rita Levi Montalcini, as well as the astrophysicist, Margherita Hack, who was already well known as a spokesperson for secular humanism. Imitating the *modus operandi* of CSICOP, its Italian counterpart, whose television programmes are now aired in other European countries, has also obtained the help of stage magicians such as Victor Balli, who claims to have replicated more than one thousand phenomena usually presented as miracles or evidence of the supernatural by religious movements and psychic groups. CICAP has also tried to create a media event by offering a prize of $100,000 to anyone who may offer unimpeachable evidence of a 'genuine' paranormal or miraculous event. It has been said that in the United States 'as a popular movement and anti-paranormal lobbying group, CSICOP has been a spectacular success'[11] Compared to CSICOP, CICAP and similar European organizations have been only a minor success, but they routinely attract media attention and have produced hundreds of news clippings.

Post-rationalist anti-cult movements are still secular rather than sectarian, but rely almost exclusively on brainwashing as a preferred explanation for the success of the 'cults'. Particularly when their leaders are not mental health professionals, they tend to look at brainwashing as something mysterious and magical and, to some extent, parallel the attitude of post-rationalist counter-cultists who attribute the spread of 'cults' to the Devil. It often happens that European movements against the cults depend heavily on an American counterpart. As CICAP depends on CSICOP, the most important European post-rationalist anti-cult movements — CCMM and ADFI in France, AIS, CROAS and Pro Juventute in Spain, FAIR in England, ARIS in Italy — although independently established, now depend, and in some cases would probably not even exist without, inspiration and materials from CAN (Cult Awareness Network) and the American Family Foundation. The Italian ARIS, for example, emphasises that it is 'a secular group' 'in contact with similar organizations in Europe and the United States' that avoids passing judgment on 'matters of doctrine or theology'.[12] 'Cults' for ARIS, are rather a 'serious problem of mental health' due to the 'sophisticated techniques of mind control' used by the new religious movements. These techniques are typically described as almost magical: 'they are capable of working on *anyone*, even on those who may think they are immune'.[13] 'Very few people' if any, join a 'cult' voluntarily; 'normally, joining a cult means only that a mind control operation has been successful'[14] In order to counter these 'mind control operations', most post-rationalist anti-cult movements, if not all, would be glad to suggest a deprogrammer and cooperate with them.

Rationalist counter-cult movements are typified in the US by the Christian Research Institute (CRI). No offence is intended by this comment, but it seems somewhat paradoxical to label its founder, Walter Martin (1928-1989), a 'rationalist'. On the contrary, in this context, 'rationalist' means that, although the background assumptions are religious, 'cults' are explained here mainly through empirical elements, including false theology and heresy, rather than by relying principally or exclusively on the Devil's activities. 'Rationalist' counter-cultists, as faithful and normally conservative Christians, of course believe in the personal existence of the Devil, and do not rule out the possibility that the Devil is pleased because of the success of the 'cults'. On the other hand, they think that an excessive interest in the Devil is unhealthy and typical of the 'cults' themselves, and first seek alternative explanations. In Europe rationalist counter-cult movements are probably less common than in the United States, but they do exist. I would include in this field the Dialog Center International — ecumenical, but Lutheran in its origin — founded by Johannes Aagaard in Denmark; and the Roman Catholic organization G.R.I.S. in Italy. Normally, because they do not immediately blame all the 'cults' on the Devil's action, these kind of movements and ministries are more interested in doing scholarly work and in reading the works of secular scholars, although of course they often do not agree with them.

I propose that we call the Christian groups whose explanation of the 'cultic' phenomena heavily involves the Devil, the *post-rationalist counter-cult movements*. These kind of movements are not well established in Europe, although some examples do exist. In Catholic circles, post-rationalist counter-cultism of the 'spiritual warfare' kind is normally discouraged. It surfaces, however, from time to time, in counter-cult authors who are members of, or influenced by, the Catholic Charismatic Renewal, which in turn is obviously influenced by trends prevailing in English-speaking Pentecostalism, where 'spiritual warfare' and 'demonization' theories have been widely discussed and partially accepted.[15] In Italy,

Tarcisio Mezzetti, an influential lay leader of the Catholic Charismatic Renewal, has lectured extensively against 'cults', the occult and the New Age, introducing many 'spiritual warfare' themes.[16] Another Catholic author who relies on demonic explanations of new religious movements is Armando Pavese of Alessandria, a specialist in parapsychology. In 1992 he devoted a book to Sathya Sai Baba, in which he suggests that Sai Baba's 'miracles' may be 'real' but produced by the Devil, and that the Indian guru may be 'a form of the Antichrist'.[17] Pavese's campaign against Sathya Sai Baba has been instrumental in convincing the Roman Catholic Church to stop the activities of Mario Mazzoleni, a Catholic priest from Bergamo, who had accepted Sai Baba as a divine incarnation and had lectured expressing his belief in Sai Baba and in reincarnation.[18] Mazzoleni was formally excommunicated in 1992, a measure rarely taken against identified individuals in today's Roman Catholic Church. But in general it is rare that the kind of arguments used by the post-rationalist counter-cult movements about 'demonic' influence in the 'cults' and 'demonization' are taken seriously by mainstream Churches in Europe.

1c. A second sub-typology may perhaps be introduced. I believe that the well-known distinction proposed by Stark and Bainbridge[19] between audience cults, client cults and cult movements, may be relevant, both for the anti-cult and also for the counter-cult movement. Some crusaders against the 'cults' seek only an *audience*: they write books and occasionally appear on television, but they do not care to organize their followers. Others seek *clients*, offering a wide range of counselling services for a fee, from the extreme 'deprogramming' to the more gentle 'exit counselling'. Finally, leaders of the crusade against the 'cults' may decide to organize social *movements*, with a newsletter, a hierarchy, and a close-knit system of beliefs and attitudes. Particularly when the movement against the 'cults' belongs to the post-rationalist group, it may exhibit the same features it attributes to 'cults' themselves. 'Many of the same arguments used against new religions can be plausibly made against the ACM [anti-cult movements] as well'.[20] Some movements against the 'cults' in fact exhibit a set of beliefs — primarily the belief in a widespread and mysterious 'cult conspiracy' — that does not appear to be shared by the society at large. When members of these movements against the 'cults' start regulating their lives on the basis of this set of beliefs they become a marginal group, devoted to, and identified by, persuasions regarded by the majority as bizarre and even deviant; they become, in their own sense of the word, 'cults'.

2. New Theatres for the Cult Wars

'Cult wars' has become the common expression to express the bitter confrontation between the 'cults' and their opponents, particularly in the 1970s and the 1980s.[21] The distinction between anti-cult and counter-cult movements, however, allows us to identify different theatres where the war has been fought and continues to be fought.

2a.   The first and most obvious theatre concerns the war between the 'cults' and their opponents. This, however, is a strange war from at least two points of view. First, not all who fight against the 'cults' agree about the identity of their enemy. It is not only a matter of a scholarly definition of 'cult' or 'new religious movement', for people who see themselves as being at war have little time for technicalities. What is relevant for them is whether certain specific groups, or categories of groups, are 'cultic' or not. The anti-cult movement — true to its programme of watching deeds, not creeds — would not care for orthodoxy or Christianity. It would also ignore the endorsement or otherwise of the mainstream Churches. The anti-cult movement cares for quantity, not for quality. When it feels that the religious pressure exerted by a group on its members is too high, it calls the group 'cultic'. Most anti-cult movements include in their list Opus Dei, notwithstanding the fact it has been endorsed by the Roman Catholic Church to the point of creating for it a special structure of canon law as a Diocese without a territory, and of beatifying its founder after a surprisingly short time in a ceremony where the Pope told a crowd of 300,000 that Opus Dei is not only a movement endorsed and recommended by the Church but 'a way towards sanctity' and a model of 'Christian humanism' for the whole Catholic community.[22] The anti-cult movement would also include groups normally recognized as legitimate by the Evangelical community. On the other hand, the anti-cult movements normally (though there are a few exceptions) would not regard Mormonism and Freemasonry as 'cults'. Particularly in the United States, they would regard them as established and mainstream institutions,while even a cursory look at the Christian counter-cult literature would show that the single most targeted group is the Mormon Church, and that serious efforts are devoted to warning Christians against Freemasonry. These are not only matters of preference. If 'cult' is defined as heresy from the standpoint of Evangelical Christianity, it becomes normal to include Mormonism. If, on the other hand, 'cult' is described secularly as a non-mainline, high-pressure group, then the inclusion of Mormonism becomes questionable, at best. Of course there is no single definition of 'orthodoxy', but in the most recent authoritative statement by the Roman Catholic magisterium — the General Report of Francis Cardinal Arinze at the Concistory of 1991 (where the Pope indicated that new religious movements and abortion were the top pastoral priorities for the 1990s) — it was suggested that Roman Catholics replace the derogatory word 'cults' with 'new religious movements'. The use of 'new religious movements' by the Catholic magisterium is not, however, the same as its use in the English-speaking scholarly literature. The statement distinguishes between various categories of 'new religious movements'. Apart from the more obvious categories, it mentions 'new religious movements of Christian background' — typified by the Mormons and Jehovah's Witnesses — and even 'new religious movements of Protestant background', to indicate the Evangelical and Pentecostal denominations particularly active in proselytization among Latin American Catholics. The project called 'New Religious Movements' of the International Federation of Catholic Universities, sponsored by four Vatican Secretariats in the years 1988-1993, routinely included among its topics discussions on Mormons and even Pentecostals. It is equally true that a number of Evangelical publications of the post-rationalist brand include the Roman Catholic Church among the 'cults', and Walter Martin was heavily criticised for not including the Catholics in his 'kingdom of the cults'.

2b. A second, and less obvious, theatre of war is slowly developing, which concerns the conflict between the anti-cult and the counter-cult movements. The anti-cult movement has not spared its efforts to secure some co-operation from the counter-cult movements and the Churches, and the small group of priests and ministers who attend anti-cult conferences are immediately publicized in news-letters and other literature as the anti-cult movement seeks to promote its image as an umbrella organization coordinating the efforts of all the groups working against the 'cults'. However, Christian counter-cultists are increasingly uncomfortable about this cooperation. Given that most counter-cultists are Evangelicals strongly opposed to secular humanism, and most anti-cultists are precisely secular humanists, they make strange bedfellows. A particularly important article summing up counter-cult criticism of the anti-cult movement was published by Johannes Aagaard in the very first issue of *Update and Dialog*, a magazine 'for associates and friends of the Dialog Center International'. 'The anti-cult movement is in trouble', wrote Aagaard. (For him, scholars also are in trouble, but we will discuss that point later.) In fact the anti-cult organiz-ations 'tend to set the truth-question aside, for they consider the cults only as a means of exploitation, having no genuine religious characteristics'. And this is only part of the story: the anti-cult organizations 'do not themselves ask the truth question.' 'The normal' attitude of parents-organisations [a definition used by Aagaard almost as a synonym of the anti-cult movement] will be that they do not care about 'creeds', only about 'deeds'. They will let people believe what they prefer to believe, and only when the creed is turned into some wrong deeds are the parents-organisations expected to react. This is of course a distinction which cannot be upheld'. 'One has to understand', insists Aagaard, 'that a *creed* is a *deed*. And if one wants to stop the evil deeds one has to react already against evil creeds. But that makes an alternative creed necessary! That is where the parent-organisations are in real trouble'. Either, according to Aagaard, they recognize that they need an 'identity', or a very dangerous tendency may develop: 'that parents against cults are also parents against Christianity'.[23] Al-though Aagaard is willing to admit that the anti-cult movements also do 'valuable' work, the question of the 'inevitability of religion' which he proposes[24] seems to make equally inevitable, in the long run, a conflict between anti-cult and counter-cult movements. There are, also, specific issues adding fuel to the fire. Although very few anti-cult movements (except perhaps in Spain, where local authorities appear strangely tolerant of such practices) will speak out openly in favour of deprogramming in the 1990s, all anti-cult groups recommend exit counselling, whereas the Evangelical counter-cult community is much less enthusiastic. In 1992 an article by the popular counter-cult writers, William M. Alnor and Ronald Enroth, was published by the *Christian Research Journal* (the publication founded by Walter Martin) and took a firm stand against exit counselling, which it described as 'a big business mingled with instances of unethical activity'. The article, which adopted the terminology distinguishing between 'anti-cult' and 'counter-cult' attitudes, charges exit counsellors with doing '»involuntary« exit counseling [a gentler word for deprogramming] using varying rationalisations to justify it', with charging outrageous fees, and with sometimes targeting Christian groups such as the Campus Crusade for Christ. Alnor and Enroth recognize that, urged by the Cult Awareness Network, exit counsellors have met to police excessive fees, but they comment that, 'for the major exit counselors to assemble and decide what their prices should be smacks of a price-fixing cartel similar to what the OPEC nations do regarding oil prices'. The basic question, however, remains the old one dividing counter-cult and anti-cult movements: exit counsellors, the article says, do not care whether their 'clients' will return to Evangelical Christianity. Christians, Alnor and Enroth say, are increasingly 'disturbed by the exit counselors' lack of concern to steer [their 'clients'] toward evangelical Christianity' and 'to guide cult members into a fuller understanding of correct biblical doctrine'. 'In many cases', Alnor and Enroth explain, 'exit counselors deal only with mind control issues, leaving the former cult members to determine *for themselves* what constitutes correct biblical doctrine'. It would be difficult to state more clearly where the problem lies between the anti-cult and the counter-cult movements. The conclusions do not foresee a very peaceful future. 'Christian ministries to cults', according to Alnor and Enroth, 'need to be wary when dealing with exit counselors... We urge caution in making research files available to most exit counselors unless assurances can be made that such information will not be used in unethical situations'. Not is the problem only ethical. 'For the Christian', write Alnor and Enroth, 'the cults represent more than merely a social or psychological problem. In a very central way they are a *spiritual* problem... A truly Christian concern proceeds from an eternal perspective. What good is accomplished if people are extricated from cults but their spiritual needs, which draw them into the cults in the first place, including the question of their eternal destiny, are left unattended?'[25] Once Evangelical counter-cultists realise that the answer of the anti-cultists to this question is very different from their own, co-operation becomes very difficult and the strange bedfellows will easily turn into future enemies.

2c. There is, also, a third theatre, opposing what I have called 'rationalist' and 'post-rationalist' opponents of the 'cults'. Within the anti-cult fold, sceptics often exert their scepticism not only against the claim of the paranormal or the 'cults', but also against the wildest claims of their fellow anti-cultists. Sceptics often do not believe in extreme theories of 'magical' brainwashing. Parallel developments have occurred in the Christian counter-cult community. I have chronicled elsewhere the bitter opposition that developed among Evangelical Christian opponents of Mormonism around the question of Devil worship secretly taking place in the Mormon temple. Post-rationalist counter-Mormon organizations have seriously argued that this is indeed the case, and have gone so far as to argue that the very shape of the Mormon temple is 'demonic' and designed to attract Satan's influence. These groups, although admittedly bizarre, are not irrelevant, and their books and cassettes have been widely disseminated in the Evangelical community, not only in the US. They have, however, encountered strong opposition from other Evangelical counter-Mormon groups which in my typology would be called 'rationalist'. Well-known Evangelical counter-Mormons such as Jerald and Sandra Tanner have made abundantly clear that they regard the whole theory of a demonic connection in the Mormon temple architecture and ceremony as ridiculous and basically stupid. The exponents of the 'demonic' theory of Mormonism have reacted very strongly. The

Tanners — key and well respected figures in the anti-Mormon community for decades — have been accused of being Mormon agents, and a fellow counter-Mormon minister has suggested that they are probably demon-possessed and should seek the services of an exorcist.[26] What is worth noting in this story is that both the Tanners and their opponents are Evangelical Christians, and there is no question that both are strongly opposed to Mormonism and have devoted most of their lives to spread counter-Mormon literature. Their bitter confrontation shows that conflicts between rationalist and post-rationalist wings of the same movements could be very real. Another area of this confrontation concerns the alleged epidemic of satanic ritual abuse in the United States and in Europe. Again, the conflict is not between the anti-cult and the counter-cult movements, but between the rationalist and the post-rationalist wings within each movement. While some anti-cult organizations have espoused the theory that there is indeed a large secret international network involved in satanic ritual abuse (though with differing degrees of emphasis), they have found their most out-spoken critics not only within the scholarly community (sociologists generally maintain that no such secret network exists) but also among the rationalist 'debunkers' and professional sceptics. One of the most harsh criticisms of the theory of the satanic conspiracy has been published by a committee with links to CSICOP.[27] Para-doxically, sceptics connected with CSICOP, on this controversy, side with some Christian counter-cultists who are vigorously criticizing other Christian counter-cultists convinced that the satanic con-spiracy indeed exists. It is interesting to note that the same Christian Research Institute (the late Walter Martin organization) which took a stand against deprogramming and exit counselling, also devoted the cover story of its magazine in winter of 1992 to *The Hard Facts about Satanic Ritual Abuse*. The story, by the well-known counter-cult Evangelical authors Bob and Gretchen Passantino, takes one by one the alleged 'proofs' of the satanic conspiracy and shows that not one of them really 'proves' anything. Books like *Michelle Remembers* and *Satan's Underground*, both classics of the conspiracy theory,[28] are heavily criticized, while the very sceptical book edited by the sociologists Richardson, Best and Bromley[29] is called 'a good reference', and studies by the anthropologist Sherrill Mulhern (also critical of the conspiracy theory) are recommended. The conclusion is that 'there is still no substantial, compelling evidence that satanic ritual abuse stories and conspiracy theories are true. Alternative hypotheses more reasonably explain social, professional and personal dynamics reflected in this contemporary satanic panic. The tragedy of broken families, traumatised children and emotionally incapacitated adults provoked by satanic ritual abuse charges is needless and destructive. Careful investigation of the stories, the alleged victims, and the proponents has given us every reason to reject the satanic conspiracy model'.[30] As it can be seen, more than one issue threatens further conflicts, not only between the anti-cult and the counter-cult movements, but also *within* each movement, between the rationalist and the post-rationalist wings. Strange alliances could also be formed, since rationalists in both groups could use similar arguments when dealing with each one's post-rationalist opponents.

2d. From time to time, it may seem that a fourth theatre of war opposes the movements against the cults and the scholars. Occasionally, this war is fought also in the Courts, as the recent US lawsuit filed — and lost — by Margaret Singer and others against a number of scholars and organizations of scholars shows. Scholars are assaulted for their detachment; rather than standing up against the cults, scholars seem to lose time in subtleties, technicalities and non-essential questions. To some extent, this criticism of the scholars is common to the anti-cult and to the counter-cult movements, but the more astute counter-cultists have now recognized that differences exist. Again the anti-cult movement accuses the scholars of downplaying the evil deeds, while the counter-cult movement criticizes the scholars because they seem not to care about evil creeds. Aagaard thinks that a number of scholars have formed what he calls an 'anti-anti-cult movement'. 'This sort of scholar', he writes, 'is in trouble. In his or her neutrality the role of an anti-anti-cult agent takes over the role of the scholar'. According to Aagaard, if 'the anti-cult movement is in trouble... the anti-anti-cult movement is in even more serious trouble by its lack of identity. Show me your hand and I shall tell you who you are. If you have no hand, you are nobody!' Aagaard has other kinds of criticism, too.

'Methodologically', he writes, 'this tends towards science for science's own sake, and this is of course 'old hat'. Like it or not you are part of the game. To pretend to stand aside having no creed of your own makes for cheating'. Here, however, one notices that Aagaard uses the same arguments against the secular anti-cult movement and against the scholarly 'anti-anti-cult movement'. In fact, he writes, 'the anti-cult movement and the anti-anti-cult movement seem to have one important point in common; they *will* and must await the truth question. They will not go for the creeds for that will hit back and force them to take up the age old question: what is truth? And to answer that they would have to take theology seriously'.[31]

3. The Question of Truth

In his 1991 article, Aagaard makes an important point: the 'question of truth' is central in the new cult wars. There are, however, different questions of truth.

3a. First, there is a question of *factual* truth. Before involving different philosophical or ethical judgments, the new cult wars are concerned about whether specific facts are true or not. For example, when post-rationalist anti-cultists and counter-cultists insist that thousands of babies are killed yearly by the satanic conspiracy, their conflict with more rationalist opponents of the cults and with scholars, is not about whether satanism is ethically acceptable or should be tolerated or condoned. The conflict arises because almost all the scholars, and many rationalist opponents of the cults as well, maintain that there is no evidence of a huge, world-wide satanic conspiracy. They do not evaluate the same data in a different way: they deny that the data offered by the theorists of the satanic conspiracy are factually true. Similarly, the controversy about the pretended worship of Satan in the Mormon temple is not about the right of Mormons to worship Satan in their temples or whether such worship should be prohibited. Critics of the 'Lucifer-God' doctrine, including the present author, simply deny that such a thing as Satan worship in Mormon temples existed in the past or exists now. Again, the question is not ethical judgment but factual truth.

Scholars are of course aware that truth is defined in very different ways by Thomas Aquinas or Karl Popper, but very few of them will maintain that propositions such as, 'Ten thousand babies are ritually sacrificed by satanists every year', or 'Mormons secretly worship Satan in their temples', could not be subject to a final and reliable assessment in terms of 'true' or 'false'.

3b. There is, also, truth about *creeds*. Here we should be very careful in order to avoid a possible misunderstanding. Take the often repeated proposition, 'Mormons today believe that Adam, the first man, and God our Father, are one and the same'. Is this proposition 'true'? 'True', here, could have two different meanings. The first meaning is again factual, although Popper warned us that factual statements about the 'World 3' of doctrines and theories are still more difficult to assess. From this point of view, at any rate, the question is, 'Do Mormons today really believe that Adam is God?' The answer is no: Brigham Young said something similar in the 19th century, but today the Adam-God doctrine is regarded as heresy and grounds for excommunication by the Mormon Church.[32] We could then conclude that when anti-Mormons claim that Mormons believe *today* in the Adam-God doctrine (as opposed to in the nineteenth century) their claim is factually false. Of course, they could qualify their statement and argue that *some* Mormons — members of splinter groups — still believe in the doctrine, but this would be a word game. It is an entirely different question whether the Adam-God doctrine is 'true' or 'false' from a theological point of view. From the standpoint of traditional Christianity (and even of contemporary Mormonism) it is certainly 'false'. The two problems — whether it is 'true' that Mormons believe it, and whether the doctrine is theologically 'true' — are obviously different. Aagaard is right when the he argues that most scholars are not interested in assessing whether the doctrines of the new religious movements are 'true' in a theological sense. However, this does not mean that the same scholars are uninterested in determining whether it is 'true' that a particular movement believes in a particular doctrine. While some anti-cult movements insist that they are only interested in deeds, scholars devote a significant amount of time to the reconstruction of each movement's creeds.

Indeed a number of anti-cult and counter-cult publications frankly recognize that they are indebted to scholars for clarifying the complicated creeds of some movements. The difference is that most scholars stop at the reconstruction of the creed, while the movements against the cults go on to brand these creeds as heretical. In this perspective it is worth noting that even the secular anti-cult movements are not as uninterested in creeds as they normally pretend. In fact, they too assess the degree of 'heresy' in the creeds, only they do not assess heresy against classical Christianity but against what they perceive as rationality and the modern world view. I would quote two key spokespersons of the secular anti-cult movement, Margaret Singer and Michael Langone. In court testimony involving ISKCON, Margaret Singer once said: 'I don't use the term 'religion' when I am studying the practices of organizations, because it's irrelevant to me what the content of the organization is'. In another paper, however, Singer stated that the doctrines of the new religious movements are 'cultic' because they are outside 'the world of science, liberalism and rationalism' and, in many cases, 'contrary to the general scientific understanding of causality'. They are impermissible because they do not 'stay within the general tenets of our larger social order which is a democracy and which operates by the theories of scientific causality'.[33] Recently Michael Langone offered a checklist to determine whether training and therapies — generally called 'products' — connected with the New Age are 'cultic'. Questions include: 'Does the product denigrate rationality?'; 'Is there a lack of scientific evidence for the product's alleged effectiveness? (distinguish between scientific evidence and pseudoscientific evidence)'; and 'Would the atheist philosopher Bertrand Russell, the Pope, Billy Graham and an orthodox rabbi agree that the product is nonsense or destructive?'[34] Here we see rationality, science, the 'principle of causality' or the consensus of a large majority (difficult to obtain if it really should include the Pope and Bertrand Russell) as criteria for a latter-day definition of heresy. From a certain point of view, the question of 'truth' is relevant for some and not relevant for others. But from another point of view there are, quite simply, different concepts of 'truth'.

3c. Finally, I would recommend taking a closer look at the question of theological or philosophical 'truth'. It would not be correct to say that 'scholars' in general are not interested in theological truth. After all, few people would deny that the progress of contemporary religious social science has been possible thanks to the contribution of both secular and deeply religious scholars. In an important essay, published as an introduction to the revised American edition of *The Transcendent Unity of Religions* by the esoteric teacher Frithjof Schuon, Huston Smith in fact argued that scholars studying religions have adopted two different attitudes, the 'theological, committed position', evaluating the other religions from the point of view of a deep religious commitment, believing that one religion is 'true'; and the 'objective, detached position', believing that all religions are subjective enterprises, equally 'true' or (according to the scholar's own preferred emphasis) equally 'false'. Huston Smith also chronicles the efforts of some scholars to find a third position, and argues that only the 'perennialist', esoteric approach, the approach of Smith himself, may have a chance of succeeding: religions are different and opposed in their exoteric surface, but united in their esoteric inner core. Apart from the difficult esoteric 'third way', Huston Smith thinks that, normally, the 'theological, committed position', at least when it is not parochial or 'funda-mentalist', guarantees a better understanding of religions than the 'objective, detached position', which is inherently relativist.[35] I have argued elsewhere that Smith's 'third way' is not convincing: the relativist would argue that, since there are as many esoteric doctrines as esoteric teachers, each 'third way' only multiplies the number of 'theological' positions available; while the follower of a particular religion would insist that the esoteric position is only another brand of relativism and the third way is only a special version of the second.[36] But, apart from the esoteric 'third way', Huston Smith is making a good point. The science of religion and the understanding of the religions of the world, old and new alike, progress because of the different points of view offered by two different kinds of scholar, the 'ideological' and the 'relativist'. Indeed, it is their continuous dialogue which adds the fuel which is necessary for the understanding of religion, including the understanding of new religious movements, to progress. Of course the 'theological' scholars are willing to confront also the issue of whether a doctrine is theologically sound or 'true'. But, for dialogue to be possible, they should recognize that even 'non-theological' scholars approach questions of truth continuously at their own non-theological level: questions of factual truth, of truth about whether a particular movement really dpes believe in a particular doctrine, historical truths, methodological truths. As Monsignor Giuseppe Casale explained in his 1993 pastoral letter, clearly a document written from a 'theological' standpoint if one wishes to adopt Huston Smith's distinction, the dialogue between scholars of different persuasions is what CESNUR is all about. The quest for factual truth and the ideal of professionalism in religious sciences are values worth promoting *per se*.[37] The dialogue could certainly include the movements against the 'cults' and the new religious movements themselves, provided that — even if they strongly disagree between themselves and with scholars on theological truth and on its importance — they are at least prepared to look for a common and fair standard of factual truth about both deeds and creeds. This is the only way to end in the 1990s the 'cult wars', whose benefits have been dubious at best for all the sides involved.

Notes

1. See M. Introvigne, *Le nuove Religioni*, Milan: SugarCo. 1989 with bibliography of J. Gordon Melton's works. I have benefited from a number of discussions with Melton on this point.

2. See for instance William M. Alnor and Ronald Enroth, 'Ethical Problems in Exit Counseling', *Christian Research Journal*, 14:3, 1992, pp. 14-19.

3. See e.g. 'Scientologists Sue Critics', *Christianity Today*, 37:2, 8 February 1993, pp.52 and 65.

4. Mons. Giuseppe Casale, *Nuova religiosità e nuova evangelizzazione*, pastoral letter of March 6, 1993, Casale Monferrato: Piemme, 1993, pp. 35-38.

5. This is still true today: see Emmanuel Feldman and Joel B. Wolowelsky (eds.), *The Conversion Crisis: Essays from the Pages of 'Tradition'*, New York: KTAV/The Rabbinical Council of America, 1990.

52   *Massimo Introvigne*

6. Cf. Natalie Isser and Lita Linzer Schwartz, *The History of Conversion and Contemporary Cults*, New York: Peter Lang, 1988; see also Lita Linzer Schwartz, 'The Historical Dimension of Cultic Techniques of Persuasion and Control', *The Cultic Studies Journal*, 8:1 1991, pp. 37-45.

7. Barbara Hargove, 'Social Sources and Consequences of the Brainwashing Controversy', in David G. Bromley and James T. Richardson (eds.), *The Brainwashing/Deprogramming Controversy: Sociological, Psychological, Legal and Historical Perspectives*, New York: Edwin Mellen, 1983, pp. 299-308, esp. p. 303.

8. Frank Peretti, *This Present Darkness*, Ventura, Cal.: Regal, 1986.

9. Robert A. Guelich, 'Spiritual Warfare: Jesus, Paul and Peretti', *Pneuma: The Journal of the Society for Pentecostal Studies*. 13:1, 1991, pp. 33-64. A sequel has suggested that large law firms and organizations like ACLU are heavily involved in the demonic cult conspiracy: F.Peretti, *Piercing the Darkness*, Wheaton, Illinois: Crossway Books, 1991.

10. On CSICOP, see J. Gordon Melton, Jerome Clark and Aidan A. Kelly, *New Age Almanac*, Detroit: Visible Ink Press, 1991, pp. 105-14.

11. *Ibid*, p.114.

12. ARIS, *Nuovi culti*, Flyer, 1992, p.4.

13. *Ibid*, p.1.

14. *Ibid*, p.3.

15. Cf. R.A. Guelich, *op. cit.*; Thomas D. Pratt, 'The Need to Dialogue: A Review of the Debate on Signs, Wonders, Miracles and Spiritual Warfare in the Literature of the Third Wave Movement', *Pneuma: The Journal of the Society for Pentecostal Studies*, 13:1, 1991, pp. 7-32.

16. See Tarcisio Mezzetti, '...Bel è coperto di confusione'...(Ger 50,2),", *I quaderni di 'Venite e Vedrete'*, n.d., 1-16.

17. Armando Pavese, *Sai Baba. Anatomia del 'Nuovo Cristo' e dei suoi miracoli attraverso la psicologia del profondo, la parapsicologia e la fede cristiana*, Casale Monferrato (Alessandria): Piemme, 1992, p. 205. The main source for the identification of Sathya Sai Baba with the Antichrist is Tal Brooke, *Lord of the Air: Tales of a Modern Antichrist*, Eugene, OR: Harvest House, 1990.

18. Don Mario Mazzoleni, *Un sacerdote incontra Sai Baba*, Milano: Armenia Editore, 1991.

19. Rodney Stark and William Sims Bainbridge, *The Future of Religion: Secularization, Revival, and Cult Formation*, Berkeley, Los Angeles and London: University of California Press, 1986.

20. Brock K. Kilbourne and James T. Richardson, 'Cultphobia', *Thought* 61(1986), pp. 258-61.

21. See for example Anson D. Shupe, Jr. and David G. Bromley, *The New Vigilantes: Deprogrammers, Anti-Cultists and the New Religions*, Beverly Hills and London: Sage, 1980; see also James A. Beckford, *Cult Controversies: The Societal Response to the New Religious Movements*, London and New York: Tavistock, 1985.

22. John Paul II, *Omelia nella Messa di Beatificazione*, May 17, 1992 (in Italian), in *17 maggio 1992. La beatificazione di José Maria Escrivá, fondatore dell'Opus Dei*, Milan: Ares, 1992. Alberto Moncada, the main spokesman for the 'cultic' nature of Opus Dei within the anti-cult movement, replied to this objection in personal correspondence with the present author arguing that the Roman Catholic Church under John Paul II is becoming itself 'increasingly cultic'. The anti-cult movements are not willing to exclude mainline Churches from their definition of 'cult' but reserve the right to enquire on a case by case basis. In 1986 the French anti-cult movement ADFI stated that the Roman Catholic Church (but in fact also its 'Protestant and Eastern Orthodox' counterparts) exhibited a number of 'cultic' features before Vatican II, including the claim 'to be the only true Church', a universal 'Catechism' with questions 'to be memorised', severe 'fasting', etc. (Alain Woodrow, 'Les Eglises sont-elles des sectes?', BULLES, 2nd quarter of 1986 pp. 6-8). By reintroducing some of the features regarded as 'cultic' by ADFI is the Roman Catholic Church becoming 'cultic' again?

23. Johannes Aagaard, 'A Christian Encounter with New Religious Movements and New Age', *Update & Dialog*, I:1, 1991, p. 21.

24. *Ibid*, p.23.

25. Alnor and Enroth, *op. cit.*

26. For the whole story and a bibliography, see the present author's 'Quand le diable se fait Mormon. Le Mormonisme comme complot diabolique: l'affaire Schnoebelen', *Politica Hermetica*, 6, 1992, pp. 36-54; and 'The Devil Makers: Contemporary Evangelical Fundamentalist Anti-Mormonism', *Dialogue: A Journal of Mormon Thought*, 27:1, 1994, pp. 153-69.

27. CSER (Committee for the Scientific Examination of Religion), *Satanism in America*, Buffalo:CSER, 1989. In a similar vein social psychologist Richard Ofshe, although a prominent spokesperson for the anticult morement, has exposed the 'strange stories of Satanic abuse' as 'pseudomemories' mostly created by therapists: see Richard Ofshe. Ethan Watters, *Making Monsters: False Memories, Psychotherapy, and Sexual Hysteria*, New York, Charles Scribner's Sons 1994, particularly pp. 177-204.

28.   Cf. Michelle Smith amd Lawrence Pazder, *Michelle Remembers*, New York: Congdon & Lattés, 1980; Lauren Stratford, *Satan's Underground*, Eugene, OR: Harvest House 1988.

29.   James T. Richardson, Joel Best and David G. Bromley (eds.), *The Satanism Scare*, New York: Aldine de Gruyter, 1991.

30.   Bob Passantino and Gretchen Passantino, 'The Hard Facts about Satanic Ritual Abuse', *Christian Research Journal*, 14:3, 1992, pp. 20-23 and 32-34.

31.   Aagaard, *op. cit.*, pp. 21-22.

32.   For a history of all these questions, see David John Buerger, 'The Adam-God Doctrine', *Dialogue: A Journal of Mormon Thought*, 15:1, 1982, pp. 14-58.

33.   Margaret Singer, testimony in George v. ISKCON, 27-75-65 Orange Country California Supreme Court, 5, 452-53;   Ead., 'Interview', *Spiritual Counterfeits Newsletter*, 2, 1984, pp. 6 and 12.

34.   Michael D. Langone, 'What is »New Age«?', *The Cult Observer*, 10:1, 1993, pp. 8-10.

35.   Huston Smith, 'Introduction to the Revised Edition', in Frithjof Schuon, *The Transcendent Unity of Religions*, 2nd American Edition, Wheaton, Illinois: The Theosophical Publishing House, 1984, pp. IX-XXVII.

36.   See M. Introvigne, *Introduzione*, in Huston Smith, *Le grandi religioni orientali*, Italian ed., Carnago (Varese): SugarCo, 1993.

37.   Casale, *op. cit.*, p.96. One notices that while the document emphasises a possible consensus between believers and non-believers on *factual* truths about both deeds and creeds, it does not mention a consensus on *ethical* truths (in the form of propositions like 'all should agree that telling lies for the sake of proselytization is wrong'). In fact, while Catholic moral theology normally argues that 'natural' moral truths may be recognized by human reason apart from their theological foundation, theologians also realize that for practical purposes it is much more difficult to find a real agreement, apart from some very broad general principles, on the 'truth' of specific moral propositions.

PART ONE

RELIGIOUS DEVELOPMENTS
IN THE FORMER
COMMUNIST BLOC

CHAPTER 3

The Evangelical Thrust into Eastern Europe in the 1990s

J. Gordon Melton

It can be argued that when the elements contributing to the present rapid religious transition being experienced by the Eastern European countries are sorted out, the Evangelical Christian community will have emerged as the most significant factor altering the shape of the religious scene in the next century. It is the only religious community which has developed a comprehensive systematic plan for filling the huge religious vacuum created by several generations of political leadership which have been hostile to religion and to public religious expression. Also, the changes in Eastern Europe coincided with the conclusion of two decades of intensive global missionary planning and mobilization, and the fall of the Berlin Wall occurred just as a call was issued throughout the Evangelical movement for a massive new missionary push during the decade of the 1990s. Thus, by coincidence or by providence, depending upon one's view, recently erected structures have quickly adjusted to take advantage of the new opportunities in Eastern Europe.[1]

Before World War II

The new push into Eastern Europe is rooted in the European Evangelical mission which began in the 1920s.[2] To be sure, during the nineteenth century and the early twentieth century, various renewal movements from Methodism to Pentecostalism had spread through various parts of Europe, but in the decade following World War I, a few American evangelicals began to question the image of Christian Europe. Based upon a different picture of Europe, that

in fact it was a Christian mission field of some importance, analogous to Africa or China, some pioneering North American mission
groups selected several communities for conversionist efforts:
Roman Catholics, Jews and Eastern Europeans. The very first
American missionary thrust was into Catholic Belgium. Immediately
after the War, as part of the relief effort, distribution of Bibles had
begun among soldiers, orphans and war victims. Ralph C. and Edith
Norton decided to launch evangelistic efforts. They founded the
Brussels Bible Institute to train Christian workers and actively
established preaching places to be eventually manned by the
school's graduates. The progress of their work was reported to
conservative Protestant churches in America through such periodi-
cals as the *Sunday School Times*. The preaching centres of the Belgian
Gospel Mission grew into congregations which eventually banded
together as the Free Evangelical Church.

A second effort in Europe began in the early 1920s. While the
war raged, G.P. Raud, an Estonian, had left for the United States
where he met Thomas MacDowell and his wife. Raud shared his
concern for his homeland, and together the three founded the
Russian and Slavonic Bible Union which began work in the Baltic
states in 1922. From its base in Estonia, Lithuania and Latvia, within
five years Raud's work spread to Poland, Czechoslovakia and the
Ukraine, and to the Roman Catholic populations in Germany,
France, Spain and Great Britain. The Union's missionaries in Eastern
Europe paid particular attention to the Jewish communities. In 1926
the name was changed to European Christian Mission, and it is now
known as the Bible Christian Union.

The Belgian Gospel Mission and the Russian and Slavonic Bible
Union were joined by a third important missionary movement in
1926. The American Bethel Mission was founded by Leon Rosen-
berg, a converted Jew who had pastored a small evangelical congregation in Odessa, Russia, through the years of the War into the
1920s. In 1922 the revolutionary government finally caught up with
him and arrested him. He left Russia and relocated, first to
Frankfurt, Germany, and then to Lodz, Poland, where he built a
vital Jewish mission which was destroyed by the Nazis shortly after
the beginning of World War II. The headquarters was subsequently
transferred to the United States.

A fourth important group founded during this period was the Slavic Gospel Association. Peter Deyneka had left Russia in 1914. Finding his way to Chicago in 1920 he was converted at the famous Moody Church and two years later entered the St. Paul Bible School. He decided to become a missionary to his people and as early as 1925 began to make evangelistic visits to the area of his birth which, due to changing boundaries after the War, had become a part of Poland. He worked for a while with the All Russian Evangelical Christian Union and the Christian and Missionary Alliance, but in 1924 organized the Russian Gospel Association. The Association continued the work in Poland and in additional targeted the many Russian communities outside the Soviet Union.

This substantial work was effectively destroyed during World War II, especially the Jewish missions which were the first to go. Political changes following the War meant that mission stations in many countries could not be re-established and as a result the headquarters was moved and missionary efforts redirected. In some cases ethnic communities in North America were the new targets. The European mission of the 1930s was gone, but never forgotten.

After World War II

The atmosphere in Europe immediately after World War II completely changed American attitudes toward the continent. Americans responded fully to Churchill's 'Iron Curtain' symbolism and watched with dread and loathing the spread of what was seen as atheism and totalitarian rule from Russia through Eastern Europe into Albania and Yugoslavia. At the same time American Christians responded to the need to rebuild Western Europe. They saw first-hand the devastation of the European Churches which had lost thousands of buildings, the displacement of millions of people by the War, and, possibly most important, the lack of support by the majority of Europeans for their religious structures and the seeming ignorance of the public to what Evangelicals defined as vital faith. As a result, Evangelical Christians serving in the European theatre called for the American Church, which had heretofore concentrated on the third world, to add Europe to their list of concerns. Immediately new agencies arose to target European audiences.

Meanwhile, changes were occurring in conservative Christianity in the United States which greatly altered the amount of attention it could give to missions in general. The 1920s and 1930s had been a time of intense turmoil, the period during which the fundamentalist-modernist controversy consumed a significant part of the attention of the evangelical Christian community. Conservative Protestant Christians wrestled for, and lost, control of the major American denominations, and their position was further wakened by the diversion of energy into the creation of new independent Church bodies such as the Orthodox Presbyterian Church and the Conservative Baptist Association. However, the 1940s were a time of re-grouping and a new wave of conservative Church leaders emerged ready to stop licking their wounds and eager to place the controversies of past decades in a secondary position. They took a positive stance toward the world and aggressively organized for evangelism and missionary work.

They dropped the designation 'Fundamentalist' and assumed the name 'evangelical' under which they created structures to embody their new perspectives. They found a leader, a young evangelist named Billy Graham; they started a periodical, *Christianity Today*; and they founded a school, Fuller Theological Seminary in Pasadena, California. Among the first organizations to embody the new enthusiasm was Youth for Christ. Founded in 1944, it quickly spread across the US and was among the first American organizations to enter Europe as World War II closed. Building on the youthful energy of its teenage membership, Youth for Christ quickly swept across Western Europe and by 1948 was ready to call its first European conference which gathered in Switzerland. Quite apart from the War, evangelicals saw Europe as a continent crippled by apathy, disunity and theological liberalism, which together had led the Church into a general state of decline. Evangelicals seized upon every negative appraisal of the Church by European Church leaders as further evidence of the need for its presence.

Among the early Youth for Christ workers was Robert Evans, a young pastor who had been a chaplain in Europe during the War. He argued that the most fruitful way to use American resources would be to concentrate on the training of European nationals to do the evangelistic work. As a result he founded the first Evangelical school, the European Bible Institute, which opened in Paris in 1950 with six students. The missionary work which grew as the extension of the school was incorporated as the Greater European Mission in 1952. A second school opened in Germany 1955 and the work has progressed from country to country ever since.

The next major step in the development of a European mission originated at that Youth for Christ meeting in 1948 in Switzerland. Among the attendees was Paul Freed, the Youth for Christ director for South Carolina. He returned home dedicated to starting missionary work in Spain. It became his passion over the next four years, when he finally was able to return to Spain to do a motion picture on protestantism in that country. The film became the vehicle for his raising the initial funds to open a radio station in Tangier. Beginning as a 2,500 watt station, the *Voice of Tangier* steadily increased its power and its range from just Spain to all of Europe and, eventually, to the Middle East. At the time, space on European radio stations was unavailable except for the very expensive time on Radio Luxembourg and Radio Monte Carlo. Licences could not be secured to erect a religious station in any of the European countries, where governments have preferred to keep control of radio frequencies. Thus the *Voice of Tangier* filled an important need.

By the end of the decade, Tangier had come under the control of the newly formed post-war government of Morocco. The Moroccan government nationalized all radio stations in the country as of the end of 1959 and the *Voice of Tangier* was shut down. In this crisis situation, European governments were again canvassed. Still no government would allow a privately operated religious station, except one, Monaco. Arrangements were finalized and a long-term lease of an abandoned radio facility built by the Germany Army secured. After being off the air for some months while money for new equipment was raised, Trans World Radio began broadcasting in October 1960.

Fifteen years of expanding Evangelical activity in Europe culminated in 1974 in the International Conference on World Evangelism which gathered at Lausanne in 1974. This conference hammered out the Lausanne Covenant which set an agenda for the Evangelical mission worldwide and established an ongoing Committee on World Evangelism with headquarters in Geneva. Lausanne focused two issues of particular importance. First, it called for a new emphasis upon 'unreached peoples'. Speakers pointed out that there were literally thousands of distinct peoples, communities distinguished by a separate language and culture, which had never been evangelized. Lausanne picked up the suggestions which had been made for a generation, that these people should be given priority over the groups which had been evangelized over the last centuries.

Secondly, action on the 'unreached peoples' required information on who they were, most being peoples of whom no-one in the West was aware. Thus a continuing project of information gathering and processing was launched, the major product to date being David Barrett's *World Christian Encyclopedia*. As each 'unreached people' group was spotted, an attempt was made to motivate one of the Bible publication groups to prepare a new translation of the Bible in their language, and for some Evangelical community to underwrite the cost of sending in missionaries. Having a strategy of targeting 'unreached peoples' immediately raised the question of legal barriers to evangelism, and the problems of conducting evangelical activities in countries which either outlawed or severely restricted the work. Such strategic planning became a distinct sub-area of missionary theoretical work. While Islamic countries were the major concern, Eastern Europe was also high on the agenda.

The Lausanne impetus gave birth to what has become the major guiding vision of contemporary evangelicalism, 'AD 2000 and Beyond'. The vision grew out of a focus on the symbolic power of the end of the second Christian millennium which emerged in a number of Christian groups and even some more secularized sources. However, it was Chinese minister, Thomas Wang, the founder of the Chinese Coordination Centre on World Evangelism in the 1970s, who articulated the vision in its most comprehensive and accepted form. From his position as the International Director of the Lausanne Committee, Wang has called for the thousands of evangelical missionary councils, movements, agencies and Churches to seize the unique opportunity to focus their efforts to reach the unreached by the year 2000, and has specified possible annual goals to be met as steps along the way. In part, AD 2000 and Beyond has been successful due to its call for co-ordinated but independent action in response to stated needs by the different evangelical groups, rather than a centralized, controlled and directed programme from Geneva or the United States, or some other umbrella agency.

Eastern Europe and AD 2000

European missions began in the early part of this century as the concern of a few. By the 1980s, Europe was very much a mission concern as were the other continents. And by the time of the fall of the Berlin Wall and the subsequent break-up of the former Soviet Union, Eastern Europe was a special part of an overall missionary planning strategy to reach the unreached. Currently, in North America several hundred missionary-sending agencies champion the cause of European missions and their work is undergirded by several non-sending organizations whose prime concern is the motivation of Evangelicals to respond to the vision of world evangelism.

The US Center for World Mission in Pasadena, California, is a complex of strategic, training and mobilization structures which sees itself as a nerve centre for the missionary enterprise. The Center works closely with AD 2000 and Beyond, an international movement centred in Singapore with the American headquarters in the San Francisco Bay area. Both organizations call for action toward the 'unreached peoples', many of which are in the territory of the former Soviet Union. Both co-operate with the 'Adopt a People Movement', headquartered at the Center, which encourages congregations to sponsor missionaries (through numerous sending agencies) to a selected unreached group.

Among the organizations which give attention primarily to Eastern Europe is Issachar, headquartered in the CIS. The Bible Christian Union has developed 'Project Winning Russia by Radio', a packet of materials to introduce Church schools to the needs and opportunities for missions in the CIS. Their effort is supplemented by the National Association of Evangelicals, the largest co-operative agency of North American Evangelicals, to mobilize and network its affiliated groups to respond to current opportunities in Eastern

Europe. Together, these and other agencies have effectively presented the vision of a Eastern Europe to be won. Currently over 400 denominational mission boards and independent missionary agencies are operating there. So vast is the scope of the work that I have selected two model areas for consideration, the Commonwealth of Independent States (with special consideration of Russia and the Ukraine) and Romania.

The Commonwealth of Independent States

Without doubt, Russia and the CIS have been the main recipients of Evangelical missionary action. Evangelicals had long resented the Soviet government's restriction on the printing and distribution of bibles, and for years have delighted in supporting programmes to smuggle bibles into the Soviet Union. Meanwhile African missionaries had produced hard data that the spread of the Church among various tribes was directly tied to the translation of the bible into their particular languages. Thus, in response to the changes of the 1980s, it was only natural that bible translation and distribution would top the missionary agenda. The effort has been impressive by any standards.

The International Bible Society headquarters in Colorado Springs, Colorado and the Evangelical Christian Publishers Association in Tempe, Arizona, launched Project Moscow which resulted in the printing and distribution of four million Russian-language New Testaments by the beginning of 1992. Terry Law Ministries of Tulsa, Oklahoma, combined efforts with International/Russian Radio/ Television headed by Hannu Haukka in Finland (now re-located to Moscow) to produce eight million New Testaments and an additional eight million 16-page children's bibles. Ironically, Law has contracted with the Chinese government in Beijing to print the bibles and ship them to Russia. Meanwhile, Haukka has opened a centre in Moscow and broadcasts regularly over the central television network throughout the country. In 1992 he began the process of distributing the bibles to his listening audience. Between 1989 and 1992, The Bible League of South Holland, Michigan, gave away eight million Russian and Ukrainian Bibles. Bibles for the

World of Wheaton, Illinois, has sent over one million bibles to Russia.

All of these efforts have been matched by the American Bible Society which has begun the distribution of 30 million bibles in 17 languages in Russia and Eastern Europe. Gideon International is now distributing 400,000 bibles per month in Russia and Eastern Europe. By 1992 the Assemblies of God had distributed five million children's bibles in Russia. Other American organizations with programmes of bible printing and/or distribution include Bibles for All, Bibles for Russia, Christian Printing Mission, Door of Hope International, Eastern European Mission and Bible Foundation, Eastern European Evangelism International World Ministries, Mission without Borders International, Open Doors with Brother Andre, Russian Bible Society and the World Bible Translation Center.

In addition, International Prison Ministry has distributed 500,000 bibles in Russian prisons. The Ukraine has been especially targeted by the Masters Foundation (Canada) which has produced one million children's bibles in Ukrainian which it distributes through the Ukrainian Union of Christians of Evangelical Pentecostal Faith. Ukrainian Family Bible Association has launched a programme to send one million bibles to the Ukraine. The Ukrainian Missionary and Bible Society has since 1988 sent one-and-a-half million bibles to the Ukraine. World Missionary Press has shipped two million scripture booklets and is preparing several million copies of the Gospel of St.Luke for Russia and the Ukraine. All of these North American efforts have been joined by additional large-scale Bible publication/distribution programmes from the United Kingdom and Western Europe.

The production of Bibles has been supplemented by the production of massive quantities of Christian literature — tracts, bible study material, hymn books and correspondence courses. For example, Gospel Literature International of Rosemead, California, recently dismantled its extensive state-of-the-art printing and publishing centre in Finland, and moved its equipment to St. Petersburg. Several agencies have in a like manner opened publishing centres in the CIS. Christian Life Ministries, the Florida-based firm which publishes *Charisma* magazine, had launched a

Russian-language counterpart in Moscow, with subscriptions paid by Americans.

Radio and Television

In spite of the several well-publicized set-backs to radio and television ministries by Jim Bakker's and Jimmy Swaggart's escapades, mass media are still seen as the most productive avenues by which to reach large groups of people. Throughout the 1970s and 1980s evangelical Christian radio and short-wave broadcasts saturated Russia and Eastern Europe through broadcasts over Trans World Radio Europe, the Far East Broadcasting Company and Radio Free Europe. They have now been joined by additional broadcasts which include Russian Christian Radio (sponsored by the Pocket Testament League) which has developed 25 hours of weekly programming for radio throughout Russia; International/Russian Radio/TV which broadcasts the CBN (Pat Robertson) children's Bible programmes over one of the national networks of Russian television. The Voice of the World Network beams 135 hours of programming per week in a variety of languages spoken in the CIS.

As a result of all of these efforts, most parts of the CIS now receive Christian broadcasts twenty-four hours a day on radio and an undetermined amount of Christian programming is carried weekly over the national Russian television networks, including prime-time weekday evening programmes.

Other

The bible distribution and the mass media evangelism efforts provide a welcoming environment in which a variety of missionary programmes can emerge. Given the massive task of evangelizing 300 million people and the experience of successful missionary programmes in the past generation, North Americans have concentrated time and energy into training indigenous leadership. Thus several groups, such as Fuller Theological Seminary in Pasadena, California, the Assemblies of God and the Gospel Missionary Union, have opened ministerial training schools in Russia, while Denver Conservative Baptist Seminary, St. James Bible College and the

Greater European Mission, have done likewise in the Ukraine. Leighton Ford Ministries regularly holds evangelism institutes in the CIS. Eastern European Evangelism and Evangelism Explosion have concentrated on lay leadership training in evangelism.

Future Russian leaders now in colleges have been targeted by organizations such as First Foundations which sends Christian books to Russian colleges and universities. InterVarsity arranges exchange programmes which place American students on Russian college campuses where they establish Christian fellowships which seek the conversion of fellow students.

There not being the same kind of issue of separation of Church and state in the CIS as in the United States, evangelical Christians have targeted the Russian public school system. CoMission, a network of Christian organizations, headquartered in Atlanta, Georgia, has established a five-year plan to place a knowledgeable Christian teacher in each of the CIS public schools. To that end they are taking hundreds of teacher-trainers to Russia to conduct workshops for public school teachers. Their effort is supplemented by the Slavic Gospel Association's programme to put a 'Faith Discovery Library' of basic Christian literature in every public school in Russia.

Leading the many efforts at direct Church-forming missionary efforts is that of Dawn Missions. Dawn pioneered the 'Discipling a Whole Nation' movement and in 1992 announced that it had combined with the United World Mission to begin a saturation Church planting effort in the 15 Republics of the former Soviet Union. The goal is to establish a Church in every village and urban neighbourhood in the immediate future, by the year 2000 if possible. Dawn is quite confident that it can motivate evangelicals to establish as many as 200,000 congregations in the CIS. This goal is similar to an earlier goal to establish 20,000 new congregations in Britain during the same time period.

Among the most important North American groups to emerge in the new Russia is YWAM (Youth with a Mission). Since its founding, YWAM has established work in over 100 countries worldwide, but in recent years it has established a Slavic ministries office, which now sends 2000 missionaries a year, most in short-term appointments with mission teams, into the CIS and Eastern

Europe. In 1992 it sponsored the first Christian Arts festival in Russia since the revolution, but its main emphasis has been on street evangelism and the founding of Discipleship Training Schools to assist young Christians to become established in their new faith.

Romania

Outside the CIS, each of the states of the former Soviet bloc and the nations of the old Warsaw Pact have experienced heightened attention, in varying degrees, from the Evangelical community. It would be fairly easy and very enlightening to detail the events in each of these nations, but time and space does not allow. Apart from the several Islamic states, Bulgaria remains the least open to outside religious influence, though even there some 27 different evangelical agencies have opened work. The greatest activity has been in Romania into which over a hundred agencies have moved since the fall of the Ceausescu government.

Romania has a distinctly different religious history from that of the CIS. Totalitarianism and active state religious persecution came only after World War II and in its greatest force with the emergence of Ceausescu in 1965. Unlike Russia, where Evangelicalism had gained only a token presence prior to the Revolution and had only a minuscule following outside the show churches in the major cities, Romania had experienced several decades of evangelism prior to the rigid regulations of the last 25 years. Outlawed for a period in the 1940s, evangelicals saw the absolute bans lifted in the 1950s, but the several groups were severely regulated and their growth slowed.

The Baptist Church began in the late nineteenth century and a Baptist Union was formed in 1919. During the Ceausescu years there were some 1,000 Baptist churches with approximately 200,000 members, but only about 150 pastors. The pentecostal Church of God (Cleveland, Tennessee) entered the country in 1922. By the 1980s it had attained the same size as the Baptists. The Seventh-day Adventists had about 50,000 members. Closely associated with the evangelical groups is The Lord's Army, a renewal group within the Orthodox Church which functions like many pietist proto-Protestant groups in previous centuries in other countries. The Lord's Army has a close relationship with the Baptists and Pentecostals and is somewhat alienated from the Orthodox hierarchy. Evangelicals gained a new respect in the post-Ceausescu years as it became known that an evangelical pastor's refusal to follow government orders was the spark that ignited the Revolution.

Bible Publication

Like Russia, Romania has become the recipient of a massive influx of bibles. The American Bible Society and Gideon International have included Romanian bibles on their multi-million bible publication/distribution programme. The International Bible Society has distributed two million bibles, and other significant efforts have been launched by Door of Hope International, the Eastern European Bible Mission and David D. Cook. International World Ministries has distributed 100,000 New Testaments and followed that effort with the establishment of bible correspondence courses in Romanian.

Radio and Television

While Romanian-language broadcasting has not reached anything near the level achieved in Russia, nevertheless Romanian programmes have been carried regularly on Trans World and Radio Free Europe stations. In addition the Romanian Missionary Society, which already produces 25 hours per week of broadcasting over Radio Free Europe, is moving to establish the first 24-hour Christian station in Romania.

Other

Because of some prime-time news coverage, the plight of Romanian orphans has assumed a unique role in Romanian evangelism. Several groups, such as Focus on Romania and Eastern Europe (FREE), have included the planting of orphanages among their missionary tasks. Ministerial training for Romanian pastors is being conducted by the European Evangelistic Society from their school in Vienna. The Church Triumphant of Pittsburg, California, has established two schools to train lay leaders in Romania and has plans to open a bible college. The International Institute for Christian Studies has moved to create departments of Christian studies at the state universities in Romania and to add supporting special collections of books at the university libraries.

Church planting activity is being done in co-ordination with the older evangelical Churches. Impact Ministries is working with the Baptist Union to found new Baptist Churches in the country. Evangelism Missions is erecting Church buildings for congregations in small towns. And Friendship Missions is sponsoring a number of short-term missions which include the establishment of summer youth camps.

Conclusions

We could continue, but enough has been said to convey the extent of the broadly co-ordinated effort to saturate Eastern Europe with Evangelical Christian ministries and workers. Sending-agencies in North America underpin the work in Europe with a vast motivational programme which emphasizes the present opportunity for Eastern European evangelism and which heightens the emphasis by noting the possibly ephemeral nature of that opportunity. And evangelicals have responded with massively concentrated publishing efforts, the provision of medical/relief programmes, the training of tens of thousands of nationals for leadership roles, and the establishment of permanent indigenous structures.

This effort suggests that, all things being equal, within the next decade in the CIS, Evangelicalism will emerge as a movement with a strength equal to, if not greater than that of, either the Orthodox Church or Roman Catholicism. It seems likely that it will gain prominence in many areas in which those two older Churches are now weak if not non-existent. It is also likely that Evangelicalism may be the entry door by which additional thousands of people discover a vital religion on their road to return to Orthodoxy and Roman Catholicism. Thus while the news is focusing upon the continued problems of the government and the economy in making the transition to capitalism, the hearts of the people may be reshaped by North American (and Western European) evangelism.

Notes

1. This essay was drawn from a large set of material published in recent years describing the new missionary thrust into Eastern Europe, especially: Sharon Linzey, M. Holt Ruffin and Mark R. Elliot, (eds), *East West Christian Organizations: A Directory of Western Christian Organizations Working in East Central Europe and the Newly Independent States Formerly Part of the Soviet Union*, Evanston, IL: Berry Publishing Services, 1993; Philip Walters, (ed.), *World Christianity: Eastern Europe*, Eastbourne: MARC, 1988; Luis Bush, (ed.), *AD2000 and Beyond Handbook*, AD2000 & Beyond, 1992; David B. Barrett and James W. Reapsome, *Seven Hundred Plans to Evangelize the World: The Rise of the Global Evangelism Movement*, Birmingham, AL; New Hope, 1988; David B. Barrett and Todd M. Johnson, *Our Globe and How to Reach It: Seeing the World Evangelized by AD 2000 and Beyond*, Birmingham, AL: New Hope, 1990. In addition, recent issues of the journals *Charisma*, *Christianity Today*, and *Mission Frontiers* have been usefully consulted. Finally, a survey of several hundred North American missionary agencies was made in 1992 by the Institute for the Study of American Religion.

2. On the history of European missions see: J. Herbert Kane, *A Global View of Christian Missions*, Grand Rapids, MI: Baker Book House, 1971, and Steve Durasoff, *Pentecost Behind the Iron Curtain*, Plainfield, NJ: Logos International, 1971.

CHAPTER 4

Pan-Baltic Identity and Religio-Cultural Expression in Contemporary Lithuania

Michael York

The Baltic states of Estonia, Latvia and Lithuania occupy the east coast of the Baltic Sea. In the thirteenth century the Teutonic Knights conquered and largely exterminated the Baltic-speaking Old Prussian peoples and organized a separate German state, later known as East Prussia. In the same century the Teutonic and Livonian Knights conquered the region comprising Estonia and Latvia and forcibly converted the inhabitants to Christianity. To defend themselves, the Lithuanians formed a strong unified state and expanded as far as the Black Sea — becoming one of the largest states of medieval Europe. While German culture predominated in the East Prussian and Livonian states and came to accept the Reformation, Lithuania drew closer to Roman Catholic Poland, and the two states fully merged in 1569 with the Union of Lublin. This led to the Polonization of the Lithuanian aristocracy and burghers, although, earlier in the fourteenth century, Christianity had been introduced into Lithuania when, through marriage, the Lithuanian Grand Duke had become King of Poland. The Estonians, a Finno-Ugric rather than a Baltic peoples, came under Swedish rule in the 16th century, but by the end of the 18th century they along with the Latvian and Lithuanian territories had all been absorbed by Russia.

However, especially in Lithuania, nationalist revival thwarted Russian efforts to obliterate national sentiment. Under German protection, Lithuania became independent in 1918, despite attacks by both Bolshevik troops and German mercenaries. By 1920 treaties with Russia accepted the independence of all three Baltic states. In the same year, Poland seized the Lithuanian capital of Vilnius and forced formal cession in 1938. In 1923 the coastal Memel Territory was ceded to Lithuania by international treaty. Smetona and his nationalist party came to power in December 1926, and by the next year a fascistic government was established in the country. With the partition of Poland in 1939, Vilnius was returned to Lithuania. The country conceded to a German ultimatum and returned Memel. The USSR occupied all three Baltic states in 1940 and, following the Germany occupation from 1941 to 1944, the Communist government returned, and the states became part of the Soviet bloc. Memel was restored to Lithuania as the city of Klaipeda.

Following the overthrow of Communism in the East European states in 1989, agitation for independence gathered momentum in the three Baltic states — including a Lithuanian referendum which prompted recognition by Iceland and the establishment of diplomatic relations. With the collapse of the Soviet coup in August of 1991 the Baltic states rapidly moved towards full political independence. The nationalist aspirations of these three countries, despite centuries of displacement and shifting borders, received much of its current support when the Romantic movement of the late nineteenth century re-kindled a deep interest in preserving indigenous folklore from extinction. Despite the Polonization of Lithuania and the domination of the Polish clergy especially in the eastern part of the country, a movement for the collection of folklore continued apace. The work prospered during the inter-war period but was largely halted by World War II and was then subsequently suppressed by Stalin. Folkloric collection, preservation and analysis, however, was resumed in the 1960s. Although there are different claims as to who was responsible, by 1967 a conscious folkloric organization was established. The underlying pagan religious revival orientation of this movement, Ramuva by name, came to be recognized by the Soviet Lithuanian government which moved to ban the organization in 1971/72. One casualty in this process was Jonas Trinkûnas who lost his university teaching position as a result and spent the next ten years making tombstones for a living. This was followed by another five years in which he joined a travelling folklore ensemble. In retrospect, Mr Trinkûnas explains, this fifteen-year period was not so bad as it afforded him greater contact with the countryside and the corresponding opportunity to gather more information on indigenous folklore and spiritual practice.

Despite the cessation of Ramuva ethnographic ensembles continued to work underground. In the aftermath of perestroika, Ramuva was re-established in 1988 (18 November) under the jurisdiction at first of the Society for Ethnic Lithuanian Culture. It now operates independently with, as of Autumn 1990, working groups in five Lithuanian cities. During a 16 December 1990 shortwave radio interview with Jonas Trinkûnas on Kalba Vilnius, the differentiation of Ramuva from ordinary ethnographic ensembles was stressed with the Ramuvan emphasis being dedicated to rekindling ancient culture on a personal and communal level rather than strictly for purposes of performance. Ramuvan members seek to collect and study and use the various elements of the folkloric tradition — tales, songs, dances and art. They also rely on the writings of the philosopher and symbolist dramatist Vilius Storosta (Vydûnas). Ancient Lithuanian culture is determinedly linked to modern ethnographic expression. Stressing aesthetics, morality, music and respect for nature, Ramuva seeks to defend Lithuanian ethnicity and culture from westernizing influence — especially those considered imposed by the Roman Catholic Church — and to offer Lithuanian cultural values to Europe and the world. More broadly, Ramuva seeks to evoke Baltic culture in general and includes concern with the Prussian and Latvian pasts as well as with that of the Byelorussians, that is, the Baltic or White Russians.

The Lithuanian name 'Ramuva' derives from the form 'Romuva', the designation for the principal Prussian pagan sanctuary as well as numerous other Baltic shrines. Romuva had been the chief sacred oak grove of the Old Prussians, located in what became East Prussia and subsequently the Kaliningrad Oblast. Romuva was also the name of the inter-war pagan sanctuary on the shores of Sartai lake in northeastern Lithuania. The Krivulê or Convention of the Ramuva Association of Lithuania affirmed the ideal of Romuva as its ultimate cultural and spiritual goal. The name 'Ramuva' has also been used for an ethnographic ensemble or folklore revival group at the University of Vilnius which refused to join the association because of personality clashes. Nevertheless, Ramuva/Lithuania, as the foremost expression of the popular Lithuanian folklore movement, works closely with other organizations such as the Children of Gediminas (school children who, after graduation, usually become members of Ramuva) and also the Lithuanian 'Society for Creative Anachronism'. The chief spheres of activity with which Ramuva is concerned consist of education, ritual and summer camps. During the summers of 1992 and 1994, in the folkloric summer camps I attended respectively near the town of Uzhuguostis and in the National Park of Zhemaitija, there was a full agenda of morning talks, afternoon craft classes and walks to sacred sites, and evening *vakaronê* gatherings of song and dance. There were also several rituals performed, including a collective offering of first fruits in a fire alter.

Concurrently with the Ramuvan developments in Lithuania, under the direction of Audrius Dundzila, an independent affiliate of Ramuva/Lithuania called Romuva/USA came into being for North America and published its first quarterly newsletter in the Autumn of 1990. Its ad hoc organizational committee of Lithuanian/ Americans operated out of the cities of Chicago, Illinois and Madison, Wisconsin. Unlike Ramuva/Lithuania. Romuva/USA focused primarily on the revival of the ancient Lithuanian religion, its world view and spiritual traditions. In one of its first statements, the North American-based movement claimed to view folklore as a 'fundamentally spiritual phenomenon'.

Romuva/USA, Ramuva/Lithuania and other Baltic spiritual folklore groups in general conform to the SPIN or segmented-poly-centric-integrated-network organization which has become characteristic of the New Age and Neo-pagan movements in general. Romuva/USA declares as its central task the networking of people interested in the ancient Lithuanian religion in particular and in Baltic spirituality in general. Its newsletter focuses on articles concerned with the indigenous Lithuanian religion, its pantheon, the celebrations, resource information and networking listings. It fosters commemoration of this spiritual understanding not only among its members but within Lithuanian ethnographic ensembles in general and other Lithuanian groups in the USA and Canada as well.

It is difficult to judge the influence that Romuva/USA has had on Ramuva/Lithuania but doubtless through financial support and moral encouragement the American network has allowed a greater confidence in the Lithuanian efforts themselves. However, in the third issue of its quarterly (Spring Equinox, 1991), Romuva/USA complained of not having any postal contact with Ramuva/ Lithuania since December 1990 due to the Soviets having stopped all press going abroad and severely restricting international mail. Telephone contact was re-established with Jonas Trinkûnas, the *seniûnas* or Elder of Ramuva, in mid-March. But with the increasing liberalization and subsequent emancipation of Lithuania itself, the more favourable political climate eventually encouraged a religious spin-off from the parent organization. While, by its third issue, Romuva/USA changed the subtitle of its newsletter from 'English Quarterly for Lithuanian Spirituality and Religion' to 'English-language Quarterly for the Old Religion and Spirituality of Lithuanians', in September 1991 several Lithuanian Ramuva groups held discussions on the formation of local Romuva groups. Ramuva by definition seeks to 'revive' Lithuanian folklore — as opposed to merely staging or teaching it. It was now felt that Ramuva had sufficiently helped rekindle the ancient Lithuanian spiritual traditions embedded in the folklore and that an organization dedicated publicly to reviving the old religion of the Liths was now necessary. Moreover, the folkloric Ramuva/Lithuania had continued to grow to the extent that following the unexpected attendance of more than 1000 people for the Ramuva summer gathering in Kelmê, Lithuania in 1990, four smaller camps were held the following year in different locations to accommodate a larger capacity. The chief ethnic celebration for Baltic peoples — whether folkloric or spiritual — appears to be the summer solstice which is called Rasa. In 1967, Ramuva celebrated Rasa in Kernavê, the former capital of medieval Lithuania. Since then, under various auspices, Rasa has been celebrated there annually, and with the granting of religious freedom by the Soviet Union in 1988, the summer solstice has become the most popular non-Christian ethno-pagan festival in Lithuania, being organized in 1991 in every Lithuanian city, while the capital Vilnius held a two-day pan-Baltic Rasa Fair. In the same year, a Rasa celebration was held at the site of the original Romuva sanctuary in the Kaliningrad Region of Russia and was attended by both local Russians and Lithuanian pagans.

Consequently, considering the growing success of Ramuva/ Lithuania and the national support of ethnographic interest and folkloric expression, the time was judged right to form a religious Romuva organization within Lithuania itself. The name of 'Romuva' had already been used for a Kaunas Vytautas Magnus University fraternity established around 1930 as well as for clandestine affiliations of Lithuanian deportees in Siberia. According to Audrius Dundzila, 'The [fraternity] seeks pan-Baltism and folklore revival but is religiously officially neutral [though] actually pro-pagan'.[1] With the contemporary desire to establish an explicitly religious affiliation, several independent and local Ramuva or folklore groups, by following the ritual and organization of Wiccan covens or Druidic groves, were judged already to be religious revival groups. While these groups met to study, learn and celebrate rituals, by contrast the typical Ramuva or folklore group studied, learned and sang folksongs to the accompaniment of traditional instruments. Following a plenary meeting of approximately ten people who met in the house of Jonas Trinkûnas, by 1992 approximately 40 people from the Vilnius Ramuva and the Shventaragis Ramuva groups registered themselves as a religious congregation called Vilnius Romuva. (The initiative group was spearheaded by Dalius Regelskis.) A similar organization was established in the city of Kaunas from among members of the Alkupis and Atgaja Ramuva groups. In Vilnius, a central figure of this development is Algis Jucevichius; in Kaunas, it is Ida Stankevichiûtê. Meanwhile, the original Ramuva assemblies have continued their work as organizations for folklore revival.

At present, Romuva/Vilnius has registered with the city of Vilnius which in turn has recommended that the national government also authorize the organization's existence. Since the former Soviet laws on religious groups are still largely in effect, the process remains a slow and twisted one. Meanwhile, Romuva/Kaunas has applied for registration in the city of Kaunas, and both organizations are considering the formation of an international union of Romuvas in which each local congregation maintains its autonomy. By the summer of 1992, there were approximately 50 active Romuvan members in Vilnius and 30 active members in Kaunas. Concurrently, Romuva/USA has registered as an unincorporated

Church with the Internal Revenue Service while state registration is pending. During the summer of 1992, Romuva/USA was deliberating its bylaws with ratification and election of trustees scheduled for the end of the summer. In the Spring of 1994, Romuva/Canada began its quarterly publication of *Sacred Serpent*.

In Lithuania, Jonas Trinkûnas has assisted the Romuva religious organization along with his continued promotion of the Ramuva folkloric movement, since November 1989 known as the Lieutuvos Ramuvos Sajunga (Ramuva Association of Lithuania). Until recently, Mr Trinkûnas headed the Department of Ethnic Culture within the Ministry of Culture and Education for the Republic of Lithuania (he now works as science collaborator for the Lithuanian Institute of Philosophy and Sociology). However, despite the greater openness of the Romuva religious organization, Mr Trinkûnas feels that he must still move with care and a degree of secrecy in the furtherance of spiritual folklore aspirations. Along with the cessation of Communism and the former Soviet control, the Roman Catholic Church has moved quickly to re-assert its former authority. For instance, under Communism, the elder Trinkûnas children were not confronted with religious teachings in School. Now these have been reinstated, and Mr and Mrs Trinkûnas have, with difficulty, arranged for their youngest daughter, aged eight, to be excused from these classes. As Mrs Trinkûnas explained to me, several other parents also do not wish their children to be subjected to the Church's teachings but have capitulated under feelings of intimidation.

In another situation, the city of Panevêzhys was forced to cancel an extra-curricular school district-wide celebration of Uzhgavienês, or the ushering out of winter, in 1992 because local Catholics complained that the holiday would disrupt preparations for Lent. A commentary in the national newspaper *Respublika* asked since when did the Church exercise a pre-Lenten Lent? The paper commented that Catholics were not obliged to keep the observance but were forcing others to adhere to their practices.

The problem for non-Catholics is exacerbated by the Roman Catholic bias of the Sajûdis national party. For instance, under its leader Vytautas Landsbergis, a non-parliamentary act was signed by the president in September 1991, which was entitled 'The Offering of Lithuania to the Heart of the Virgin Mary'. In the name of all Lithuania, the act promised to profess only Catholicism, to obey the Pope, and to propagate Christianity in Lithuania. Additionally, under the Sajûdis the state did not require the Catholic Church to adhere to the requirements set forth in the Soviet inspired 'Rules for Religious Unions'. The Church's exemption from these rules allows Catholic congregations to accept infants as members, whereas non-Catholic groups could only accept people who were 18 or older. Under the Sajûdis, the Lithuanian government required the Kaunas Evangelical Baptist congregation to provide copies of all members' passports, despite the legal invalidity of passport copies.

With the advent of a national constitution, paragraph 30 of the Temporary Basic Law grants the individual the right to realize his or her religious interests. Paragraph 31 allows for freedom of thought, conscience and belief; equal rights for all to profess, express and propagate convictions; and the granting of corporate status to religious congregations and the right to administer their internal affairs without outside influence. Nevertheless, the Soviet Lithuanian 'Rules for Religious Unions' continue to restrict congregations in various ways. For instance, when Kaunas Romuva submitted its documents to the government, its membership was not allowed to include either minors up to 17 years of age or people not living in Kaunas proper. Moreover, the group was required to submit a creed since the government claimed that creedless congregations can hypnotize youths, lead them astray, or even physically abuse them.

In October of 1992, the Sajûdis national party was defeated in general elections, and the former communists, now as a socialist party, came to power. Nevertheless, Sajûdis continues to operate, both as the opposition, and also through various organizations such as the Lithuanian National Cultural Center of Kaunas which promotes Catholized Lithuanian national culture. This centre publishes a journal called *Vydija* in which its editor-in-Chief, Algirdas Patackas, has blamed 'new-age anti-Christian satanism' for reviving 'the demon of the bastard Pagan religion'. Patackas, along with another leader of the organization, Aleksandras Zharskus, discourages students from studying such wayward influences as Maria Gimbutas or Dundulienê.

The conflict between the Roman Catholic Church and the Ramuva/Romuva movement in particular, and the general interest in folklore of the population at large which exists in Lithuania is not to be found in the Baltic state of Latvia to the north. As a result of the influence and control of the Livonian and Teutonic Knights, the country is now largely Lutheran. But at the same time, due to collectivization and re-settlement, most Latvians live in the city of Riga and few are left in the countryside, with the result that Latvia is without the rich and living folkloric tradition found in Lithuania. Nevertheless, an ethno-cultural movement with a spiritual emphasis similar to that which operates for her southern neighbours does exist in Latvia. One expression of this movement is the cultural association known as Paganis Europa, or Paganian Europe, which was founded in September 1990. This group parallels the Lithuanian Ramuva. Within Latvia, however, the big pagan group is known as Dievturi, or Dievturiba, literally, the 'god-holders' or 'god-bearers'. Dievturi has an American affiliation as well.

In an article entitled 'The ancient Latvian religion — Dievturiba',[2] Tupeshu Janis explains that, following the collection of Latvian Dainas as their main source of orally transmitted wisdom and traditional values, a group of intellectuals, writers and artists decided that, 'instead of syncretising the ancient Latvian wisdom within the Christian dogma, the uniquely Latvian encounter with the sacred is worthy enough to carve its own destiny. Starting with a small group of convinced enthusiasts, the movement gained momentum in the mid-thirties and is very much alive today'.[3] The main ideologue of the Dievturi movement as a unique Latvian religion was Brastinu Ernests. Although officially Christianized in the thirteenth century, Latvia did not accept Christianity until the eighteenth and nineteenth centuries, and then only superficially since the ruling German nobility did not accept the indigenous populations as equals. Moreover, Latvians could not understand the Latin and German which was used in the pulpits. Although no longer true today, for approximately 600 years the Latvian culture was that of the peasant class.

Tupeshu Janis sums up a post-modern sentiment for Dievturi which is applicable to native Baltic spirituality in general. Accepting an *Encyclopedia Britannica* definition of religion as 'man's relation to that which he regards as holy',[4] Tupeshu concludes: 'The hard-line and fundamentalist Christian will consider the Latvian religion as pagan, pantheistic and polytheistic and in many respects it is. But to assign a value-judgment in this pluralistic, data base and information age is extremely problematic. Who is to say that the modern scientific age with all its answers has a better paradigm for survival and well-being than the perennial Wisdom and value system in the Sacred Dainas!'[5] Ramuva/Lithuania cooperates closely with the Latvian Church Dievturi.

At present, however, the Latvian group divides essentially into two factions: the old guard and the younger members. The old guard are hierarchical and centralized and insist on things being done the way they were before the War. The newer and younger members are opposed to the rigid structures favoured by the older faction. They, in contrast, believe in or accept the idea of rein-carnation. In Latvia an uneasy alliance exists between the two factions and the younger members expect to inherit the mantle of leadership in time. In America, on the other hand, due to the dominance of the old guard there has been little attraction for younger people of Latvian-American descent. The American Dievturi branch at present appears to be moribund.

At the Romuva gathering held in Uzhuguostis in August 1992, which I visited, several Byelorussians also attended. The Lithu-anians were most pleased with their presence and recognized the strong affinity between Baltic and Balto-Russian folkloric spirituality. During a talk given by Sergei Sanka, who heads ethnic research for the cultural museum of Minsk, the living non-Christian traditions of Byelorussia were expounded, and there was mention of pagan sanctuaries continuing until well into this century. With a fairly even balance between the Roman Catholic Church and the Russian Orthodox Church in White Russia, it was thought that ethno-cultural spirituality did not face the same monolithic obstacle as the Lithuanian pagans must confront, and, consequently, they were in a more favourable position to prosper and further their efforts.

Among others who attended the Uzhuguostis camp were delegates from Latvia and Estonia, and one Russian, who was the uncle, though older by four months, of one of the Latvians. The majority of attendees were in their late teens and early twenties, but older people also were conspicuously present, as well as children. Although some arrived earlier and others remained afterward, the 'official' gathering itself was for five days (15-19 August) with a perpetually rotating attendance that approximated about 60 people at any given moment. Some delegates from other countries were unable to locate the camp site. Among the Lithuanians, apart form Romuva itself, there were also pagan members of at least two ecological groups: from Atgaja ('Rebirth') and from Zaliojo Taika ('Green Peace'), collectively, the Lithuanian Greens. There was one Lithuanian Sai Baba pagan, and one of the Latvian pagan leaders described himself as a Theosophist. Also present was a Wiccan priestess from Germany and a Wiccan priest from the UK. The latter writes under the name of 'Robert' and is one of the few remaining people who was initiated by Gerald Gardner himself. In fact, it was chiefly through Robert's efforts on behalf of the UK-based Pagan Federation that British contacts with Ramuva and related Baltic spiritual folklore movements were first established.

While attending the Ramuva/Romuva summer gathering, Robert's efforts could almost be described as a form of 'subdued proselytizing'. It was difficult to assess how successful he may have been, since the modestly favourable response expressed by one lady may have been more the result of Lithuanian politeness. In general, I judged that the consensus supports the attitude expressed by the Trustees of Romuva/USA in their journal's eighth issue. Under the heading 'Principals [sic] of Authenticity', the following statement was made:

In any matters concerning creed, doctrine, and similar matters, Romuva/ USA advocates an accurate authentic perpetuation and reconstruction of Baltic beliefs and practices. Although Romuva/USA supports everyone's right to interpret the Old Religion in a way meaningful to themselves, the old beliefs should not be made to conform to any interpretations or principals [sic] of Western magical and religious thought.

Romuva/USA is especially worried that the concept of male/female dualism and the idea that all Deities are merely names for different aspects of 'The Goddess and The God' might be established as normative. This appears to have already happened in Latvian Dievturyba. All the evidence of surviving Pagan traditions and recorded beliefs from ancient religions indicates that these viewpoints were NOT characteristic of original Paganism and therefore should not be the standard for Romuva.

The value of Baltic Paganism lies in enlightening and restoring the worship of Pagan deities, not in conforming to a standard based on faulty reconstruction, wishful thinking, and modern political or social agendas, not to mention Christian concepts of Deity.

Romuva should be based on what lasted for millennia, not on light and transitory causes.

With this affirmation, along with the consensus of sentiment within Romuva/Lithuania, Romuva/USA is making a distinction between original paganism and the Neo-paganism which has come to characterize Western development. Romuva identifies with the aspirations of such related groups as the Sodalicium Romanum in the USA, various branches of the Asatru, Odinists and Vanirists in North America and Britain, and several of the different Druidic Orders. They are all to be contrasted from the bi-theism of Wicca as well as the monotheism inherent in contemporary forms of Goddess Spirituality. As Audrius Dundzila, editor of *Romuva/USA*, states, 'Lithuanian Paganism differs from American Neo-Paganism'. In the same issue, Dundzila continues:

Most Lithuanians accept Lithuanian Pagans and their festivals as something natural and folkloric. In spite of their current professed Christianity, Lithuanians are staunchly proud of their Pagan past. When asked about religion, they always boast that they were the last Pagans of Europe to be christianized. Most Lithuanians eagerly participate in ethnic Pagan festivals and rituals because they consider it part of their cultural heritage.[6]

I myself witnessed the casual non-reaction bystanders would reveal in the presence of, for instance, a circle dance around a lit fire altar in the Kainu Park of Vilnius. As Irena Egle Laumenskaite has pointed out,[7] in Lithuania, Catholicism socially consolidated itself only as late as the seventeenth and eighteenth centuries, and in the ideologization of commonness which has become its legacy, there exists a current dialectic between respect for the Church and fear of clericalism. Laumenskaite considers there to be three types of religiosity among intellectuals in present-day Lithuania: (1) cultural religiosity which is characteristic of a cultural pantheism or transcendent humanism, that is, image-belief with no personal obligation; (2) seasonal Catholicism, that is, acceptance of such religious ceremonies as baptisms, weddings and funerals as necessary, although generally not accompanied by belief in the Christian concept of God; and (3) implicit religiosity with its focus on the sacred, if only the mysterious self and its identity.

In 1990, with the exception of Denmark and France, belief in the supernatural in Lithuania was slightly lower than it was for other West European counties in 1981. Laumenskaite argues that, 'The orientation to transcendence, more characteristic of Catholicism, at a time when the experience of Christian transcendency has been weakened, made it possible to raise the nation and the national state to the level of sacred things and to attach independence and statehood to the dimension of the transcendent'.[8] Whether the source of Lithuanian nationalism can be attributed solely to a Roman Catholic heritage might be doubtful, but even within the ranks of the spiritual folkloric circles, I encountered an understandable nationalistic fervour that came close to expressing itself in unpalatable terms of racism and fascism. The Lithuanian state was indeed considered sacred and transcendent and possibly even superior, even when its indigenous and pagan roots were recognized. For Laumenskaite, the solution is straightforward: '... a reconstruction of society and moral order will hardly be possible without appealing to moral meanings and the ultimate Christian values, i.e. without a revival of a conscious religious belief'.[9] She appears to be unaware of the religious dimensions, and of the possible contribution toward reconstruction inherent in the Ramuva/Romuva movement and affiliated interests.

Unofficially released information received through a seminarian suggests that the Church claims that 80% of the Lithuanian population are baptised Roman Catholics, though it admits that only 10% of the country attend services regularly. Many less than the 80% attend even the high festivals such as Easter. Moreover, there are self-proclaimed atheists within this 80% figure; in fact, it has been claimed that as many as 40% of the population are atheists, although this figure is doubtful. Laumenskaite found that 38% of her sample could be regarded as observing traditional Catholic religion (Church attendance outside Christmas and Easter, and self-description as a religious person). On the other hand, 57% of her sample declared themselves to be Roman Catholics. Among the remaining 20% that the Church at least unofficially accepts as non-Roman Catholic, the Evangelical Reform and the Lutheran Churches are the largest. Religions which have existed in Lithuania since the Middle Ages and which have at least five congregations include the Jewish, Muslim and the Karait (Jews who accept only the Torah). Altogether there are 19 new religious movements at present, including Zen Buddhists, ISKCON, Sai Baba, Baptists and Word of Faith. The laws of the Lithuanian Republic allow all religious groups to take two days off work for religious celebration, although, as minority religionists point out, Roman Catholics get all their days off.

In contrast to Laumenskaite, in an article entitled, 'The devil's invasion: cultural changes in early modern Lithuania',[10] Vytautas Kavolis blames the cultural decline of Lithuania on Roman Catholic domination. He argues that in the sixteenth and seventeenth centuries, the peak of Lithuanian power, there was more equilibrium and a balance between different confessions, and that, for Lithuania to become a liberal democratic society, it must take care not to have one dominant form in religion, philosophy or culture. Despite the past association of Lithuania with totalitarianism, or the present-day fascistic outspokenness of Sajûdis which seeks to outlaw Romuva as well as all other minority religions, and despite the bristling animosity often burning just beneath the surface against the one lone Russian present, the Romuva Summer Gatherings were expressions of the multi-culturalism that is increasing becoming characteristic of a pluralistic and cosmopolitan society. With the enthusiastic encouragement of ethnic diversity and exchange on the part of such leaders as Jonas Trinkûnas, the spiritual folkloric tradition may come to play a significant role in the promotion of future cultural harmony in place of factional divisiveness.

Notes

1. Private letter dated 8 September 1992.
2. *Lituanus*, 33.3, 1987, pp. 46-61.
3. *Op. cit.*, p. 48.
4. 15th edition, 1986, 1016, vol. IX.
5. *Op. cit.*, p. 61.
6. No. 8, Sambariai 1992, p. 4.
7. *Religion Today*, 7,3.
8. *Op. cit.*, p. 9.
9. *Op. cit.*, p. 11.
10. *Lituanus*, 35, 1989, pp. 5-26.

CHAPTER 5

The New Religious Landscape in Romania

Silvia Chiţimia

To provide complete information, any comment about the new religious landscape in Romania has to begin with the larger frame of religious life during the 45 years of communism. Several characteristic aspects can be identified: 1) The latent persecution of religious practice (this was seen even at a linguistic level, with words and phrases such as angel, Holy Spirit, sacredness, and 'to be blessed' being prohibited. 2) The culpable non-involvement of the Orthodox Church in the struggle with the dictatorship, and in some cases complicity with the police, meant that the spiritual life was reduced to little more than administration. 3) The demolition of churches offered dramatic proof of the low level of militancy of the Orthodox Church; the only real protests came from architects, art historians and writers. 4) Despite all of this, religious life has survived. The knowledge that the Church was there provided for many people a frail shelter against the brutal interference of the regime in their private lives.

On the first level, we must note the existence of an underground Orthodox life (80% of the Romanian people are Orthodox), with the private observance of the Christian holy days, and of the ceremonies of christenings, weddings and burials. On the other hand, we observe also the underground activity of Christian sects, such as the Pentecostal Church, the Jehovah's Witnesses and the Adventists, which on occasions gave rise to official persecution and political protests.

Occurring against this background, the 1989 revolution has produced a profound religious impact because of the sacrificial involvement, i.e. the martyrdom, of the so many young people.

Many religious symbols (the cross, the lighted candle, the cenotaph) and rituals (prayers, and frequent death-wakes in the streets) have together created a kind of New Religious Movement. The death of so many innocent people during the revolution has produced a massive, though short-lived, Orthodox revival at all social levels. Generally speaking we can see here elements of a new religious movement:

1. The revolution broke out near a protestant church near Timisoara.
2. The sacrifice of the young people was akin to the massacre of the Holy Innocents.
3. Young people faced physical violence with lighted candles in their hands.
4. The death-wakes and prayers during the nights of fighting.
5. On the main streets of Bucharest and Timisoara burial processions and death offerings appeared.
6. On the morning of 22 December, when the people found the dictator had fled, people knelt down in the main streets of Bucharest and the church bells started to ring.
7. There followed the creation of an Association of the Heroes of the Revolution, with periodic meetings.

After 1990, with the new freedom gained, some other religious movements have appeared. A National Centre of the Baha'i community was created, and Jehovah's Witnesses, who before were prohibited, now have the opportunity to practise openly, and they have in Bucharest their own edition of *The Watchtower*.

We can find also the Sahaja Yoga teachings, especially in intellectual circles, the Grail movement, the arrival of Mormons as 'Brothers from the USA', and the Archives of the Guardian Angel.

So, in the three years following the revolution, we can see an increase in the activity of religious sects, especially of protestant ones. The Baptist and Pentecostal Churches have extended their activity, as have the Eastern-inspired groups such as Sahaja Yoga, Raja Yoga and Tantra Yoga. But the new religious movement which has had the biggest impact on the mass media has been the Church of the New Jerusalem, also called the Pucioasa Phenomenon.

The Church of the New Jerusalem Settlement: Description and Plan

The settlement of the New Jerusalem was built near the town of Pucioasa in a rural region not far from Bucharest. The church was built in three months, according to the instructions received by revelation. It has the appearance of a monastery. The whole place is surrounded by a concrete wall, 1000 metres. Seen from above, it looks like a lotus flower with a cross on the top, and all the mortar is brilliant white.

The Symbolism of the New Jerusalem

To the members of the Church, the settlement is rich in symbolic significance:

1. The Great Church that is the New Jerusalem is Romania itself.
2. The settlement is the altar of the Church.
3. The Gate is catapeteasma, or the alter screen.
4. The building with cupolas in the middle of the garden is the altar table.
5. The garden is laid out as a stylized representation of the geographical map of Romania.

The foundation of the building is in the form of a cross, 12 metres by 12 metres. It is 12 metres up to the dome, which has 33 smaller cupolas. The building also has 12 doors which represent the 12 tribes who follow the teachings of Jesus Christ. The foundation stones symbolize the 12 Apostles, and 33 is the age of Jesus.

The Paintings in the Interior

The theme of the paintings in the interior is the Descent of Heaven, and the walls are painted with images of saints without bodies, only wings, thus representing the angelic state. All the paintings were revealed to the main members, and were painted by young artists.

The Gate in Carved Wood

The entrance to the New Jerusalem garden is dominated by a large gate in carved wood. The main symbolic elements were also given by revelation. In the foundations of the building was buried a revealed text, which consecrated the place.

The Community of the New Jerusalem

The settlement of the New Jerusalem is occupied by 14 members, seven men and seven women, who consider themselves to be a special monastic community 'chosen by the Holy Spirit' to serve at the altar of the Great Church at the time of the second arrival of Jesus Christ. The community was founded by the great Prophetess Virginia through whom the Holy Spirit initiated its workings. The members call each other 'brother' and 'sister', and their activities include working within the community, taking care of the settlement, and participating in the esoteric meetings which have a ritual character. During these meetings the Holy Spirit speaks to the participants. The communication is said to be like a whisper or a murmur heard in their ears — like an inside voice. The community has the role of guardian of the holy messages, and it should be noted that these messages all concern real aspects of the political, social and cultural life of Romanian society. Most of the messages are secret, and only some of them may be communicated to other, non-initiated, people.

The main revelation of the community is that, 'The people of the world will worship the New Jerusalem born in Romania, under the royalty of King Michael', the 'King' representing a principle, rather than a real person. Generally speaking, their utterances are messianic, and members seem to be living in an atmosphere of perpetual expectancy. Their appearance is unusual, the men wearing a long white shirt, long hair and an untrimmed beard, the women wearing a long black skirt, white blouse and a white kerchief.

The Prophetess Virginia

The history of the New Jerusalem is strongly linked with the life and activity of the Prophetess Virginia. She was born in 1923 near the town of Pucioasa and died in 1980. She was illiterate and she never read the Bible. From 1955, Virginia manifested special states of a mystical nature. When she fell 'asleep' she would receive messages, the Holy Spirit speaking through her mouth. The house of Virginia was a place of pilgrimage for many disciples who talked about religious matters while waiting for Virginia to fall into a trance. During her 'sleep', after uttering a ritual formula, Virginia would start to speak and answer questions. Her disciples say that in these moments a halo appeared around her head. It is reported that she predicted the earthquake of 1977, the revolution of 1989 and the advent of King Michael. It is said also that she informed Ceausescu that he would have a tragic end. She was arrested several times by the secret police and she was sent to psychiatric clinics.

The Leaders of the Community

New religious movements are rarely initiated by committees, as Eileen Barker has observed, and most movements have, or have had, a founder or leader who is believed to possess some special powers or knowledge. In the present case it was the Prophetess Virginia. Later, the main leaders of the New Jerusalem were the 'Sister Michaela', Marian Zidaru, and his wife Victoria. The official guarantor was Bishop Irineu Bistrițeanu. Marian Zidaru is a plastic artist and author of the plans of the Church and the settlement. These plans were revealed to him in a kind of visionary light. Sister Michaela has a central position within the community, reminiscent of a sacerdotal hypostasis. It seems that, beginning with Virginia, women have played a central role in the community. The members consider themselves to be elected by the Holy Spirit and keep a close daily contact with each other by telephone.

The Degree of Public Perception

The inhabitants of the district surrounding New Jerusalem perceive the Church as a strange presence with magical attributes. Some consider it malevolent, others say it is good because they hear the beautiful hymns and prayers. Some villagers believe that ritual sacrifice takes place there, although nothing is known for sure and the members keep up the mystery. The Pucioasa phenomenon that is the New Jerusalem has been widely spread through the mass media of television, newspapers, and magazines.

The Contradictory Dialogues With The Romanian Orthodox Church

The New Jerusalem phenomenon has aroused a strong reaction inside the Orthodox hierarchy. Any Christian religious movement needs the recognition of the Romanian Orthodox Church. For eight years the Pucioasa phenomenon was studied by Father Irineu, the Bishop and *locum tenens* of Cluj. In 1992 he published an affirmation of the movement, recognizing it as belonging to traditional Christian Orthodoxy. The Holy Synod debated the 'heresy' of this well-known bishop, and later, in the presence of the Assembly of the Great Synod, this Bishop denied his earlier affirmations. The main objection of the Orthodox Church was of a canonical order, that it does not admit the existence of prophets, except those of the Old Testament. After Jesus Christ no further revelation is accepted. The adherents of the New Jerusalem assert, on the contrary, that revelation is not finished with Jesus Christ and may continue with everyone who meditates upon the words of the Lord. Another objection concerns the non-canonical, unusual form of the Church, but members of the community assert that with the words of the Lord, who had descended in 1955 in Pucioasa, nothing new was added to Holy Scriptures.

Influences from the West

Comments on New Jerusalem Movement have pointed out its resemblance to some western religious sects. For instance, it is customary among sectarians to choose as titles for their movements the names of saints, citadels or holy lands. Also, they frequently pay great attention to apocryphal books, such as the Gospel of Thomas, which is the case for this group. Attention has been drawn also to the similarity between the beliefs of New Jerusalem Movement and the alarmist apocalyptical vision common to millenarian sects such as the Pentecostalists, Jehovah's Witnesses and Adventists, who prophesy the second coming of the Saviour. Other parallels have been drawn with Rowenists, reformed Adventists: devotees should not take meat, drugs or alcohol, and notably present in the movement are 'chosen' prophetesses such as Helen White and Margaret Rowen. Included in the same category is Jacob Wirtz, who in Switzerland at the end of the nineteenth century, founded a Nazarean Community, in which members lived as brothers and sisters (and it is worth noting here the metaphor of the family, present also in New Jerusalem Movement). Wirtz claimed to have messages from angels, and saw God and the Holy Spirit who dictated to him inspired texts; Secretary Sisters transcribed his dreams and prophetic revelations. He claimed that God had conveyed to him the Spirit of Melchizedek in order that he might found a New Church, immaculate, pure and distinct from the compromising official churches.

Another comparison may be drawn with Betanists, a nineteenth century reformed Church, which was organized in closed communities, and which considered all other people to be sinful and marked by the devil. They led strictly ascetic lives, were pious, lived isolated from the world so as not to endanger their salvation. They considered themselves to be the successors of the elected people and struggled to renew the whole reformed church.

Influences from the East

The old Russian chronicles mention the 'Heralds of the Advent', a sect named 'HLISTII' founded by Daniile Filipovici in the sixteenth century. Daniile had a prophetic dream that he had been called for the salvation of mankind. He organized a group of prophets and they went from one village to another working wonders. They claimed a permanent communication between heaven and earth. The groups were named 'ships and arks' and the adherents were the 'brothers and sisters of the Lord'.

The SCAPETII movement, or the 'servants of the soul', was founded in 1800 by an illiterate peasant, Selivanov, delegated by 'one from heaven' to gather believers and found the kingdom of the saviour of Russia. It is said that the Apocalyptic Angel itself appeared to Selivanov. The sisters and brothers of the SCAPETII sect used to travel all over Russia, gathering believers and many devotees. They penetrated also into Romania and they set up communities in Iasi and Bucharest. In 1990 they numbered 1600.

But the most interesting similarities with the New Jerusalem Movement can be observed among the INOKENTISTS. Inokenti was a monk who performed miracles to substantial audiences in Moldavia. He was surrounded by a great number of devotees, monks, pilgrims and peasants who claimed that the Holy Spirit had descended onto Inokenti. The Inokentists built in Lipetkoe a settlement called 'The New Jerusalem', which was called also 'The Garden of Paradise'. The community consisted of 'brothers and sisters' who declared themselves free from ecclesiastical authority. They claimed that the preaching brothers embodied the archangels, and they worshipped Inokenti.

Similarities between the New Jerusalem Movement and the Baha'i religion have been neglected until now, but some parallels are obvious. First, there is the form of the settlement, or house of worship, which in the both cases is a stylized lotus flower. The Baha'i temple allows access from all parts, having nine doors, the doors symbolize the nine heavens which are open to believers. Secondly, there are the duties to be fulfilled by the adherents: daily praying, prohibition of meat, alcohol, drugs, an idea of an ethical and moral way of life, cleanliness and purity of body and soul, and an ecological attitude towards the world.

Finally, it is important to note that in contemporary times New Jerusalems have been built in different parts of the world.

In Poland, the visionary Carl, guided by the Holy Spirit, has raised a New Jerusalem.

In Florida, near Disneyland, a Jew has built a Jerusalem, expecting the future coming of Jesus Christ. Near Moscow, a 'White Jerusalem' is being built now by Archbishop Ivan, who came from a catacomb church, and who has been receiving his revelations from the Virgin Mary since 1984. He also founded the Church of the Virgin Mary, registered at the World Congress of Churches in Canada.

Quotations from the Community

What is the New Jerusalem?

Marian Zidaru (the leader): 'In this place it is Heaven, since the moment when the Church was built, we guard it, so that no one can enter. Here is the Holy Place for the Unification of World Religions. That is why it has a non-canonical form'.

How do you live here?

'God's plan for the planetary renovation is of an ecological nature, here we live in conformity with the ecological norms'.

What do you think about the future of the New Jerusalem?

'Here is the Holy Place. The New Jerusalem will not be a place of pilgrimage. It must be kept aloof from the interference of the evil spirits'.

PART TWO

REACTIONS AND RESPONSES TO NEW RELIGIOUS MOVEMENTS

CHAPTER 6

Cults, Conflicts and Journalists[1]

James A. Beckford

One of the reasons why some rationalists dislike religion is that it is apparently inseparable from violent conflict.[2] The history of religious wars in Europe and Latin America in particular has often served as a justification for abandoning religion altogether. In fact, many heirs of the various Enlightenments have confidently believed that the demise of religious belief and practice would entail a lessening of social conflict. Indeed, there is an expectation that religion will cease to be a source of conflict in a largely secular society. But I want to argue, on the contrary, that the very opposite has occurred in countries where reported levels of religious beliefs and belonging have been declining for many decades but where unconventional new religious movements have developed.

My argument is paradoxical. It suggests that some aspects of religion have become more controversial and conflictual for the very reason that general levels of religious understanding and practice are so low. Unconventional forms of religion have become especially problematic at a time when large numbers of people find even the most conventional religion alien. In these circumstances, it is the new and unusual kinds of religious groups which encounter most hostility. In their turn, these controversial groups have sometimes exaccerbated matters by responding with even more hostility towards their detractors. This vicious spiral has occasionally erupted into massive conflicts and bloodshed. Jonestown in 1978 and Waco in 1993 are the most tragic examples. But I believe that there are also echoes of this process to be heard in the suspicions frequently voiced by the nominally Christian public in the UK about non-Christian minorities. Tariq Modood' s characterization of this phenomenon as 'cultural racism' is challenging but not unproblematic.[3] I shall focus this paper, however, on the part played by journalists in conflicts involving so-called cults, i.e. those new religious movements which have been outstandingly controversial since their emergence in the West in the 1960s. A central theme will be that there are connections between the low-level prejudice displayed against so-called cults in everyday journalism and the spectacular conflicts which erupt from time to time around controversial new religious movements.

Controversial Cults

It is not difficult to see why many of the new religious movements which emerged in the USA and Western Europe in the 1960s, such as Scientology, the Unification Church ('Moonies'), the International Society for Krishna Consciousnesss ('Hare Krishna') and the Children of God (now called 'the Family'), quickly became controversial. First, the simple fact that so many of them seemed to arrive at roughly the same time was enough to persuade some people that a new 'invasion of the body snatchers' had occurred. Secondly, the movements which drew on Asian philosophies and cultures tended to arouse suspicions merely for being foreign and therefore perceived as threatening. Thirdly, the people who were targeted by the new movements were mainly young, relatively well educated, middle-class students. They were not down-and-outs or obviously deprived. This meant that their aggrieved relatives and former friends tended to have the money, connections and confidence required to make their complaints heard in centres of influence and power, at least at local levels.[4]

The list of complaints voiced against controversial new religious movements grew so long that anti-cult organizations began to emerge in the early 1970s to combat what they considered to be a major menace to young people. Allegations of economic exploitation, mental cruelty, the deliberate alienation of recruits from their families, deceptive recruiting practices, harmful diets and lifestyles, sexual abuse and, of course, brainwashing were widespread. The high-water mark of anti-cult feeling probably occurred in the late 1970s following the death of more than 900 followers of the

Revd Jim Jones at Jonestown, Guyana. This was also the period of
the most rapid growth in membership of the most notorious cults.

Yet, for all the hostility and suspicion expressed towards the
new religious movements at that time, only a tiny proportion of the
population of any Western country had ever had any direct contact
with any of the movements. Of course, some people came to know
about them in the course of trying to 'rescue' relatives or friends
from the movements' clutches. But very few people attended new
religious movement meeetings or read their literature. Nevertheless,
the movements' notoriety was confirmed many times by opinion
polls which showed cult leaders to be among the most strongly
disliked celebrities of their time.[5]

My own research into cult controversies was able to confirm that
even people directly affected by new religious movements relied
for their information overwhelmingly on the mass media. Very few
people managed or tried to contact the movements directly. Instead,
they preferred to contact journalists who had published stories
about the movements. Indeed, the secretiveness or defensiveness
of most controversial cults helped journalists to play a crucial role
as go-betweens and arbitrators between new religious movements,
their members and angry outsiders. Only ex-members could rival
the privileged position of a few investigative journalists; but most
ex-members were understandably reluctant to talk freely about their
former commitments. In these circumstances, the role of groups in
the anti-cult movement has assumed significant proportions.[6] Cult
controversies cannot be properly understood unless the symbiotic
relationship between these anti-cult groups and journalists is taken
into account.

The Anti-Cult Movement

Some anti-cult movement organizations have become influential and
materially secure over the past twenty years. They are now
powerful enough to have the sympathetic ear of politicians, leading
Church representatives and sections of the medical and psychiatric
establishments. National-level organizations have consolidated
themselves, and cross-national links are slowly emerging. In short,
today's anti-cult movement is much more substantial and effective

than its predecessors in the long-running struggle between mainstream and marginal versions of Christianity.[7] Moreover, Jehovah's Witnesses and Christian Scientists, for example, have always been the target of critical attacks mounted by representatives of mainstream churches, and these large sectarian organizations have also had to contend with the aggressive criticism that disgruntled ex-members have showered on them. Yet, these 'established sects'[8] have never had to cope with the incessant barrage of highly public and politicized attacks that the anti-cult movement now routinely directs against new religious movements.

The fact that the anti-cult movement's dismissal of new religious movements is not based on primarily theological considerations and that the aim is not to convert members into mainstream Christians enhances the movement's appeal to journalists. The latter find the anti-cult movement useful precisely because it attacks the very existence and *modus operandi* of new religious movements without appearing to draw on doctrinal issues. It is actually common for the anti-cult movement's activists to disclaim any 'religious' intent or any animus against religion as such. They prefer the strategy of exposing alleged illegality and exploitation in new religious movements. In other words, the critics' aim is to disqualify 'cults' from the category of 'religion' altogether, thereby framing cult-related problems as 'economic', 'political' or 'psychological'.

As I argued earlier, part of the success of the anti-cult movement is due to the high degree of religious illiteracy, or the simple lack of familiarity with things religious, among the nominally Christian sections of most advanced industrial societies. It can therefore trade on fear of the unknown at a time when so few young adults have any experience of 'normal' religion with which they can realistically compare new religious movements. As a result, it is not difficult to catch the popular imagination with allegations of a sci-fi nature about the supposedly weird and dangerous goings-on inside cults. Journalists find this approach to the movements virtually irresistible, even though, according to McDonnell, 'Religion does not fit easily into the dominant world-view of most contemporary broadcasters who are often ill prepared to deal with religion, being indifferent, or occasionally, actively hostile'.[9] At least, sensational stories about new religious movements require no knowledge of religion on the part of their audience. The focus on the non-religious aspects of the movements means that there is no need to tackle issues of religious belief or experience. And the parallels that are emphasized with stories of fraud and exploitation in politics, business and crime provide the audience with a recognizable script. In short, the anti-cult movement presents journalists with material which needs very little adaptation before it can be easily digested by audiences with no taste for religion — let alone religious controversies. In this sense, it is not difficult for journalists to deal with religion (*pace* McDonnell), especially when they concentrate on expressions of religion which challenge conventional ideas or practices. Indeed, the very controversial character of some religious phenomena makes the journalists' life relatively easy in so far as conflict can easily be made to serve as the thematic 'line' of a story. Thus, although journalists may feel uncomfortable having to report on, for example, angry protests against publication of *The Satanic Verses*, which call their own professional objectivity into question, the story-line conforms readily with the 'script' of social and cultural conflicts.

I shall now analyse, with examples, the ways in which the mass media's tendency to portray new religious movements as contro-versial helps to generate and perpetuate conflict.[10]

The Portrayal of New Religious Movements in the Mass Media

Conflict and newsworthiness

The most elementary observation about print and broadcast media's portrayal of new religious movements is that the movements' activities are newsworthy only when conflicts are involved. In the quarter of a century that I have been studying the movements in Western Europe, North America and Japan I have rarely found articles or programmes which did not use conflict as (a) the main occasion for the portrayal, and (b) the principal means of structur-ing the account. Even those accounts which aspire towards a balanced, i.e. two-sided, presentation of the issues tend nevertheless to allow the conflictual aspects to predominate. 'Cults are problema-tic' is the inescapable refrain of this type of journalism. The audi-ence very rarely has the opportunity to receive information about new religious movements which is unrelated to conflict. The movements are only in the news when conflict is involved; and conflict concerning *one* movement is pounced on as an excuse for investigating *all* the others. The aftermath of Waco was full of stories along the lines of the *Boston Globe*'s, 'If you think Waco, Texas was bad, consider who could be next'.[11]

These stories about the so-called cult menace are as much about speculation as about news. They use events relating to one particular movement as a platform from which to launch 'scare' stories about the possible threat that the entire category of cults represents for other people in other places. This was an especially noticeable feature of reporting in Western European papers about the siege at Waco. In the absence, day after day, of new facts about the Branch Davidians, journalists from various countries turned to the questions of whether a comparable problem could occur in their own countries and whether the authorities there ought to be taking pre-emptive steps to avert such a possibility. Opinions were divided, but the view which prevailed was that the problem of armed cultists was a uniquely American phenomenon. Nevertheless, there was also a strong note of warning against the risk of allowing a similar conflict to develop in European countries. Vigilance was the order of the day. The virtual globalization of mass communications thereby helps journalists to frame new religious movements as primarily conflictual even in countries where the movements are virtually unknown or unproblematic.

Conflict as the Leitmotiv

Conflict is the *Leitmotiv* which connects journalistic portrayals of new religious movements together. This is evident in the extensive use that journalists and programme producers make of the 'negative summary event'.[12] This is the practice of creating continuity between episodic (especially slow-moving) stories by adding a capsule summary of the negative features of the phenomenon in focus. This reminds the audience of the sequence of reported events into which the current story can be slotted. It also stamps a particular 'mood' on the story even if the very latest episode has not been primarily about conflict. For example, brief news reports about the attempts of new religious movements to buy residential property or to open new centres are often accompanied by longer 'reminders' of the movements' past conflicts and problems. What should be the most bland and innocent news items are thereby framed in a threatening fashion.

Cross-references to conflict

A third aspect of the journalistic construction of cult conflicts is that stories are frequently cross-referenced to other mass media items. Television programmes, for example, use still shots of newspaper and magazine headlines as devices for emphasizing shock and horror. Similarly, the still photographs of cult leaders which are sometimes used in television programmes are shown staring out of the pages of the print media. Presumably the intention is to try to enhance the sense of realism and veracity by showing that stories about a particular movement or leader have already appeared in the print media and must therefore be true. Since the information and images that are 'quoted' in this way between different stories and/or media tend to be overwhelmingly unflattering and critical, the effect is likely to reinforce the generally negative image of new religious movements. In turn, this hardens public opinion against the movements and fuels the anti-cult campaigns.

An allied feature of the reporting of cult-related conflicts in which the journalists have difficulty gaining access to relevant material is that they tend to substitute their own operation for the ostensibly central subject. This was especially clear in the case of Waco where access to the Branch Davidian compound was denied to journalists. The focus of many stories therefore became the media circus on the compound's perimeter. The fact that so many journalists were present seemed to guarantee the importance of the event at moments when nothing significant appeared to be happening. Writing stories about the stories being written by other journalists took the place of direct reports on the siege of the Branch Davidians. Perhaps this practice also helps journalists to cope with the competition for customers between different publications or programmes. They can keep a story running despite the lack of directly relevant material.

Conflict feeds on stories of conflict

The next point is that, just as anti-cult activists commonly supply journalists with negative copy about new religious movements, the hostile depictions of the movements in the mass media are then recycled as further evidence in anti-cult propaganda campaigns.[13] There is in fact a mutually beneficial and reinforcing dynamic at work. It is difficult for the leaders of the movements or for disinterested parties to break into this cosy circle in order to challenge or correct the dominant imagery. Given the public's heavy reliance on the mass media for information about unconventional religion, the close alliance between the anti-cult movements and journalists makes it unlikely that non-controversial and favourable material about new religious movements could be published or broadcast.

The logic of suspicion which turns many investigative journalists into allies of the anti-cult movement helps to set the scene for the official agents of control. Knowing that the public has a very poor opinion of new religious movements, largely as a result of stereotyping in the mass media, police officers are not taking much of a risk if they take high-handed action against these unpopular movements. Journalists function as the principal gatekeepers of public opinion especially on matters with which the person-in-the-street is not normally familiar. Their overwhelmingly critical portrayal of the movements can therefore contribute indirectly towards the latter's control. Indeed, as many informed commentators on the *débâcle* at Waco have pointed out, the FBI, the US Department of Justice, journalists and programme maker all tended to favour the testimony of psychological experts whose anti-cult views were well known in advance. One of the many scandalous aspects of the whole affair was the studied refusal to give credence to the testimony of sociological, anthropological, historical and theological experts on controversial new religious movements. It is unlikely that any of these scholars with first-hand experience of researching these movements in their natural settings over many years would have advocated or supported the strategy and tactics adopted by the Bureau of Alcohol, Tobacco and Firearms (BATF) and the FBI. Instead, the authorities gave credence selectively to opinions rooted in individualistic abnormal psychology. This is always newsworthy, as was shown by the all-consuming fascination with the psychological condition of David Koresh. By contrast, the strictly social dynamics of exclusive, high-demand religious groups and the cultural force of apocalyptic millennialism were deliberately screened out of the mass media coverage.

Conflicts, journalists and control

If the mass media portrayals of new religious movements, based mainly on the one-sided evidence supplied by activists in the anti-cult movement, are sufficiently numerous and disturbing, there is a strong probability that social control agents will have to be seen to respond. Legislators and police officials in particular find themselves under pressure to say what they intend to do about the alleged wrongdoings and outrages perpetrated by cults. 'Could Jonestown happen in Britain?' or 'What are you doing to prevent another Waco happening here?' are the kind of questions put with monotonous frequency to officials in the wake of those two tragedies. Journalists seem to be relatively uninterested in the specific circumstances which led to such spectacular disasters. Instead, all the emphasis is on the presumed and unquestioned resemblance between the People's Temple or the Branch Davidians and cults in the UK. The authorities are forced to respond to these leading questions and are not given the opportunity to express doubts or reservations about the practice of 'lumping all cults together'.[14]

This dramatization of the situation increases public nervousness and official defensiveness, neither of which is conducive to clear thinking and fairness. There is a danger, then, that inadvisable panic reactions may follow. In the case of the Branch Davidians, for example,

The ante at Waco was upped because of the intervention of television reporting. Lives were endangered because the story line was created and embedded in a pernicious dualism which legitimated the 'authorities' and discouraged unconventional perspectives and opinions. The shared mentality — the corporate mentality — was served as the cultural mainstream [and] was reinforced, not challenged.

Waco's Branch Davidians, then, were victims of a media-induced disaster, executed before the eyes of the nation on television. The polarization that led to the catastrophe at Waco was inherent in neither the religious group itself — nor even in the FBI.[15]

Numerous commentators have blamed the Editor of the *Waco Tribune-Herald* for running the first episode of a hard-hitting exposé of the Branch Davidians immediately prior to the BATF' s assault on the compound. This allegedly broke an agreement with the BATF to withhold publication; and it probably forced the Bureau to take its ill-conceived action earlier than it had intended. On the other hand, it seems that the FBI placed considerably tighter restrictions on journalists covering the siege than is normal in similar events. In other words, the trade-off between journalists and authorities worked to the greater advantage of the latter.

Not enough attention has been given to the consequences of sensationalist depictions of religion in a secular age. To adapt the old adage, I am not trying to blame the messenger for bringing bad news but I am, indeed, accusing the messenger of fermenting mischief by relentlessly peddling negative stereotypes of new religious movements.

One conflict can hide another

Journalists' fascination with the tragedies of Jonestown and Waco stemmed not only from the exotic and improbable details of the two communities' ways of life but also from the suspicion that the cult controversies were only the tip of the iceberg. Investigative journalists had a field day with their inquiries into the possibility, either that people in authority had bungled the operations to prevent loss of life, and/or that attempts had been made afterwards to cover up the errors made by the forces of order. In other words, cult-related conflicts were connected with broader concerns about the use and misuse of state power.

Other examples of stories linking cults with conflicts against the state include the bombing by police of the anarcho-ecology group, MOVE, in Philadelphia; the killing by police in 1983 of all six followers of Lindberg Sanders, a self-styled 'Black Jesus', in a shoot-out in Memphis; and various armed assaults on dissident Mormons in Utah. The result is usually a polarization of journalistic and public opinion between, on the one hand, the view that agents of the state acted negligently or illegally and, on the other, the view that the same agents should have acted more decisively to suppress the movement in question before the problem had become unmanageable by peaceful means. But both cases illustrate the more general point that it is invariably the conflicts associated with new religious movements which make them newsworthy even when responsibility for the conflicts is attributed to the state.

An interesting twist to this theme quickly emerged in European print-media accounts of Waco. The long and slow-moving story of the siege provided an opportunity for journalists to investigate in depth the issues of gun ownership and control in the USA. In fact, the amount of attention devoted to this context of the action taken against the Branch Davidians sometimes outweighed reports of events at Waco. The conflictual image of cults was thereby reinforced by linking them with a separate conflict about firearms. One conflict was 'nested' in another.

Conclusion

This is not the place to analyse in detail the full repertoire of journalistic devices for depicting new religious movements. Elsewhere I have summarized the tendency for the mass media to characterize or caricature the movements as threatening, strange, exploitative, oppressive and provocative.[16] A content analysis of selected British print-media between 1975 and 1985 showed how this sensationalist approach helps to cement the public perception of cults as, at best, weird, and, at worst, destructive.[17] There is strong confirmation of this analysis from the USA.[18]

On the other hand, it is clear that the reasons for the biased presentation of new religious movements in the mass media are rooted in commercial pressures, cultural stereotypes and the lack of time for journalists to take a more nuanced and longer-term view of the movements.[19] It should also be recognized that some journalists have exposed the criminal activities of a few cult leaders and have therefore been helpful in checking abuses.[20] Indeed, the public is heavily dependent on the mass media for information about unconventional and sometimes secretive religious movements. My purpose is definitely not to denigrate these positive benefits of investigative journalism, for a healthy democracy depends in part on a combative press.

At the same time, however, it seems to me that the public is right to expect that journalists should be more methodical, discriminating, careful and open-minded than they normally are when it comes to portraying new religious movements. Their knee-jerk categorization of the movements as problematic and conflictual is not only prejudiced and lazy but it also feeds directly into public ignorance and a less than evenhanded attitude towards the movements on the part of social control agencies. The cosy relationship that many journalists have with the anti-cult movement can be an excuse for them not to do their research properly.

Notes

1. A slightly revised version of this chapter has appeared in *ISKCON Communications Journal*, 4, 1994, pp. 17-24

2. C. Candland, *The Spirit of Violence. An Interdisciplinary Bibliography of Religion and Violence* (Occasional Papers No. 6), New York: Harry Frank Guggenheim Foundation, 1992.

3. T. Modood, *Racial Equality. Colour, Culture and Justice*, London: Institute for Public Policy Research, 1994.

4. J. A. Beckford, *Cult Controversies. Societal Responses to New Religious Movements*, London: Tavistock, 1985.

5. J. T. Richardson, 'Public opinion and the tax evasion trial of Reverend Moon', *Behavioral Sciences and Law*, 10, 1, pp. 39-52.

6. Beckford, 1985, *op. cit.*, and D. G. Bromley and A. Shupe, 'Organized opposition to new religious movements', in D. G. Bromley and J. K. Hadden (eds), *The Handbook on Cults and Sects in America*, Greenwich, CT: JAI Press, 1993, pp. 177-98.

7. As examples of mainstream Christian antipathy towards marginal movements, see H. Davies, *Christian Deviations*, London: SCM Press, 1954; K. Hutten, *Seher, Grübler, Enthusiasten*, Stuttgart: Quellverlag, 1950; A. Hoekema, *The Four Major Cults*, Exeter: The Paternoster Press, 1969; W. R. Martin, *The Rise of the Cults*, Grand Rapids: Zondervan, 1955.

8. J. M. Yinger, *The Scientific Study of Religion*, New York: Macmillan, 1970.

9. J. McDonnell, 'Religion, education and the communication of values', in C. Arthur (ed.), *Religion and the Media*, Cardiff: The University of Wales Press, p. 92.

10. My analysis is based partly on a systematic scrutiny of print-media items about new religious movements in selected newspapers and magazines in the UK between 1975 and 1985, and partly on a thorough but more impressionistic study of the portrayal of the movements in British, American and French newspapers and magazines since 1985.

11. Quoted in I. L. Maffett, 'Waco and the *War of the Worlds*: media fantasy and modern reality', in R. J. Lewis (ed.), *From the Ashes: Making Sense of Waco*, Lanham, Md: Rowman and Little, 1994, p. 159.

12. K. E. Rosengren, P. Arviddsson and C. Winick, 'The Barsebäck »panic«: a case of media deviance', in C. Winick (ed.), *Deviance and Mass Media*, Beverley Hills: Sage, 1978, pp. 131-49; Beckford, 1985, *op. cit.*

13. The regular Newsletter of FAIR, the main anti-cult movement in Britain, devotes a great deal of space to print and broadcast reports of problems concerning movements. There is no evidence that these reports are checked for accuracy or bias. It is enough that they have appeared in print.

14. E. V. Barker, *New Religious Movement: A Practical Introduction*, London: HMSO, 1989.

15. C. A. Jones and G. Baker, 'Television and metaphysics at Waco', in Lewis, *op. cit.*, p. 151.

16. Beckford, *op. cit.*

17. J. A. Beckford and M. Cole, 'British and American responses to new religious movements', *Bulletin of the John Rylands Library of Manchester*, 70, 3, 1988, pp. 209-04.

18. B. van Driel and J. van Belzen, 'The downfall of Rajneeshpuram in the print media: a cross-national study', *Journal for the Scientific Study of Religion*, 29, 1, 1990, pp. 37-61; B. van Driel and J. T. Richardson, 'Print media coverage of new religious movements: a longitudinal study', *Journal of Communications*, 38, 3, 1988, pp. 37-61; B. van Driel and J. T. Richardson, 'The categorization of new religious movements in American print media', *Sociological Analysis*, 49, 2, 1988, pp. 171-83.

19. J. A. Beckford, 'The media and new religious movements', in Lewis, *op. cit.*

20. D. C. Mitchell, C. Mitchell and R. Ofshe, *The Light on Synanon*, New York: Seaview Books, 1980.

CHAPTER 7

The Christian Receptions of the New Age

Richard Bergeron

The New Age Movement, which took birth in North America, did not arrive alone and by itself in Europe. Like any other historical movement coming from outside, the New Age movement came to Europe bringing with it signs of the reception it received in the USA. As a matter of fact, many people had already heard about New Age from people outside the movement before they themselves had the chance to come into contact with the New Age in one or more of its manifestations. For some people, without even meeting a new-ager, without even reading new age literature, without even coming into contact with anything New Age, their first contact had been through material written by outsiders.

We have to admit, then, that most people receive the New Age through the reception of another. It follows that the personal reception of a socio-cultural and religious movement such as the New Age is a very delicate and tricky procedure. The personal reception must take into account:

1. That one has to be aware of the reception that other people have made of the New Age, based on their own keys of interpretation, or their own interests, sympathies or fears.
2. That one has to be clear about one's own personal convictions as well as one's own prejudices, insecurities and resistances.
3. That one should be prudent, and not make too hasty a judgement; instead, one should take one's time to study New Age with an open mind and with spiritual sympathy.

The focus of interest in this paper is the reception that French-

speaking Christians of Europe and Canada have accorded to the
New Age. This reception has taken three forms: the model of
refusal, the model of accepting, and the model of a dialectical union
of refusal and accepting.

1. The Refusal Model

The reception characterized as refusal has been elaborated by the
American Pentecostal and Evangelical congregations and churches
in the USA. These groups have expressed their response to the New
Age in an abundant literature, in precise pastoral practices, in
pamphlets, in articles appearing in Christian newspapers, and in
the mass media under the control of evangelicals and pentecostals.
Because of the silence of the great historic Churches (the Roman
Catholic church and the mainstream protestant Churches), the evangelical-fundamentalist response has come to be considered as 'Christian'. This vibrant and dynamic reception, marked by a zeal to defend Christianity and to denounce the perverse errors crossing its
borders, has often been pretentiously put forward as '*the* Christian
reception' of the New Age. In any event, it was the only available
model of Christian reception. This model accompanied the coming
of the New Age to French-speaking countries, and we have proof
of this in the French translations of several of these American books.

The evangelical-fundamentalist model of reception rests on three
basic principles:

1. There is no salvation outside the explicit belief in Christ and
    conversion to Jesus acknowledged as the only Saviour and
    mediator between God and human beings;
2. All teaching not found in the Bible is against the Bible, and
    hence heretical, the Biblical text being the only and last judge
    of all doctrine and practice;
3. Prophecy is the ultimate key of interpretation in understanding
    the historical events underlying the plan of salvation and a pre-
    millenarist conception of eschatology. With the help of
    prophecy, especially that of the Apocalypse, it is possible to
    discern in history signs which show the accomplishment of
    God's plan for the earth.

These three basic attitudes determine the understanding of the New Age which is widely circulated in evangelical-fundamentalist circles. The New Age is seen as:

1. A road leading to damnation, even if it does contain some elements of a search for the transcendent;
2. A mixture of heresies, errors and false beliefs about God, Christ and Salvation; a return to paganism, with pretensions to achieving divinity;
3. A predestined sign of the general apostasy which is supposed to precede the return of Christ and the end of the world;
4. A conspiracy of Satan under the direction of the Anti-Christ, to impose neo-fascism and destroy the kingdom of Christ. The books by Cumby, by Marrs and by Larson are extreme illustrations of this conspiratorial interpretation.

The model calls for a very characteristic response:

1. By rejecting the phenomenon as a whole, especially its doctrinal aspects, not least because of its esoteric occult practices;
2. By a challenging attitude which seeks to denounce the errors of New Age and to illustrate the truths of evangelical Christianity;
3. By a conversion strategy, using all energies to pull people away from the New Age.

This is the type of die-hard attitude which is shared by the great majority of evangelical and pentecostal fundamentalists in French speaking Europe and Quebec. The Pentecostal groups are the most aggressive. Their pastors cannot tolerate any involvement with error, for they see themselves as being accountable to God for uprightness in doctrine. They positively pride themselves on putting down the New Age. The Pentecostalists believe that the gifts of the Spirit flow in their communities. The pastors and the members of their congregations feel that these gifts have been entrusted to them, especially the gift of discernment, and this gives them the right to judge between what is good and bad, black and white, true and false. Their discernment comes from the power of the Spirit, and thus they feel they have the right to denounce without weighing things and without any involvement.

This attitude is somewhat softer in some evangelical groups which reject a conspiracy theory but which retain the apologetical dimension of this model of reception which invites all Christians to try their best to convert new-agers.

The pentecost-evangelical model of reception has succeeded in penetrating the great Christian Churches, both Catholic and Protestant, in the French-speaking world, where in some instances it seems to be in favour of new-agers: the New Age, it is said, has good intentions, but is off-track from the truth.

The Roman Catholic Church and the great Protestant Churches have developed no apostolic strategy towards New Age, and therefore it is difficult to define a particular reception of the New Age coming from these churches.

A good number of Catholics and Protestants, even among regular church-goers, have been influenced by ideas and practices proposed by the New Age. Belief in reincarnation, positive thinking, the quest for psycho-spiritual experiences, body-therapies, and much more from the market of the new religiosity has invaded the spiritual fields of many Catholics, who more and more are composing for themselves a Christianity *à la carte* by reinterpreting certain components of the Christian heritage and by taking skin grafts from cosmic religions, from esoteric thinking, or from transpersonal psychology. From all these elements, they have created a personal synthesis in which the internal coherence stems necessarily from an emotional logic, rather than from theoretical reasoning. People are less willing to accept ideas because they are true and in conformity with the magisterium, or with an outside authority, but only because they touch emotions, they are doing good, they are comforting or effective. The proven, the felt, the experiential become the measuring-stick of truth, and the basics from which new Christian coherence is made. Although many Catholics assume certain beliefs and practices of New Age, very few are converted to the project, to the paradigm, to the world vision of New Age. They have not yet accomplished the psycho-spiritual and epistemological conversion which goes hand in hand with entering into the New Age. Because many people touch the periphery of the New Age, we believe that the New Age is widespread, even among practising Christians.

In this situation, pastoral agents — priests, pastors and lay people — have often assumed an attitude influenced by the negative reception coming from the pentecostal-evangelicals. This approach has been used also in charismatic circles in the Catholic church. The charismatic community of the Lion of Judas in France is a good example. The negative attitude is developed without any preliminary theological reflection and under outside influence, without any planned approach. It expresses itself as a refusal, based on the incompatibility between New Age and Christianity, and takes pleasure in reaffirming its Christian faith, sometimes in the most traditional and conservative terms.

As for Jean Vernette, this kind of refusal seems to go with a certain form of acceptance. In fact his attitude, even if it goes under the banner of discernment, is still an apologetical endeavour, where the New Age is very subtly disqualified, to the advantage of Christianity, which has all the answers. Vernette proposes a method which may be summarized in three steps: exorcize, discern and evangelize. The exorcism is done by denouncing the New Age as neo-paganism, neo-gnostic syncretism, pantheism, monism. For Vernette the New Age is seen as a 'concoction' of techniques, practices and beliefs, as a 'bulimia of mystical experiences, as a new form of hedonism in a society over-heated by tranquilisers' etc.[1]

Once the New Age has been exorcized, then one may use discernment. Thus, for Vernette, discern means 'separate the grain from the husks',[2] and this can be done only by choosing a point of comparison from where one can discriminate. Vernette takes several points of comparison, according to each case: the Bible, Catholic dogma, the Apostolic tradition, the mystical masters, the Pope's words, Father Godin. His discernment consists of comparing the New Age doctrines with one of these measures with the aim, says the author, of showing that because of 'fundamental points of difference'[3] with Christianity, the new-ager is 'radically outside of Christianity'.[4]

Once the exorcism is accomplished, and the sorting out is realized, the third step is to evangelize by using the kerygma that proclaims that 'salvation is given by faith to the God of Jesus Christ'.[5]

This evangelization, reduced to the proclamation of the kerygma, aims either to convert the new-ager to Christianity, or to give to the New Age 'a reply coming from inside of Christianity itself'.[6]

With a few variations, we find this Vernette apologetical approach in Bernard Bastien,[7] and in the pastoral letter of Cardinal Danneels, Archbishop of Malines-Bruxelles. Even if the exorcism of the New Age is done with a very low profile, this letter aims particularly at showing the difference between the New Age and Christianity, and reaffirms that the Christian faith in an incarnate God is the answer to the New Age.

2. Acceptance

Just as the refusal model does not entirely exclude open-heartedness and acknowledgement of what is good and true in New Age, so the acceptance attitude does not exclude criticism and reasons for not receiving the New Age. Those in favour of an acceptance attitude do not miss the chance, on occasions, to criticize the New Age, to denounce commercialization and abusive practices, sometimes to such a degree that the great patron of New Age in Quebec, J. Languirand, has said, 'I have been de-frocked by the New Age', while at the same time remaining an ardent new-ager.

A minority of both French-speaking Catholics and Protestants take this attitude to a point of even sometimes declaring themselves to be new-age Christians. This liberal attitude is influenced by the Dominican theologian, Matthew Fox, who attempts to reinterpret Christianity using elements of the New Age paradigm. Based on the doctrine of the original blessing, on the monist principle and on the primacy of the cosmic on history, Fox seeks to elaborate a creation theology of the Cosmic Christ that integrates the intentions, feelings and values of New Age. Inspired by his thought, a minority of Catholics are searching through New Age for a new model of Christianity.

The best example of this liberal attitude in French-speaking society is perhaps the Protestant theologian from Switzerland, Carl Keller. In his book, *New Age*, Keller proposes the hypothesis, 'that the original melody of the New Age is the chant of Christ himself who sings his own glory';[8] he thinks that 'the yeast which makes the movement rise is the essence of Christianity itself, in other words, Jesus Christ is its Life and its Survival'.[9] According to him, 'the guru who leads the Aquarian children to perfection is none other than Christ who works anonymously. Authentic followers of New Age seek Christ without even knowing it; they are anonymous Christians, because they ignore the true identity of their inner dimensions'.[10] In summary, the Cosmic Consciousness which is spoken of in New Age is the Christ-Logos who created the universe and whose energy operates in all things. Thus the spirit of whom the New Age speaks is, in fact, the Spirit of the God of Christians. In a word, Keller perceives the theo-cosmo-anthropic Christ in the Cosmic Consciousness and the universal energy that the New Age speaks about. 'By calling for a change of paradigm which will re-establish the primacy of the spirit/consciousness/energy on matter, the New Age asserts implicitly the primacy of Christ/conscious-ness/energy on all phenomena of creation'.[11] This viewpoint, in-spired by the inclusivist model of theology, is built on interesting intuitions, and insists on the convergence of, and the similarities between, Christianity and the New Age. But does it not run the risk of dangerous misinterpretations, and of falling into comparisons which ignore the differences? And if the differences are covered up, would it still be possible to have a real dialogue? Isn't there a dis-guised Christian imperialism pretending that the New Age ignores what it adores, and that only Christianity is able to name and identify the liberator principle at work in its experience? And will the new-ager be happy to wear the label, 'Christian', and have others define his or her identity? I do not guarantee that this pro-posed attitude will bear as much fruit as may appear possible at first glance.

3. The Dialectical Union of Rejection and Acceptance

It seems to me that one has to find a response in which rejection and acceptance are held together in a dialectical union; a method which allows us to establish, in the same movement, a dynamic of acceptance and refusal. This does not mean accepting what is acceptable and refusing what is not acceptable, from the Christian standpoint. It means, rather, an attitude which maintains in a dynamic tension of refusal and acceptance at the same time. In a same action, one welcomes the New Age integrally and one refuses it integrally. That is to say that, on the one hand one recognises the New Age as an emerging spiritual reality, and, as such, one can only welcome it as it presents itself with all its specific components, true or false, with its greatness and its limits; on the other hand, one refuses it, meaning that one sees it as being something else, in its differences and distortions.

We assume, that is, that the dynamic typology proposed by Tillich in *Christianity and the Encounter of the World Religions* allows us to realise this dialectic union of acceptance and refusal. I have shown the validity of this method for treating new religions in my book *Le Cortège des fous de Dieu*, and its validity for treating the New Age in *Le Nouvel Âge en question*. This is the standard adopted by the 'Centre d'Information sur les Nouvelles Religions de Montrêal', and it has also been recommended to the Bishops of Quebec. I am happy to see that, during a Congress held in Geneva in May 1991, the Swiss theologian, Schwartz, explicitly declared that the method put forward in *Le Cortège des fous de Dieu* is the most appropriate approach for Christians in their encounter with New Age.

The dynamic typological attitude requires a certain elaboration of religious types, that is the Christian type and the New Age type. Each religious type articulates in its own way the great polarities found in every religious model. Here is an incomplete list: God/man, one/many, immanence/transcendence, faith/knowledge, mystic/ethic, reason/mystery, historic/cosmic, time/eternity, experience/belief, origin/end, action/contemplation, liberty/ destiny, life/death, nature/grace, personal/impersonal, good/evil. In each pair of polarities, the poles are in contrast and in tension. Tillich writes:

Types stand beside each other and seem to have no interrelation. They seem to be static, leaving the dynamics to the individual things, and the individual things, movements, situations, persons (e.g., each of us) resist the attempt to be subordinated to a definite type. Yet types are not necessarily static; there are tensions in every type which drive it beyond itself. Dialetical thought has discovered this and has shown the immense fertility of the dialectial descripton of tensions in seemingly static structures. The kind of dialectics which, I believe, is most adequate to typologial inquiries is the description of contrasting poles within one structure. A polar relation is a relation of inter-dependent elements, each of which is necessary for the other one and for the whole, although it is in tension with the opposite element. The tension drives both to conflicts and beyond the conflicts to possible unions of the polar elements. Described in this way, types lose their static rigidity, and the individual things and persons can transcend the type to which they belong, without losing their definite character.[12]

Thus, according to the method of dynamic typologies, the decisive point in the meeting of religions is not situated in historical structures (doctrinal, cultural, social), but in the way each religion understands and organizes the elements that are common to all religious models. The particular understanding of these common elements, and the particular way that they are organized around their constitutive poles, determines the specificity of religious types.

Reciprocal Interpellation

According to the dynamic typological method, the meeting of Christianity with the New Age takes, in the first place, the form of a reciprocal 'interpellation'[13] where the other is recognized in its specific difference. Interpellation does not occur at the level of doctrines and beliefs, but at the level of the constitutive poles of each spiritual and religious model, and is done thus: first the New Age questions the Christian Church on its manner of articulating, *hic et nunc*, the great poles of the Christian model; once this question is accepted, the Church, in its turn, can question the New Age. The New Age invites the Christian Church to consider critically the religious polarities as they are currently articulated in Christianity. Western history, the coming of modernity and scientific rationality, the triumph of technique and efficiency, have unbalanced the tensions between polarities to the advantage of certain poles: the historic to the detriment of the cosmic, action to the detriment of contemplation, sin to the detriment of goodness, the magisterial to the detriment of experiential, redemption to the deteriment of creation, transcendence to the detriment of immanence, the prophetic to the detriment of the mystic. The New Age challenges the Christian Church to severe self-appraisal and to a serious re-balancing of the tensions beween the poles.

On the other side, Christianity can also challenge the New Age on the balance of tensions which is particular to the New Age model. Does it not privilege the one over the many, the cosmic over the historic, the impersonal over the personal, the mystic over the ethic, the magic over the rational, immanence over transcendence, etc.? Christianity should question the New Age about its tendency to resolve tensions by negating certain polarities, which can lead to painful absolutizations and to a spiritual shrinking which can be very harmful.

The Confrontation

The second element of Christian reception of the New Age is confrontation, not in the sense of a quarrel, but in the sense of a head-to-head dialogue, establishing which elements are identical, and which are different. This is a dialogue in which similarities are recognized through confronting differences, a dialogue which refuses to skip over the differences and to go for unity at all costs. The confrontation is not at the level of spiritual paths and the great polarities of the types, but at the level of emphases and standpoints. I would like here to note three important points: the ambiguous relationship between New Age and modernity and rationality, the confusion between the spiritual and the psychic, and the refusal to acknowledge suffering as a factor in spiritual growth.

Ambiguous Relationship to Modernity

The New Age seeks to transcend modernity by returning to the archaic, archaic being understood as a model of understanding where the individual is anchored in a world-order dominated by forces and energies that eventually one can seize, orientate, and turn away by appropriate techniques, shamanic rituals, magic and occult practices, the use of objects said to possess mysterious powers, crystals, channelling, etc. By these practices one tries to create a Disney-world. The New Age is post-modern in the sense that it comes after modernity; it is pre-modern because it returns to traditional teachings and re-animates archaic principles. This retro-futurism seems to be an indication of the ambiguous way in which the New Age is situated in relation to modernity, particularly in relation to the rationalist ideal which is its principal regulator.

The New Age should be challanged on its relationship to analytical and technical rationality. If it is true that modern and scientific rationality ends in a *cul-de-sac*, it is an illusion to believe, as the New Age seems to, that one can correct the confusion and contradictions caused by reason by dismissing analytic rationality itself. It is not by doing away with rationality, but by stripping it of its pretentions to an absolute standard of knowledge that one may hope to find a way between the spiritual infertilty of modern rationality and the damaging credulity born of the denial of all forms of critical approach. It is only through minimizing the requirements of the critical spirit and of the *Aufklärung* that the world of wonder can be recreated.

Confusion Between the Psychic and the Spiritual

In the New Age, the words 'spiritual', 'spirituality' and 'spirit' carry a vague meaning. One thing is certain: the New Age tends to identify the spiritual with the psychic or para-psychic. Some authors, for example, Placide Gaboury, have drawn attention to this irritating confusion. As a result of this misunderstanding, the New Age encourages the psychic and para-psychic and adds to their strength. Even if exploration of the psychic leads towards a spiritual path, there remains the possibility that, in practice, it diverts people away from such a path because it ascribes to techniques and therapies a role and powers they do not really possess.

Because of this confusion what is best in the New Age, i.e. its spiritual research, runs the risk of degernating into a psychic side-product in search of happiness, psycho-corporeal well-being, and even a power-trip.

Concerning Suffering

The New Age is incapable of integrating suffering into its approach, as noted by Placide Gaboury and Matthew Fox. Yet we know that suffering forms an integral part of love, just as it is part of growth; whoever refuses to suffer, refuses also to love and to grow. To become, entails suffering; to reject suffering is to refuse to become. There is no short-cut along the spiritual path, and he who wants to avoid suffering has opted for spiritual atrophy. The New Age is false when it forgets that there is a serpent in paradise, and that happiness and abundance are not the sole aspects of spiritual growth. 'Spiritual growth', writes Placide Gaboury, 'demands a courage, a strength and faith that have nothing to do with crystals, ecstasies, out-of-body experiences, well-being and all that those therapies are supposed to bring. I believe that all of that does not prepare people for the terrible meeting with their own demons, when they find themselves alone, without explanation, without consolation, without any object to lean on. We do not prepare people by cradling them with angelic lullabies, astral-music (which avoids completely all discordancies and shocks), caressing and floating-baths. All these are mothering. There is one essential element missing, I say the »essential«.'[14]

The Criticism

This third approach to the Christain reception of the New Age contains the possibility of denouncing abuses of trust and the exloitation of the naivety of people in distress. Unwarranted commercialization risks stifling the dynamism of the New Age, reducing it to mere trendiness or to something simply commercial. Marketing means that all products may be labelled New Age, be they glasses, furniture, or clothes. Especially when we deal with psycho-spiritual therapies, we are often 'in the presence of »by-products« where one finds them here and there, applied by »thera-peutics« who sometimes are charlatans, sometimes »charismatics«, sometimes »humanists« or »Jungians«, or just vaguely »oriental«'.[15]

There is good reason to call for prudence and discernment. One does not entrust one's soul to just any Tom, Dick or Harry.

In conclusion, we can say, in the spirit of Vatican II, that the attitude to the New Age should be one of dialogue. This implies that each of us, secure in his own beliefs, should be willing to listen and to learn, even if it is only to gain in precision and flexibility when reaffirming our own convictions. New-agers who display a 'new-convert' mentality are not always disposed to enter into dialogue because, having rejected the faith of their childhood, they feel they have nothing to learn from the Church. In reality, the New Age counts more sympathizers than adepts, and many of the sympathizers are Christians, even practising Christians. Some of the sympathies are the result of misunderstandings of Christian faith and also of the New Age. The dialogue approach may be of particular help in enabling sympathizers to realize what the New Age is really saying and what the Christian Church is really teaching. The New Age may be a positive stimulus if we take it for what is: a spiritual quest in the heart of authentic humanity.

Notes

1. *Le Nouvel Âge*, p. 207.
2. *Op. cit.*, p. 4.
3. *Ibid.*, p. 182.
4. *Ibid.*, p. 181.
5. *Ibid.*, pp. 179-208.
6. *La Vie chrétienne*, July-August 1992, p. 4.
7. *The New Age: Where is it Coming From?*
8. P. 77.
9. P. 78.
10. P. 67.
11. P. 87.
12. Tillich, *op. cit.*, p. 55.
13. Interpellate: '(In foreign, esp. French, Chamber) interrupt order of day by demanding explanation from (Minister concerned)', *Concise Oxford Dictionary* [Ed.].
14. *Renaître des cendres*, Libre Expression, 1991, pp. 76-77.
15. Pierre Pelletier, *Les Dieux que nous sommes*, Montreal: Fides, 1992, p. 50.

CHAPTER 8

New Age: The Religion of the Future?

Reender Kranenborg

The West is experiencing three developments, among others, with respect to religion. First, there is the rise of New Age. For years there was talk of a coming secularization: more and more people were abandoning the Church and Christian belief and going their own way. This development was often viewed as unique to religion: one could now, it seemed, speak of a-religious or post-religious humanity for the first time in the history of religions. The last decade, however, has made it clear that this view was mistaken. The secularized, the a-religious, person did not appear to exist. In fact, it is just the opposite: the modern person appears to be religious in the extreme, to be interested in the deeper questions of life and non-observable ultimate reality. This trend can be seen in what is presently known as the New Age movement. Even though it is not a unified movement, it can be characterized as a religion coming into being within Western culture.[1]

The second development concerns an earlier, but still important, trend: the continuing movement away from the Church. It is no longer correct to see this as secularization in the strict sense of not being religious or subscribing to any belief, since those who are now leaving the Church are not always non-religious. On the contrary, as we have seen, many feel sympathy with New Age thinking. This abandonment of the Church is still continuing in Europe. If we look at the established Churches, it does not appear to be levelling off — the tempo is picking up rather than slowing down.

A third trend can be detected between the first two: one can note increasingly that New Age ideas and influences are making inroads into the Church, with the result that within the Church a new spirituality has arisen. Without sensing any need to break with the Church, many members are accepting ideas and practices of New Age and related schools of thought, through which the official Church doctrines and traditional Christian teachings are being interpreted in an entirely different way. In addition to the independent development of New Age outside the Church and Christian belief, we also see its development within the Churches themselves.

With these three developments, the following question is raised: What will be the religion of the future in the West? Does the future belong to New Age? After all, the New Age movement is growing, while the Church is declining, and within the Churches an increasingly New Age mentality can be seen. Is it not obvious, therefore, that, in the United Europe of the twenty-first century, Christianity will probably be nothing more than a marginal group, differing greatly from traditional Christianity? A few traditional Christians and Churches will continue to exist, but these, in the new age of a United Europe, will be as unimportant as the diverse small sects now. In short, it might be claimed that New Age — the religion of holism, solidarity and unity — can be seen as the religion of a new united Europe (and America). In other words, New Age is not only the new world religion but also the religion of the new world.[2]

Here I wish to analyze more closely the above-mentioned expectations and trends. It is, of course, impossible to predict the future of religion in the Europe of the twenty-first century, but on the basis of specific developments some conclusions can be made which may give us an idea of the future.

New Age's Attitude to Christianity and Christian Faith

If one wants to speak of New Age and Christianity one has first to deal with the question of how each views the other, how each responds to the other, and what they expect from each other. Do the views that each has of the other reflect the trends mentioned above?

We will look first at the views of Christianity within New Age. In order to understand this properly, it is necessary to ask how New Age views religion generally, since the specific view of Christianity fits with the framework of its view of all world religions. With respect to this, theosophy has been determinative for New Age, since New Age has taken over views that theosophy displayed from its beginnings in 1875. It is believed that there existed in the beginning a universal world and life view, a primal religion that preceded all the world religions. The latter are seen as formalistic and fossilized. They have lost touch with their original universal inspiration, were under the supervision of priests who no longer had any knowledge of the origin, so that what was once a living experience was cocked in cut-and-dried dogmas.

Because these dogmas were seen as eterna truths, differences between the religions arose on an increasing scale. The dogmas later received further elaboration, through which the differences increased and the original inspiration receded further into the background.

Theosophy held that the original universal religion must be rediscovered. If this could be done, the petrified religions could return to their roof. This original religion was (and is) the secret, esoteric religion. Although this knowledge of the esoteric truths was generally lost within the world religions, there have always been small groups of initiates who held fast to these in secret and who have been present throughout all ages.[3] Now, that is, in 1875, the time has come that this carefully preserved esoteric teaching can become universally known; it is now revealed and visible in theosophy.

This view of the esoteric nucleus of the world religions has a corrollary view of the future of religion. In any case, it not for nothing that this can be made fully known in 1875. It indicates that the time is now ripe and that people are now in a position to orient themselves to the original intention. From this point on, people will now increasingly give up the dogmas of the churches and religions and search for this living experience. In the course of time the dogmatic religions will disappear entirely, which is what we see happening now in the West at the end of the 20th century.

There are many authors belonging to the New Age movement who expound this position in one way or another, applying it to Christianity. Well-known here are Capra and Ferguson or, already in the sixties, Spangler in England. In their writings we see a continual resistance to the dogmatic side of Christian belief. In particular, they object to the idea of an exclusive revelation, in which there is no salvation outside of the Bible, the church or Jesus Christ. The notion that Jesus Christ is the mediator, the only Redeemer or the Reconciliator is rejected. This view is exclusive and too negative with respect to other spiritual leaders and traditions in the history of religion. Further, there is a strong resistance to the position of priest (and the pope) as a clery that considers itself to be in a position to decide what people may or may not believe. Biblicism is also a point of difficulty: here too one can see the absoluteness of Christianity that allows no space to other views. The monolithic character of the Church, through which there is no room for new and other views and development is excluded is also deplored. Difficulty is also expressed with respect to the dualism of Christian faith, in particular the posing of God and humans over against each other. Finally, there is disagreement with the conviction that the revelation or speaking of God to humans is closed off in Jesus or the Bible.

From the so-called original esoteric view a further clear distinction is made between what the chruches on the one hand have made of it and teach and what on the other hand, according to the theosophic interpretation, is still present of the original view. One does not throw the baby (content) out with the bathwater (church). Thus the Bible is respected as an important book, as a source of inspiration for belief and thought, even as the Bhagavad Gita or the words of the Buddha. Jesus also is respect as an important religious personality, comparable to other great figures from the world religions, such as Buddha, Zarathustra, Lao Tse or Pythagoras. Jesus is of interest within New Age, different sides of which are illuminated. Sometimes Jesus is the inspiring example or he is the model of what every person can be. In other cases, Jesus is he who raised the evolution of humanity to a higher level, or he is an avatara, in whom the divine revealed itself in order to show people at the time the true way. Sometimes Jesus is the Gnostic or the one who gave people the liberating gnosis. Again, others speak of the Christ principle or the Christ energy that was manifested in Jesus and which is present in every person. One must become aware of this Christ spirit.

Another point is yet made: revelation has not been closed. What occurred in biblical times and of which we can read in the Bible occurs also now. Now as well, there is address from the other world and also now people can have contact with God.

The New Age critics of Christianity are of the opinion that traditional Christianity is doomed but that the essential elements will remain and constitute an integral part of the universal religion that is New Age.

Reactions to New Age from the Churches

Reactions to New Age from the churches are forthcoming. Almost everywhere we see that Christians and theologians are becoming occupied with this new spirituality. This is striking, for the churches did not react or in very minor ways to a previous challenge, that of the so-called 'sects' or new religious movements. Pastoral letters appeared, warnings were issued here and there, but basically the Church did not feel challenged and there was no necessity to enter into dialogue with one or more of these groups. This is different with respect to New Age. We can ascertain some reasons for this.

In the first place, over against sects, New Age is indeed competition. The sects were (or are) small, separate, often extreme, had peculiar ideas and seemed to give people little room. In New Age this is not the case. That which restrained people from joining sects is missing here. New Age seems to be more attractive.

In the second place, sects were complete, for the most part thought in black-and-white terms and not much freedom was to be found. Here again it is different with New Age. Here one can find 'associative thinking', one's own ideas are praised as being an alternative and academically solid. The emphasis is on the living experience. Moreover, New Age presents itself as complementary: next to one's own belief, a New Age method can be experienced as enriching.

In the third place, connected to the above, New Age is not absent from the Churches. People increasingly experience the fact that church members appropriate central New Age ideas without much difficulty, attempt to combine these with Christian belief and remain within the Church. Indeed, sometimes they present themselves as 'New Age missionaries'. The Church feels called upon to respond to that which occurs within her space.

Fourthly, one sees, in connection with the above, that New Age affects christian belief, often in fundamental ways. Non-Christian New Age circles often give an image of Christian belief that is not recognizable and within New Age groups associated with the churches, one sees a Christianity arise that no longer resembles what was learned previously. The churches feel themselves affected with respect to their identity. This necessitates response.

New Age as the Realm of the Opponent

One of the first responses is that of right-wing Christianity — evangelicals, Pentecostals, charismatics (both Protestant and Catholic) and the strict confessional or fundamentalist Churches or groups within the Churches.[4] The responses coming from these circles are chiefly characterized by a lack of openness towards New Age. They do not ask whether one can learn something from this movement, nor why people are attracted to it; they opt for an all-out confrontation with New Age, giving no quarter and admitting no subtle nuances. For the rest, it is not always clear what the various writers see as belonging to New Age. Some include within New Age everything not in agreement with their own views — such as the other world religions, Marxism, all alternative healing methods, sects, the World Council of Churches and the United Europe. Others are more restricted, and exclude only certain things. Thus, they view certain forms of alternative healing, such as homeopathy, as not falling under the category of New Age and do not oppose it. Nonetheless, however extensive or limited they define the scope of New Age, in every case it is to be rejected.

Two motives play a central role in this rejection. The first is the conviction that these are 'the last days' and the expectation that Jesus Christ will return in the near future. They read in the Bible that the return of Jesus will be preceded by a great falling away from the faith and that Satan will make a last attempt to establish his power. For that purpose the antichrist will appear before the end to establish his kingdom on earth and through his preaching and activity will cause many to fall away from the faith. The antichrist will present himself as child of light, who will perform special signs and wonders, through which people will be converted to him. He will attempt to bring the whole world into his power and his symbol in the Bible is the number 666.

For these groups, it is clear that the Bible is speaking of New Age. After all, within New Age there is talk of a new era or a new kingdom, an attempt to unite all people. Its philosophy is one of holism and New Age adherents also speak about light in various ways. Peculiar things happen in different therapies or in contacts with the other world. It is clear that there is much in New Age that is cause for wonder. Its right-wing critics also point out that New Age does speak about Jesus but in an entirely different and non-Christian way. It is striking, in addition, that the New Age symbol, as used by Ferguson, as well as others, can be seen as three sixes revolving around one another. These circles, moreover, emphasize that New Age is anti-Church and anti-Christian, citing various quotes as evidence. The term 'conspiracy' is thus also a clear indication that a dark force is at work here, attempting to alienate people from Jesus in all sorts of ways. Thus Cumbey writes:

Authoritative figures of the New Age movement (Alice Bailey, David Spangler, Nicholas Roerich, etc.) have threatened a world war against the world religions and even the annihilation of Christians, Jews, Moslems and others who refuse to accept Maitreya as 'the Christus'.

Such a fate awaits those who refuse to be converted to the 'new world religion'.[5]

A second motive is one of 'practical dualism'. Although the Christian Church and theology have never recognized a dualism between good and evil in the sense that an eternal God exists over against an eternal evil, in practice, especially among 'rightist' Christians, one often comes across mention of a practical dualism. Reality has broken into two: a kingdom of God and a kingdom of Satan. There is a continual struggle between the two and both are present in this world in which Christians also live. Because of grace and repentance, Christians are on the right side, but this entails their feeling even more intensely the power of the evil kingdom. Their lives are therefore engaged in continual struggle against the devil and his kingdom. Where is this kingdom of the devil to be found? While Satan attacks on many fronts, it is the occult that is the serpent's domain. The latter is, as it were, his kingdom proper, the anti-kingdom that stands over against Jesus Christ. One is thus required expressly to reject the occult — in fact, one must fight against it wholeheartedly and guard oneself against all contact with it. Contact with the occult, once made, can infect one for the rest of one's life and cause difficulties.

The occult is defined as comprising everything that God has explicitly forbidden: meddling with idols and idolatry, becoming involved with astrology, taking up contact with spirits, the dead or beings from the other worlds, espousing magic and the power of evil, making use of powers that do not come from God. The attempt to liberate oneself without God's grace can also be called occult. Thus, it is clear that New Age belongs to the domain of the occult. In New Age people do work with powers and with magic, they do seek contact with other worlds and heed the stars. They attempt to predict the future and speak of self-realization. New Age is thus seen as nothing else than a new shoot from the root of the occult, which in modern dress and by new methods, including an appeal to 'science', attempts to pass on the old message of esotericism. In short, New Age is to be rejected as part of the kingdom of Satan. It is also striking that the critique of New Age coming from these Christian groups was found prior to its actual appearance, and before the term 'New Age' came into common parlance. One can find the same arguments in older literature which opposed spiritism and esotericism.[6]

Without evaluating this attitude as such, we wish to make a few remarks. First, this response clearly demonstrates that the ideas of New Age are not neutral (insofar as ideas can be neutral) but are explicitly coloured by a specific philosophy. Even though New Age does speak of God, Jesus Christ and humanity, the way in which this is done clearly stems from a specific tradition which differs from the generally accepted Christian faith. In this evangelical response we can see clearly where the differences lie and sense precisely where the changes occur. In the second place, this response points to the fact that the practices in which New Age engages are themselves not neutral. An anthropology lies behind the various kinds of therapies and/or techniques. Even though this is not always expressed within the therapy group, it is present, and a Christian critique helps to bring this to one's attention. It is also shown that people are changed by these groups and techniques, and that participation in such New Age activities is not without strings attached, and not always healthy. Through New Age, people can become involved in situations which they did not anticipate, and can also find that their own Christian faith has been lost, or interpreted so differently that it no longer resembles the original. Thus this evangelical circle also explicitly poses the question of mental/ psychological/spiritual health.

In short, this response, however one-sidedly applied in an occult-demonic framework, clearly interprets New Age as rejecting Christianity. In addition, one should note that many of the books published in this circle — nomatter how incorrect — offer extensive information about New Age. With respect to that which rejects Christianity, the authors are for the most part well-informed, although very one-sided.

New Age as an Instrument for Reflection

More nuanced approaches can be found within the established Churches. The interpretive framework of eschatology and the occult is lacking, there is a willingness to listen to New Age, and to inquire why people feel themselves attracted to it. The representatives of this response are prepared, by means of New Age, to pay attention again to the essentials of Church and faith and to reflect on their central aspects. At the same time, they clearly reject New Age in principle. It is not accepted theologically, and several fundamentally incompatible aspects are noted. It is also criticized over several points. A number of different reactions can be distinguished.

We can best illustrate the first response by reference to the Belgian Cardinal Danneels,[7] who maintains, on theological grounds, that New Age and Christian faith can never be fully compatible. His view reflects that of several Roman Catholics, such as many in the charismatic wing, to which Danneels feels sympathetic. On the one hand, Danneels can understand the attraction. He also sees the good in New Age — the ideas of universal brotherhood and peace, the use of all powers for good, certain yoga and relaxation techniques. He does not see New Age as the work of the devil against which people must anxiously guard themselves. He also gives an analysis of the origin and the nature of New Age. He indicates its roots in the modern natural sciences, Eastern religions, new psychology and the already older esotericism and astrology. New Age for him is ultimately a form of syncretism. In his response he clearly accentuates the fundamental differences. God and people will never converge — God is the Other. Prayer involves a relationship, not a form of losing oneself in meditation. People are dependent on grace for liberation and here Jesus Christ is the redeemer. Also, Christ cannot be seen as an idea or an ethereal divine being manifested in Jesus. Jesus Christ is the Son of God. Within New Age, the reality of suffering and death are finally denied and people are burdened with the heavy task of freeing themselves through redemption techniques, in contradiction to the Christian faith, in which God liberates humans through the sacrifice of Jesus Christ, and evil is seen as evil. Furthermore, in New Age, belief becomes a form of self-experience, which it is not. Moreover, humans are unique individuals, and the notion of redemption via many lives is to be rejected. Danneels also refers clearly to the idea of responsibility for one's neighbour, an idea that, according to him, is disappearing in New Age. In short, New Age is indeed a challenge but does not offer anything new. Rather, New Age is a temptation for the person; the essential and the true are to be found in Christianity.

A related Protestant response asserts just as emphatically that New Age and Christian faith are finally incompatible. Central to this response is the theological thought of Barth. Barth maintained that religion is unbelief, and therefore the establishment of New Age as a religion, in the full sense of the word, means that New Age is not enriching. After all, religion is the work of proud humans, in which they fashion their own gods, assert themselves over against God, and in which they are searching only for themselves. Faith concerns openness to God, the recognition that God is the Wholly Other, and that God must reveal this to people. New Age is therefore also a factory of gods, a good illustration of the depraved nature of religion. It is the very epitome of religion and is therefore to be rejected and combatted. For the rest, the representatives of this response are prepared to pursue the question as to why people feel attracted to New Age, but are quick to see this as emerging from the innate nature of humans as tending to devise their own religion without God.

Apart from its connections with Barth, this response finds an ally in the 'Sceptical Movement'. This organization, which is not associated with any Church or religion, but wishes to be purely scientific, is set on exposing the irrational aspect of phenomena of various sorts, in particular the paranormal and the occult, and New Age is included within this. People are in danger of losing their healthy powers of judgement and becoming wrapped up in irrationalism.[8]

The Christians here also strongly emphasize the consequences of New Age for practical living. Here they refer also to irrationalism, the lack of critical insight, through which people can run into difficulties, become psychologically confused or dependent on shrewd leaders.

In addition to this, the objection is also raised against New Age that people are distracted from the concrete world and their fellow human beings. In New Age the higher world is ultimately more important, and the development of oneself takes priority over the encounter with the other. The world is abandoned to its fate and there is no interest in, or devotion to, this world: problems such as poverty, underdevelopment, etc. are no longer tackled. In this connection it is expressly noted that the prophetic element is lacking, that is, no critical voice is raised against the powers of this world and the developments that occur in it. On the contrary, one sees much more of an absolutization or divinization of this world: all that is related to the divine. Everything is holistically connected to everything else, and thus has its own place, in relation to which little can be changed.

This leads to a further criticism, that within New Age, it is claimed, evil has no place, since in principle it is good. In New Age, good and evil are relative concepts, for what is bad on our level can be good on a higher level. This is connected to the view that evil has a function and meaning. A person can learn and grow from what happens to him, he can develop through experience. The consequences of this view are listed: the terminal illness that someone contracts is due to her own choice and has a purpose; the premature child that dies has itself willed to die, the parents have chosen its death, and the entire experience helps the parents to develop spiritually. These ideas are associated with so-called positive thinking, which maintains that consciousness determines the physical state of a person, that thinking can affect and rectify situations, including situations of sickness. This is considered to be a harsh and cruel way to think. Here Christians are joined by the sceptics, since they also note the loveless consequences of such a way of thinking. Finally, great difficulty is also experienced with the fact that death is seen as something positive, as an entrance to a new and better existence, as the beginning of a higher phase of life. Death is trivialized, the struggle against death loses its impetus, and it is impractical to grieve over the mortality of oneself or another. In short, this Christian group is of the opinion that New Age undermines human life and devalues human beings. The human being is no longer a human being.

New Age as an Instrument for Depth

We encounter still another kind of response within the Churches. Here agreement is expressed in principle with the responses described above, that there is a fundamental difference between New Age and Christian faith. In this case, however, it is held that Church, theology and Christian thinking can change. It is possible to reformulate certain aspects, or to supplement or deepen one's own thought. New Age exposes the shortcomings of the Church and theology and it becomes clear that they have often been limited and one-sided. For Christian faith, New Age is a rich source of opportunities to come to new formulations and a further deepening and enrichment. We can encounter this approach in Sudbrack, for example. In the Netherlands one could mention Veenhof.[9] The latter sees New Age as providing a challenge and corrective to the shortcomings of the Church and theology. New Age has exposed the cultural crisis, apparent in environmental destruction, in the one-sided rationalistic approach in the West. New Age provides a new paradigm that is holistic, evolutionary and dynamic and which no longer recognizes the one-sidedness of the past. Veenhof wishes to reflect further on this and arrives at five issues where Church and theology can follow new directions. First, he asks that attention be paid to the significance of meditation. Even though this would have a different content within a Christian framework, one could learn much from New Age with respect to form and method. Next, Veenhof finds the holistic approach to human beings appealing: the human being is a unity and must not be viewed in a dualistic way as has often happened in theology. Thirdly, Veenhof wishes to reconsider the relationship between God and the world. Even though one must retain the difference between the two, they could be related more closely to each other: God dwells in the world through his Spirit. Veenhof argues for 'panentheism' (God dwells in the world he has made, and the world exists in him). Fourthly, he questions more explicitly the relationship between God and human beings. In the past, God and humanity were seen too much in opposition to each other (humans were small and sinful), but God is not far from any of us. Even though the distinction between God and humanity remains, the relationship with, and indwelling of, God could be more emphasized. Finally, he refers to the concept of God. God was too often thought of as the Wholly Other, and New Age brings the Church back to the ideas of covenant and relationship. God is the Other, the Thou, but in a close, loving relationship.

New Age as a Perspective of the Future

There are also groups within Christianity that see new opportunities for Christian faith in New Age. A few presuppositions are almost always present here. In the first place, the conviction exists that we are indeed living on the faultline between two ages. The old Age of Pisces is passing away, while the new Age of Aquarius has still not fully dawned. In view of evolution, these groups are convinced that the New Age will dawn shortly and it can now be perceived. This new era is seen for the most part as the coming of God's kingdom. Secondly, these circles generally hold to universalism: the view that all religions ultimately refer to the same reality. The Church has been too limited in this respect and has shown itself to be closed. This view is mistaken because Christian faith is also concerned with the same universal wisdom. Thirdly, it is believed that there are messages from the other, higher world (the spheres) at this time. These messages can be considered to be revelations of the God of the Bible. God also speaks today to modern human beings.

For these reasons, they listen to New Age and are prepared not only to learn but also to take New Age thinking into their own Christian faith, or to give this Christian faith an entirely different content. They see the old Christian concepts assume a new clarity, and recover their original meaning in New Age. In this sense, these circles associate themselves with the theosophical view of the previous century. New Age is thus seen as an enrichment; it is Christianity as it was meant to be, and as it will function in the future. These groups explicitly consider themselves to be Christian, even in this New Age interpretation of Christianity. After all, precisely because New Age lays bare the true meaning and gives back to Christianity its proper content, they can see themselves as the true, although different and modernized, Christians. Apart from this, these groups bring their own emphases with respect to the whole of the New Age movement. In many instances more emphasis is laid on Jesus Christ than is the case in New Age generally. In that sense, there is a historical parallel with anthroposophy, in which Jesus receives a more central place than in theosophy.

Douven,[10] in particular, is associated with this view in the Netherlands. Inspired by certain New Age spokesmen, he has developed a new Christian theology. Prominent in this view is the idea that we are living in a period of transition and that the new era is about to dawn. Douven considers this development to be the result of evolution. Humanity as a whole, as well as each individual, is evolving towards higher levels spiritually. At the level of the world this is evident in the advent of a new era; we are more developed spiritually than was the case 2000 years ago. Characteristic of the present is that God is engaging in new revelations. In channelings and other transmissions, God is speaking new things to people and the revelation of the Bible is being advanced in concrete ways. In this time, more than previously, people are occupied with realizing their divinization. God is entering more strongly into the hearts of people, people are uniting themselves with him. In this connection he can speak of the 'the Christ', or the Christ energy, that manifested itself in Jesus of Nazareth and which is becoming stronger in people today. Through this Christ energy, humans are more and more conforming to the image of God. For Douven it is clear that this development involves several lives — it does not proceed without reincarnation. The concept of karma is also central here: we learn through what overcomes us, it helps us to develop spiritually. Finally, Douven likes to appeal to the secret tradition of Jesus, which agrees in principle with what had always been taught in esotericism. The Church no longer understood this, but this secret teaching is now becoming known once again.

Douven does not stand alone. There are many Christians who find themselves in agreement: Christians who have had contact with the other world, believe in reincarnation, work on their karma, and await the new age with joy. It is clear that this response also evokes criticism within the Churches. Missing here are the fundamental rejection of New Age and the critical insight. Nonetheless, those who follow this line are certain that their view can be called Christian.

To Whom Does the Future Belong?

Having considered all this, we can now ask: What will the future bring? It is clear, of course, that nobody knows with certainty; indeed, religion has always been full of surprises. Nevertheless, a few threads can be pulled together and a few considerations brought to the foreground.

Christianity is not disappearing

As we saw, one of the beliefs of several New Age groups is that Christianity, as a religion of the old Age of Pisces, will no longer exist in this form. If there will be something called Christianity in the Age of Aquarius, it will be entirely different. The question then arises of whether Christians of today will recognize the Christianity of the new era.

The question, however, is whether this idea is not too schematic. Does history work in this way? After all, when Christianity began as the religion of the new Age of Pisces (to keep to the New Age terminology), the religion that originated in the previous age, i.e., Judaism, did not disappear. As everyone knows, Judaism has continued to exist in its various forms right up to the present and does not give any impression of becoming a relic of the past. There is something else as well. Christianity did indeed begin at the beginning of what New Age calls the Age of Pisces, but it was not the only religion to do so. At about the same time Gnosticism came into existence, while at the end of the first century Mithraism also arose as a new religion which was highly attractive. Christianity was finally victorious in the fourth century, and the other religions disappeared or went underground. But why did this take 400 years to occur? Was Christianity that which fitted best with the Age of Pisces? For the rest, we must keep in mind that we are dealing exclusively with the Western world, the world of the Roman Empire. The cultures and religions of the East, from Persia to China, do not fit into this scheme at all. It is striking, moreover, that the religion that also arose in the West, Gnosticism, disappeared, but is now reviving, precisely at the beginning of the Age of Aquarius. How could a religion that had such a great influence, and which, according to many, answered a general human need (though it did not fit into that earlier age), function at the time? Or was it ahead of its time? That seems improbable, since Gnosticism has always existed underground in one form or another.

But we can turn to an entirely different case. Islam does not fit at all into the framework of world eras. How could a religion arise from nothing, as it were, seven centuries after the beginning of the Age of Pisces and have so much influence, defeating and out-flanking Christianity on several fronts? It is not coincidental that Islam (with the exception of the mystical sufis) plays no role at all in New Age thinking. The idea that a new religion begins with the advent of a new age, and that the old religions will disappear, is not borne out by the historical facts. There is no reason, therefore, to expect that the Christian religion will no longer exist in the next century.

For the rest, one should think in global terms. New Age often thinks too regionally and pays too much attention to developments in Europe and North America, where there is indeed an abandoning of Church and Christian faith. Globally, however, this does not appear to be the case. In Africa, Christianity is one of the two fastest growing religions, and in Latin America, Christianity is growing quite rapidly in the form of Pentecostalism and Protestant groups. The decline of Christian faith in the West is being compensated by growth elsewhere in the world. New Age, on the other hand, can scarcely be detected in other parts of the world. Viewed globally, Christianity will enter and survive the next century largely intact.

What, however, are the prospects for the West? Will the Christian faith disappear in the West? On the one hand, those who are informed in the history of religions know that religions which are not associated with specific peoples seldom disappear. They can be driven from a specific area, but still continue to exist, either as a remnant or by re-establishing themselves elsewhere. The Buddhists were driven from India but have become prominent in Southeast Asia and are re-emerging in India. Christians, sometimes in large numbers, disappeared from Turkey, the Middle East and North Africa but, as is well known, exist everywhere else in the world. The Persian religion was driven from Persia but Parsis exist today in India. The most sombre scenario for the West would be that the majority take their leave of the Christian faith and a minority remains. However, if we ask ourselves what sort of a minority this will be, we can see that this will consist of different segments. In the first place, Pentecostals, evangelicals, fundamentalists, orthodox Catholics and Protestants, and groups that are largely insensitive to the concerns of New Age will continue to exist. These groups have by no means become any weaker in the West — on the contrary, some are growing. Secondly, besides the above-mentioned more fundamentalist groups, there will undoubtedly be many other Churches and Christians that, inspired by Christian faith, will simply adhere to their own convictions without being fundamentally influenced by New Age or related movements. They will be critical, sometimes sceptical, emphasizing human responsibility and adhering to their fundamental religious convictions. This attitude is not disappearing among Christians. In addition, there will be a third group of Christians, as can be expected in a pluriform society, who allow themselves to be influenced by New Age. Nothing further can be said about the scope of this group.

For the rest, anyone who discusses the future of religion and wishes to know what are the possibilities for religion, needs to widen the circle. Both Islam and the Eastern religions are factors. Religion as a whole in the Europe of the twenty-first century will be quite varied and extremely pluriform. New Age will also be an element here. Whether it will be the most significant, whether it will take the place of current Christianity, and whether it will be in competition with other religions, is very much the question. The claim that New Age will be the religion of the future comes, in fact, from its own strong missionary faith.

Christianity has not disappeared

We could say that Christianity has withstood similar challenges. The emergence of New Age is, within New Age circles, compared to the Renaissance and Romanticism. In the fifteenth century, too, a new understanding of life accompanied the Renaissance, with a different view of God, humanity and the world. Hermetic gnosticism was discovered and people saw a new age dawning. The Christian thinking of the time was viewed as outmoded and new ways were sought. If one asks whether New Age is to be compared with a cultural movement like the Renaissance, then there are indeed correspondences. But the sixteenth century Renaissance ideas with respect to religion were not determinative of the religion of the future. In Europe, the future proved to belong, on the one hand, to the Reformation, which because of the Renaissance trend to return to the sources, rediscovered the Bible in the original languages and thus received a new impetus, and, on the other, to the Counter-Reformation. The Christianity that appeared in Europe after the Renaissance was anything but coloured by the religious ideals of the Renaissance. On the contrary, it was representative of a period prior to the Renaissance, and the ideals that were so enthusiastically adhered to with respect to religion almost completely disappeared.[11]

Something similar could be claimed with respect to Romanticism, which arose at the end of the eighteenth century. Here we also see, as a reaction to rationalism and the Enlightenment, a search for a different religiosity. The East came into view, and people paid attention to the soul and their inner selves. The experience of nature was of great importance and secret powers were explored. Nothing was expected of a fossilized and dogmatic Christianity. But the religious ideals of Romanticism finally did not determine the future of religion in Europe. Neither did Christian faith disappear. Romanticism did, indeed, give rise to stimuli in the religious life that still exist, such as spiritism, and the esotericism that would later appear in the form of theosophy, but in the nineteenth century these remained marginal. Within Christianity, Romanticism gave rise to the Reveil, which signified a revival of Christian faith. The Reveil took over the emphasis on emotions but remained orthodox with respect to content. In Catholicism, Romanticism led to the rise and strengthening of conservatism. In addition, as a response to Romanticism, several Protestant theologians, such as Schleiermacher, initially laid heavy emphasis on the element of experience, but after some time turned toward a more biblically inspired faith. In short, Romanticism did not lead to another religion in the West, but was in many ways a stimulus for, and a strengthening of, Christianity.

While history does not repeat itself, some developments do return. Therefore, New Age must take account of the fact that, while it may inspire Christianity on a formal basis, this does not have to the case materially. The so-called challenge of New Age could mean that a stronger, more self-conscious, Christianity re-emerges. For the rest, this does not mean that New Age will disappear but that its position is much weaker than is recognized.

The Inherent Paradoxicality of New Age

There is yet another question that must be asked: Can New Age function as the religion of the future in a structured, organized way? After all, a religion that wishes to have influence and to retain its adherents requires a sound structure. This inevitably raises the question, what is New Age? From the beginning this has been unclear. As is well known, New Age is more a designation for a certain way of feeling than for an organization. Some feel sym-

pathetic to religion on a number of points, and feel they have discovered a common, alternative orientation. Nevertheless, there is
no mention of a fundamental unity, and no mention of one
organization. The thesis that the specific character of New Age lies
in the fact that it is organized like a network, and is thus much
stronger than any other organization, suggests a sort of unity that
is not actually present. The network does not exist, unless it exists
spiritually. But one cannot build an organization on that. Furthermore, we must take note of the fact that, in the Age of Aquarius,
the new religion is said to have no need of organization, because
the inner self of the human will be present and it is not manageable.
This could be feasible, but up until the present it has been the case
that ideas have not been able to survive without organization of
some sort. The strength of New Age is at the same time its
weakness. Its strength lies in the fact that it can embrace various
ideas in its understanding of unity, through which it seems to be
unified. Its weakness is that this unity collapses as soon as it is in
actual fact organized.

A New Age religion of the future will need to define its doctrine
in one way or another, need to create something that can bind
people to it. Whenever they take up the question of what should
be included or excluded from this body of doctrine, New Age will
split into diverse groups and there will be no unity. Furthermore,
as soon as New Age arrives at a formulation of its doctrine (though
the expression 'doctrine' is abhorrent within New Age thought) it
also defines and limits itself. It then becomes a group with specific
ideas, ideas which either will no longer be attractive to many, or
with which disagreement is expressed, with the result that a
separate independent group is formed. It can be seen already that
what is called New Age is actually a conglomerate of groups, each
of which goes its own way. Thus it is inconceivable that New Age
can be the religion of the future in that sense. Either New Age
remains as it is, a loose collection of ideas to which various people
adhere to a greater or lesser extent, or it becomes organized and
perhaps becomes a larger group. In the first case, it will dissipate
over time, and in the second, it will become too small to include
everything, and lose its holistic and universalistic character. In
short, the prospect can be that, in the new Europe, New Age could

be a religion, but one that exists alongside many other schools of thought.

Notes

1.   As is well-known, 'New Age' is not a unity. There is no New Age movement existing as an organization, even less a New Age philosophy. Nonetheless, one can find a number of points held in common by the many groups who see themselves as belonging under the umbrella of New Age.

2.   See the title of the book by a leading Dutch New Age channeler *Op weg naar de nieuwe wereldreligie* [*On the Way to the New World Religion*]; in the writings of Creme, for example, we can find the same idea, see *Maitreya's Mission*, London, 1986; see also A. A. Bailey, *Education in the New Age*, New York: Lucis Trust, 1954.

3.   Here they have in mind the gnostic undercurrent, the Cathari, alchemy, the legendary Rosecrucians, the Free Masons, etc.

4.   Important authors are C. Cumbey, T. Marrs, D. Hunt & T. A. MacMahon. See on this subject I. Hexham, 'The evangelical response to the New Age' in J. R. Lewis & J. Gordon Melton, *Perspectives on the New Age*, New York, 1992, pp. 152-65.

5.   Cumbey, *The hidden dangers of the Rainbow*, p. 241.

6.   So, K. Koch, *Christian Counseling and Occultism*, Grand Rapids, 1972, and *Between Christ and Satan*, Grand Rapids, 1961, and *Okkultes ABC*, Basel; in the Netherlands, see W. J. Ouweneel, *Het domein van de slang*, Amsterdam, 1978.

7.   G. Danneels, *Christus of de Waterman*, Mechelen, 1990.

8.   The 'sceptical movement' is known as 'The Committee for the Scientific Investigation of Claims of the Paranormal' (CSICOP), with the journal, *Skeptical Enquirer*. In the Netherlands it is known as 'Stichting Skepsis' with the journal, *Skepter*.

9.   Cf. 'New Age, uitdaging voor kerk en theologie', *Gereformeerd Theologish Tijdschrift*, 90, 1990.

10.   Douven is compared with M. Fox, author of *Original Blessing*, Santa Fe, 1983, and *Creation and Spirituality*, Santa Fe, 1991, but is more theosophically influenced. Douven is very much inspired by G. MacGregor, an Anglican priest and author of *Reincarnation in Christianity*, Wheaton, Ill., 1978, *Gnosis, a Renaissance in Christian Thought*, 1979, and *The Christening of Karma*, 1984.

11.   Apart from that, many of the religious ideals of the Renaissance continued to exist within the more esoteric tradition, such as alchemy, the Freemasons, etc.

CHAPTER 9

Ritual Abuse Accusations and Incitement to Religious Hatred: Pagans and Christians in Court

Graham Harvey

Readers of the 'Satanism' article in *Encyclopedia of Religion and Ethics*,[1] might be forgiven for believing they were in fact reading an article about propaganda against Freemasons. If someone wanted a precedent for 'survivors' 'disclosing' details of an otherwise hidden Satanic conspiracy, that article would be a good place to begin. It concerns claims made in the first two decades of the last century that ex-Freemasons were disclosing information about Satanic deeds.

Nothing that they said then would be out of place in the books being produced by the evangelical Christians who claim to be survivors of abuse in modern Satanic cults.[2] Even the language of 'survivors' and 'disclosure' continues.[3] Indeed, nothing that these modern 'survivors' allege cannot be documented in earlier accusations. The 'rituals' in which children are allegedly abused, and sometimes sacrificed, were described in fuller detail in the last century. Even then, the allegations were only a repetition of those previously made against Jews and 'witches'.[4] Similar accusations have been made against Catholics and Communists.[5] They are being made yet again. It is not my purpose to detail the history of these allegations, ancient or modern, but to note the context in which they occur.

To understand the role played by accusations of 'ritual abuse' — the alleged organized abuse and sexual abuse of children and teenagers by a conspiracy of satanists — it is important to know that no evidence has been produced for its existence in this country or anywhere else. The reason for this lack of evidence is that there is no such conspiracy, and no such *ritual* abuse. To put it positively, there is evidence that these allegations are unfounded. All cases which have come to court have resulted in those accused being found not guilty, and have often provoked strong comments against the accusers.[6]

I feel it is necessary to make the point clearly that the accusation of 'Ritual Abuse' has made it much harder for the courts to deal with the already difficult issue of child abuse and child sexual abuse. These things undoubtedly happen and are crimes, rightly so. There are considerable problems in dealing with both victims and perpetrators (most often close relatives) of such crimes.[7] The addition of the word 'ritual' does nothing to help.[8] Rituals are not illegal, while child (sexual) abuse is.

Clearly the word 'ritual' masks the more emotive and less widely acceptable word 'satanic'. If a vicar were to abuse a choirboy in a church, it would almost certainly not be labelled 'ritual abuse'. The media would probably present it as closer to comedy than horror. If such a case came to court if would rightly be tried as a case of child abuse. If there are Satanists who abuse children, their crime, too, is child abuse, in whatever context they commit the crime.[9] It is ridiculous to suggest that a ritual context makes such a crime worse. All this is said by way of introduction. My concern is with the presentation of modern Paganism by evangelical Christians. In the following sections I sketch Pagan belief and action;[10] then I explore the way evangelical Christians portray Paganism; and in a final section I discuss some suggested ways of dealing with the most severely negative portrayals.

Paganism from the Inside

Pagans in Britain consider themselves to be heirs to pre- and non-Christian spiritualities. 'Pagan', or its North European equivalent, Heathen, is a widely used self-designation. Pagans associate the name with 'country-dweller', more than with its Christian usage, 'non-Christian'. Many come to some form of Paganism through an interest in ecology. It is hard to estimate exactly how many people in Britain consider themselves to be Pagan, but anything up to one million has been suggested to me.

Other names are used in addition to Pagan, which then function as the name of a kind of spirituality further defined by more specific names. Alongside reconstructions of ancient religions, such as Druidry,[11] and theories about medieval alternative movements, such as Murray's 'witchcraft',[12] Pagans frequently make much of modern non-Christian traditions, especially those from primal religions.[13]

Few of these diverse subdivisions are mutually exclusive (a Witch can also be a Druid) and many people belong to no organization at all. Respect for nature is central to all the varieties, and people are most frequently attracted to Paganism because they see it as a more ecological way of relating to the earth than either Christianity or modern secular world-views.

Almost all Pagans share a calendar of eight annual festivals. These, the main ritual occasions of Paganism, are celebrations of nature, especially of the four seasons. The Pagan year starts with the beginning of winter, celebrated on November eve in Britain. Spring begins on February eve, summer on May eve and autumn on August eve. The midpoints of the seasons are marked by the two solstices and the two equinoxes. Lunar festivals are also important to many Pagans, especially to those who call themselves Witches or Wiccans.

Each of these festivals is associated with a theme such as birth, initiation, marriage, sexuality, death, rebirth. Such themes are celebrated at suitable times of year, death with the onset of winter, initiation with the onset of spring, for example. Some Pagans celebrate the festivals out-of-doors, around a fire, while many prefer to celebrate with a candle-lit ritual and meal in their own home. In such celebrations divinities are sometimes invited to 'bless' the participants and the occasion, but often more is said about elemental and ancestral beings than about divinities.[14]

These seasonal celebrations are times of feasting and dancing, of meditation and communion. The 'ritual' element is often less significant than that in Christian celebrations. Paganism does not condone or encourage killing beyond what is necessary for eating (and many Pagans are vegetarian or vegan). Sacrifice, when not understood in purely metaphorical terms (i.e. as something akin to temporary abstinence), must be willingly made and cannot involve a 'victim'. The sacrifice can only be something belonging to the sacrificer. No Pagan divinity *demands* worship, let alone sacrifice. Sexuality is celebrated in Paganism as a natural part of life. Ritual nudity is rare and sex-magic rarer, though significant in some magical and tantric groups.[15]

It is important to note that no Pagan tradition has a place for a devil, demons or any concept of ontological evil in permanent opposition to some all-good entity. As nature includes death as well as birth, healing herbs as well as poisonous snakes, so a respect for nature must find some way of honouring all these *natural* things.[16]

There are a few people who call themselves 'Satanists', though they mean by this something different to the Dennis Wheatley stereotype. Some undoubtedly use the name deliberately to spoof Christianity or to upset Christians — it seems the name itself is effective for this purpose, without any unpleasant activities. For others, Satanism is basically a self-religion, rejecting 'faith' as un-thinking allegiance to another, with no sense of a quest for know-ledge and experience. In short, most modern Satanists are trying to follow the advice, 'know thyself' and 'to yourself be true'.[17]

Evangelical Christian Presentations of Paganism

Evangelical Christians present Pagan celebrations as satanic rituals, occasions for (child) sexual abuse and other criminal activities.

I do not intend to present an exhaustive description of the accusations made. Unless you share the evangelical world-view, the whole thing can sound comical, ridiculous and badly scripted. My purpose in dealing with the issue at all is that, far from being comical, the accusations have led to some grave injustices and real abuse of children and parents.[18] Ultimately, my purpose is to indi-cate that this issue is not fundamentally dealing with the real prob-lem of child (sexual) abuse. It is a religious issue, an interesting one, in that it undercuts efforts made towards mutual understanding between the faith communities of modern Britain, but a disturbing one in its intolerance and in the pain it causes.

In that light I will present a brief summary of what some evangelical Christians allege constitutes 'ritual abuse' and 'satanism'.[19]

It is alleged that there is a conspiracy of satanists who are to be found in every profession and every part of Britain.[20] Parents conceive and bring up children purely for abuse and sacrifice to Satan. Satanist child care workers abuse children, provide others with victims, and confuse the children so they do not betray their abusers. Satanists in hospitals and abortion clinics dispose of human remains and provide sacrifices. Satanist police offers refuse to investigate allegations or destroy evidence. Blood and semen are drunk, and excrement eaten, in a parody of Christian ritual. Churches and graveyards are desecrated. Satanists corrupt teenagers with role playing games and heavy metal music with subliminal and overt satanic messages. Younger children are corrupted through occult symbolism cunningly disguised as Care Bears and Smurfs, as fairy tales such as Snow White, and in films like Teenage Ninja Turtles.[21] Satanists attack the family and other divinely sanctioned life-styles, by homosexuality, bestiality, oral sex, infidelity, necrophilia, rape, foul language, parent murder and suicide.[22]

I should make it clear that not all Christians share this world view. Some have rejected the idea of a personal satan or devil. There are Christians happily dialoguing with Pagans about many issues, especially ecology, in the same way that they and others dialogue with Jews, Buddhists and others. However, in saying positive things about Pagans, such Christians open themselves to criticism from some evangelicals as condoning 'Satanism' or themselves being Satanists.[23]

Beneath the accusations there are three truths, though they are not of the essence of matter. Firstly, child (sexual) abuse does take place, in 'religious' families as much as elsewhere.[24] Secondly, many people in Britain are not Christians. Thirdly, some people indulge in what might be called 'un-American' practices in memory of a previous 'witch hunt'.

It is arguable that ending this 'satanism scare' would enable the relevant authorities to get on with the job of dealing with real cases of child (sexual) abuse.[25]

The evangelical groups who write about Satanists also tend to be very negative about any world-view other than their own.[26]

There are other, less intolerant, ways in which Christians can understand other religions. These have their problems,[27] but are a significant aspect of many Christians' lives. The majority of the Churches have, for example, publicly stated that their former views of Jews and Judaism were wrong.[28] Similar comments might be made about what these evangelicals see as 'un-natural or 'ungodly' lifestyles.

If there are other ways of dealing with the three truths buried beneath the polemic, less can be said for the polemic itself. When the issue is clearly described, and it is noted that a) there is no evidence, and b) the allegations have been made against other groups for centuries (also without evidence), it is surprising that it gained a hearing. However, a number of cases have reached the courts: somehow the 'scare' has persuaded far too many people.

The effect of these accusations, amounting to a 'satanism scare' and 'witch hunt' in some cases, can be briefly described. Parents have been arrested, children have been kidnapped ('taken to a place of safety'), subjected to repeated physical examinations and 'disclosure interviews', and trials have taken place — all on the basis of belief, not evidence.[29] Clearly, there must be some urgency in dealing with a suspicion of child (sexual) abuse, but these cases frequently ignore the recommendations of the Cleveland Report, especially in its advice about the inappropriateness of 'disclosure interviews' and repeated medical examinations.[30]

During panics, initiated by evangelical Christians, at least two 'New Age', 'magical' or 'occult' bookshops have been firebombed.[31] People have lost their jobs and had to move from their homes because their Paganism is portrayed as 'evil' and dangerous.[32]

There may not necessarily be a conspiracy of evangelical Christians trying to persuade us of the veracity of their 'ritual abuse' allegations, but there is certainly something less organized — a 'scare' infecting a far wider population. Equally certainly, there is an evangelical attack on Paganism being carried on behind the banner of eradicating 'satanic abuse'.

Halloween is the eve of a Christian festival, 'All Hallows', honouring those ancestors now known as 'saints', followed the next day with the honouring of other 'souls'. It occurs at the time of the (much older) Pagan new year festival, Samhain, during which

Pagan ancestors are honoured. Each year, efforts are made to portray Halloween/Samhain as a dangerous and satanic event. Literature is sent to schools, 'informing them of the dangers of continuing the practice of celebrating "Halloween (Samhain)" with young children.[33] Videos are also available, though some of these are 'not suitable for children'.[34]

'Witchcraft, Spiritualism and other occult based religious cults are part of the satanic religion and are roots [sic] through which many victims find themselves entrapped in fear'. More than fear, there is 'ritualistic child abuse', including the sacrifice and cannibalism of newborn babies, which is endemic to 'SATANISM'.[35]

Pagan festivals are frequently listed as 'satanic sabbats'.[36] (It is perhaps worth noting that many Pagans do indeed call their celebrations 'sabbats', despite the the fact that the term was used originally by the earlier 'witch-hunters' when they linked 'witchcraft' and heresy with Judaism, which was always always under attack from Christians.) John Celia (Apostle) says, 'We have just had a full moon which meant that I have just spent a whole night counselling three new victims [presumably of 'ritualistic child abuse'] from sunset to sunrise. On Halloween (Samhain) night I expect to be sitting up through the hours of darkness with at least eleven victims'.[37]

In one evangelical work which manages to say some positive things about Paganism, it is still portrayed as something which can (will?) lead children deep into 'destructive occults', i.e. satanism[38] and is therefore something to beware of.

In seeking to protect children from abuse, Geoffrey Dickens MP has implied that the Witchcraft Act 1735 (repealed and replaced by the Fraudulent Mediums Act 1951) should be re-instituted, in order to 'check the spread of witchcraft, satanism and other worrying occults'.[39]

In tracts and books, lectures and sermons, Paganism is misrepresented and portrayed as something inherently evil and deliberately anti-Christian.[40] The only truth here is that Pagans just are not Christian. Few evangelicals are explicit about their opposition to all other religions, though Yoga and other meditative techniques, too, are sometimes portrayed as satanic.[41] This is bad enough when it is done within the confines of the Church, but it is considerably more harmful when it gets into courts, the media and social work training as 'the truth'.

Incitement to Religious Hatred

How should such accusations and allegations be deal with? Some Pagans conduct an information campaign to explain exactly what Paganism is, and to present their view of the 'satanism' allegations.[42] It is hard to know how useful such a campaign has been or could be in the future.

It is arguable that there should be some recourse to law in this situation. The issues are similar to those faced by other religious groups in this country. Only Anglican beliefs are protected by the Blasphemy Law, which is increasingly out of place in this multi-faith country. When the Muslim community feel aggrieved there is little they can do.[43] Not every such situation is covered by racial discrimination, especially when it is the Muslim community rather than, say, the Arab community which is affected.

Religious insults could be dealt with as slander or libel if an individual were named or implicated, but such cases are too expensive for most (Pagan) individuals, and would require one person to attempt to prove he or she had been particularly victimized.

Some Pagans are now pressing for legal recognition as a religious minority, with protection from infringement of religious freedom. Many Pagans, however, are extremely wary of such moves, seeing them as an attempt by a few to gain personal power as priests or priestesses with wide authority. The major objection is that many people are attracted to Paganism precisely because it is about experience and exploring each person's place in the web of things. There can be no central authority. Even within a Pagan organization, leaders are respected while they are ahead of their followers, and can only base their authority on what they give out. There could be no certainty that if the Pagan world did become one organized religion, rather than a wide spectrum of spiritualities, it would be given legal recognition anyway.[44]

In Northern Ireland it is illegal to incite religious hatred.[45] It has been argued that this law should be widened to cover the whole of the UK, and all religious communities.[46] The most desirable effect of such a law would be that people would have to think before they say or write the kind of thing we have been discussing. It might provoke evangelical Christians to change tack, and, rather than present others as 'evil', they might stress what is good and valuable about their own tradition. There would be no automatic cover for Pagans in such a law, and the issue of legal recognition would still have to be dealt with in some way. Perhaps conferences such as this might be persuasive in showing that traditional western definitions, descriptions and discussions of 'religion' are (and have always been) inadequate.[47]

Notes

1. B. S. Hartland, 'Satanism', in *The Encyclopedia of Religion and Ethics*, 11, 1920, pp. 203-7.
2. Indeed these very allegations against Masons and others are still believed and repeated. See A. Boyd, *Blasphemous Rumours: Is Satanic Ritual Abuse Fact or Fantasy? An Investigation*, London: Fount, 1991, p. 112.
3. See, for example, Boyd, *op. cit.*, D. Core, *Chasing Satan*, Gunter Books, 1991; A. Harper and H. Pugh, *Dance with the Devil*, Eastbourne: Kingsway, 1990; K. Logan, *Paganism and the Occult*, Eastbourne: Kingsway, 1988; J. Parker, *At the Heart of Darkness* London: Sidgwick & Jackson, 1993; B. and G. Passantino, *When the Devil Dares your Kids* Guildford: Eagle, 1991; I. Tate, *Children for the Devil*, London: Methuen, 1991. Tim Tate's book has been withdrawn after a High Court action, but remains influential among many evangelicals (whether they know of its withdrawal or not). For comments on the inappropriateness of 'disclosure', see *Report of the Enquiry into Child Abuse in Cleveland*, London: HMSO, 1988.
4. N. Cohn, *Europe's Inner Demons: A Inquiry Inspired by the Great Witch-hunt*, New York: Basic Books, 1975; R. P. Hsia, *The Myth of Ritual Murder: Jews and Magic in Reformation Germany*, New Haven: Yale University Press, 1988; R. I. Moore, *The Formation of a Persecuting Society: Power and Deviance in Western Europe 950-1250*, Oxford: Blackwell, 1987. See also Montague Summers's approving introduction to *Malleus Maleficarum*, London: Arrow, 1971 (first published 1928). The Salem 'witch' hunt of 1692 is instructive here as in so many other areas. Accusations against the Jews as 'child sacrificers' are still being made, see, e.g., 'CPS may prosecute leaflet publisher', *Independent*, 1 September 1990, p. 3.

5. P. Jenkins and D. Maier-Katkin, 'Occult Survivors: the Making of Myth', in J. I. Richardson, J. Best and D. G. Bromley (eds), *The Satanism Scare*, New York: de Gruyter, 1991, pp. 127-44. The same accusations were also made against Christians by the Romans in considerable detail. I am indebted to my colleague Brian Yherm for drawing my attention to this material in his unpublished essay, 'Sex, Violence and Intrigue: Pagan Perspectives on the Early Christians'.

6. See the comments of Mr Justice Scott Barker in, *The Times Law Reports*, 2 April 1990, pp. 270-73. Rosie Waterhouse of *The Independent* is worth reading on this whole issue; see various articles between 12 August 1990 ('The Making of a Satanic Myth', p. 8) and 26 February 1992 ('Legal Threat to Channel 4', p. 7), though I may have missed earlier or later articles. She is not alone among journalists concerned with the issue, of course. See also Nick Anning, 'Court Out?', *New Statesman and Society*, 29 November 1991, p. 14. See, also, J. LaFontaine, *The Extent and Nature of Organised and Ritual Abuse*, London: HMSO, 1994.

7. Among others, see *Report of the Inquiry into Child Abuse in Cleveland; Child Abuse: A Study of Inquiry Reports 1973-1981*, London: HMSO, 1982; *Working Together*, London: HMSO, 1988; J. S. LaFontaine, 'Child sexual abuse and the incest taboo: practical problems and theoretical issues', *Man*, 23, 1988, pp. 1-18.

8. For example, it misdirects police, judges, journalists and everyone else, away from investigating child (sexual) abuse, into investigating murder and conspiracy allegations. See Anning, 'Court Out?'. For the use and avoidance of the words 'ritual' and 'satanic', see R. Waterhouse, 'NSPCC questions led to Satan cases', *Independent on Sunday*, 30 September 1990, p. 8.

9. The Revd Kevin Logan has sent me a copy of a report in The *Daily Telegraph*, 3 July 1992, about a man convicted of sexual abuse of his great-niece, adding, 'this fulfils quite a few of the criteria that we are using to define ritual abuse'. If this were so, all sex offences must be seen as 'ritual' ones. In the report, and the reported case, the defendant was found guilty of 'sexual abuse'. Frequently, the 'evidence' used by evangelical Christians for 'ritual abuse' has been read very differently by others. See, J. T. Richardson, 'Satanism in the Courts: from Murder to Heavy Metal', in Richardson, Best, Bromley (eds), *The Satanism Scare*, pp. 205-17.

10. C. Hardman and G. Harvey (eds.), *Paganism Today*, London: Aquarian Press 1996; G. Harvey, *Paganism in Britain*, London; Hurst, 1996.

11. P. Carr-Gomm, *The Elements of the Druid Tradition*, Shaftesbury: Element Books, 1991, and *Druid Way*, Shaftesbury: Element Books, 1993.

12. M. Murray, *God of the Witches*, Oxford: OUP, 1971.

13. M. Eliade, *Shamanism: Archaic Techniques of Ecstasy*, London: Routledge and Kegan Paul, 1964.

14. Harvey, Gods and Hedgehogs in the Greenwood, in G. Flood, *Mapping Invisible Worlds*, Edinburgh: Edinburgh University Press, 1993, pp. 89-93.

15. For Ritual Nudity, or going 'skyclad', see V. Crowley, *Wicca: the Old Religion in the New Age*, London: Aquarian, 1989. See also, T. Luhrmann, *Persuasions of the Witch's Craft*, Oxford: Blackwell, 1989, pp. 48-49.

16. G. Harvey, 'Avalon from the Mists: the contemporary teaching of Goddess Spirituality'; *Religion Today*, 8.2 (1993) pp. 10-13. G. Harvey, 'The Roots of Pagan Ecology', *Reliogion Today* 9.3 (1994) pp. 38-41. T. P. Tawhai, 'Maori Religion', in S. Sutherland *et al.* (eds), *The World's Religions*, London: Routledge, 1988, pp. 854-63.

17. See G. Harvey, 'Satanism in Britain', *Journal of Contemporary Religion*, forthcoming.

18. See below.

19. In addition to those evangelical books already noted (a small percentage of the books produced by evangelicals worldwide), I have drawn on literature and leaflets produced by organizations such as The Christian Response to the Occult, Reachout Trust, The Christian Rescue Service. I have also corresponded and had discussions with a number of interested clergy and other Christians. National and local newspapers often carry articles and letters about such views.

20. If this sounds like the popular image of Freemasons, this is possibly because some Christians believe there are Masonic Satanists. See Boyd, *op. cit.*, pp. 128 and 167; Logan, *op. cit.*, p. 150.

21. Passantino, *op. cit.*, pp. 125, 126 & 214; J. Best, 'Endangered Children in Antisatanist Rhetoric', in Richardson, Best, and Bromley (eds), *op. cit.*, p. 103.

22. Passantino, *op. cit.*, p.128.

23. Evangelicals have objected, for example, to the 'creation liturgies' and 'festivals of creation' held in Winchester, Coventry and Gloucester cathedrals. For a similar objection to an inter-faith 'prayer for peace' gathering at Assisi ('demons had in effect been recognised as deities on an equivalent level with the God of the Bible') see L. Gassman, 'Occultism, Eastern Religions and the New Age Movement', *Gospel*, 3, 1991, pp. 65-83. For satanic priests see Boyd, *op. cit.*, p. 80.

24. For physical and emotional abuse and religion (including Christianity), and abuse of children by religious (including Christian) parents, see D. Capps, 'Religion and Child Abuse: Perfect Together', *Journal for the Scientific Study of Religion*, 31, 1, 1992, pp. 1-14. Also

see H. Cashman, *Christianity and child sexual abuse*, London: SPCK, 1993.

25. My research into modern Paganism suggests that Pagans are concerned with two dangers of the 'satan scare': one is a 'witch hunt' which could destroy many people's lives; the other is that child abuse goes on while the authorities are following the false trail of a satanic conspiracy. There is also the possibility that when people keep hearing the more fanciful allegations they might eventually reject all talk of child abuse. See C. Dunkley, 'Perverse appetite for mumbo jumbo', *Financial Times*, 25 March 1992, p. 17.

26. The Christian Response to the Occult (CRO) publish a leaflet which condemns any other tradition but evangelical Christianity, denigrates many of them with the title 'cults', and sees them as centred in one form of abuse or another.

27. See the present author's, 'Jewish-Christians: Jesus and now', *Theology*, forthcoming.

28. M. Braybrooke (ed.), *Jews and Christians: what do the churches say?* London: Council of Christians and Jews, 1992.

29. There is a strange (and disturbing) paragraph in Boyd (*op. cit.* p. 31), which turns this on its head, and asserts that the existence of 'ritual abuse' should not be presented as an article of truth: 'the weight of empirical evidence [permits] observations [and] evidence'. Evangelicals often cite as 'evidence' Court cases where, in fact, a 'not guilty' verdict has been returned. Somehow they know better.

30. See D. H. S.Reid, *Orkney Child Abuse Scandal: Suffer Little Children*, Napier Press, 1992; also, *Report of the Inquiry into Child Abuse in Cleveland*, 1988.

31. *Lincolnshire Echo*, 28 January 1992, p. 1.

32. Personal communications. Opposition of one sort or another from evangelicals is a frequent Pagan experience.

33. Letter from John Celia (Apostle) to Charity Commission, 29 October 1991.

34. The Reachout Trust's 'Resources' catalogue. Sunrise Video Productions, in conjunction with CRO and supported by the Evangelical Alliance, produced and distribute a video called *Doorways to Danger*. On the video, Judith Dawson endorses the allegations about 'Ritual Abuse' and makes her own evangelical position very clear, contradicting her claim that her Nottingham social work team is 'secular' and 'does not believe in the Devil or God' (J. Dawson, 'Vortex of Evil', *New Statesman and Society*, 5 October 1990, pp. 12-14).

35. Letter from John Celia (Apostle) to Charity Commission, 29 October 1991, p.5.

36. Boyd, *op. cit.*, p. 144.

37. Letter from John Celia (Apostle) to Charity Commission, 29 October 1991, p. 5.

38. Passantino, *op. cit.*, pp. 33-62 and 221.

39. *Hansard*, 132, cols. 485-88, recording the adjournment debate of 27 April 1988.

40. Paganism is not inherently anti-Christian, anymore than are Judaism, Buddhism or Islam. In fact, some Druids and Magicians are also Christians, although not evangelicals.

41. The Christian Response to the Occult (CRO) produce a leaflet called 'Set Free!' which includes Yoga among many other dangerous 'occult' activities and groups (including even the Baha'is).

42. The Pagan Federation, and the Sub-Cultures Alternatives Freedom Foundation (SAFF) related to the Sorcerer's Apprentice bookshop in Leeds, produce a wealth of such information.

43. When their inability to gain a hearing in the Salman Rushdie situation had gone on for 'too long', Muslims in Bradford publicly burned copies of *Satanic Verses*, which guaranteed them a hearing with considerable malice. See D. G. Bowen (ed.), *The Satanic Verses: Bradford Responses*, Ilkley: Bradford and Ilkley Community College, 1992.

44. Scientology is a religion according to the Australian High Court, but not according to Lord Denning, for whom it is a 'philosophy but not a religion', see S. Lee, 'Religion and the Ways Forward', in Bowen, *op. cit.*, p. 74.

45. Public Order (Northern Ireland) Order 1987.

46. Lee, *op. cit.*, pp. 73-78.

47. See the comments of K. M. Morrison, 'Beyond the Supernatural: Language and Religious Action', *Religion*, 22, 1992, pp. 201-05.

CHAPTER 10

Descriptions of Sabbats and Rituals in Contemporary Anti-Satanic Fears

Véronique Campion-Vincent

The legend of the evil activities of Satan's disciples seemed to be dying out in the 1950s, but it has been relaunched in the wake of the renewal of interest in heterodox and occult currents that characterized the counter-culture at the end of the 1960s. The main social forces which support the legend are the Churches, especially the fundamentalist sects on the rise in the United States, although the Catholic Church has also recently emphasized the permanence and ubiquity of the menace posed by the devil. The police play their part in supporting the legend, as do seminars exposing the dangers of satanism which are are very successful. Finally, certain psychiatrists and therapists confer scientific legitimacy on the tales of 'survivors'.

This paper focuses on the description of satanic rites and the role they play in these accusations. It extends a earlier analysis that focused on the notion of demonologies.[1]

Since the 1980s, denunciations of the monstrous activities attributed to satanic sects have been steadily growing in the United States. These denunciations have multiple dimensions.

a. Warnings against popular culture, declared to be a medium of corruption of youth under the influence of satanists. Satanists stuff rock-lyrics with occult messages that can be spotted only if the song is heard backwards: it is the technique of backward-masking. They also implant traps in fantasy role-playing games that turn the players into controlled robots.

b. Identification of satanic sites on the edges of towns, in meadows, woods and hills, and in graveyards or sheds, barns, farms, factories and houses that have been abandoned. These sites are revealed through signs: thus dead animals or graffiti with satanic symbols are considered indisputable proof of satanists' activities.

c. Affirmation of a conspiracy of the elites, corrupted by satanism. The high social position of these sects' secret members is often emphasised, giving a populist overtone to the accusations. Big companies also are accused of owing their commercial success to a diabolical pact, a fact betrayed by their logos, which are loaded with satanic symbols.

d. Testimonies and statements of 'survivors', mainly women, who publicly relate in seminars aimed at therapists, and in television programmes that draw a wide audience, the horrors endured during their youth. These horrors, they say, were inflicted by their next-of-kin, memories of which were recalled under hypnosis. Analogous statements are made by very young children, who recall under treatment the memories of abuse endured in day-care centres. These cases raise considerable collective emotion and, although the trials that follow only exceptionally lead to guilty verdicts, they leave in their wake hurt and suspicion-ridden local communities.

The anti-satanist movement of psychiatrists and therapists has been extensively analyzed by Sherrill Mulhern,[2] who has emphasized its triple link to:

1. A redefinition of dissociative personality disorders that swept the United States and led to the rediscovery of pathological multiple personality disorder (MPD) as a clinical entity that entered the DSM-III diagnostic manual of the American Psychiatry Association in 1980.
2. The uncritical use of hypnosis and abreaction in therapy by therapists unaware of the risks of suggestion inherent in these techniques, especially among highly susceptible subjects who unconsciously fabricate, following therapists' suggestions when they are subjected to hypnotic treatment.

3. Growing public concern with physical child abuse, incest and child sexual abuse that encouraged therapists to postulate the existence of childhood abuse as a master key to explain all their adult patients' disorders.

This movement is evidently of central importance: it is the scientific legitimacy conferred by these secular professionals that has transformed a set of tales (that were traditional but hardly credible and limited to marginal sectors of society) into a real social scare.

e. Four levels of satanic activity, marked by increasing secrecy, have been presented in awareness-raising seminars organized by police officers: (1) *Dabblers*, 'teenagers or very young adults who, in an unsophisticated fashion, play with satanic bits and pieces'. They start with fantasy role-playing games and listen to rock music, but find themselves branded by satanism and commit suicide or become killers; (2) *Self-styled satanists*, psychopaths and criminals, adopting a satanic 'ideology that helps them to reconcile their crimes with their consciences'; (3) *Publicly organized satanists*, belonging to groups such as the Church of Satan or the Temple of Seth, who attract dangerous people and must be watched closely; (4) *Traditional satanists*, 'an international underground, tightly organized and covert, responsible for upwards of 50,000 human sacrifices a year'.[3]

About the evil deeds of satanists, stereotyped tales follow each other, echo and mingle, organizing themselves into a legendary series whose elements mutually reinforce each other and have consequences for behaviour.

Thus: Adolescents who engage in mainly harmless deviant games — allowing them to express and resolve conflict with their parents as well as to oppose the dominant adult culture — adopt the scripts of satanism whose symbols they flaunt through their dress as well as through graffiti.
Thus: They are drawn towards this adoption by popular culture that multiplies horror movies with satanic themes (*Rosemary's Baby*, *The*

Exorcist I, II, etc., The Believers), or rock groups with a satanic look
to their names (*Black Sabbath*, or *Judas' Priest* for example), their garb
and their lyrics.

Thus: Criminals and psychopaths also draw from popular culture
to 'contextualize and rationalize their violent acts by framing them
with the mass popularized paraphernalia of the satanic cult-world
as a justification for ostensive narration: telling the story by actually
doing it'. They thus show a paradoxically conformist acceptance
of the day's norms, 'criminals as well as psychotics always commit
their anti-social deed adjusted to normative rules of social behaviour and the trivia of the day'.[4]

The role of the media is central. Television has given a resonance
to the 'survivors' tales that has given rise to several episodes of
rumour/panic in American small towns. The press has relayed the
accusations and charges (charges which are generally dropped),
directed against day-care organizations or against the parents of
survivors. It has also relayed the declarations of sceptics refuting
these claims.

In Great Britain, fears about satanists had spread by the end of
the 1980s and resulted in action by social workers in 1990 and 1991.
Tales of disturbed children were interpreted as proof of atrocious
satanic activities in their families, and the children were forcibly
taken into care. Six cases involving 69 children received great publicity,[5] and the survey undertaken by Jean La Fontaine, of the London
School of Economics, and Bernard Gallagher, of Manchester University, found 84 cases in which allegations of ritual abuse had been
presented.[6] After having echoed the accusations in the first phase,
the press (the quality press as well as popular press — although
they are strongly contrasting sectors, both are very influential in
Great Britain) generally shows hostility towards the assertions of
the social workers and towards their actions against the suspected
families. By the end of 1991, the fear of 'ritual abuse' was discredited, and the population of believers had become scarce. The accused
population of social workers, however, still supported the
allegations.

Anti-satanic fears hardly touch France, where the existence of
satanists is not denied, but its meaning is considered far from

ominous. The treatment of the subject in the French media shows that satanists are mostly considered to be 'picturesque' groups, mobilizing consenting adults whose orgies harm no-one. Worries are sometimes expressed about the authoritarian and fascist tendencies of some group leaders, or about the expansion of magical practices of African or Caribbean origin involving animal sacrifices or the use of human cadavers; these, however, are not considered to be major problems.

Explaining this differential impact, not only in comparison with the United States but also with Great Britain, is difficult, as many complex factors are involved, but I will attempt to offer some possible explanations.

Two of the groups strongly involved in spreading anti-satanic fears are very different in France, where the influence of evangelical movements is quite weak, and where the therapeutic milieu is different, being dominated by psychoanalytical currents which disagree among themselves and oppose one another, mainly with reference to the thought of Freud, who remains the major influence.

In France, two opposed traditions co-exist and strongly influence the cultural outlook: that of Roman Catholicism, the major religion (in which the presence of the Evil One is not denied, but treated through the intervention of exorcists controlled by the Church), and that of atheism and rationalism, prevalent amongst many intellectuals, in which alarming tales about evil satanists belong in the realm of old wive's tales, branding those who spread them as backward and ignorant.

France is not an island, and the Catholic Church has seen its influence decline markedly: Church practice has weakened, and religious values become confused, one index of which is the growing proportion of adults who assert in polls both that they are Christians, and also that they believe in reincarnation. The same evolution can be seen in the main Protestant denominations, while evangelical movements also spread. Probably mainly through the influence of popular culture, interest in the Devil has increased in recent years. Exorcists barely existed fifteen years ago, but now their association numbers over fifty priests, and five books were published by or about exorcists in the first half of 1993.[7] These books are generally rather sceptical, and present the exorcist as a colleague of the psychiatrist, to whom belong most of the 'cases' he is called upon to treat. However, the reality of the Evil One cannot be doubted, even if authentic possessions are considered exceptional, and two of these authors, Amorth and Morand, present themselves in their sensationalist books as soldiers of Christ rather than as auxiliaries of psychiatry. The rationalist tradition was represented during the same period by a sixth successful book, the sceptical *Histoire générale du diable*,[8] whose author, a journalist who directs the influential popular science magazine, *Science et Vie*, credits the creation of the Devil to the followers of Zoroaster in the sixth century BC He hypothesizes that this creation was transmitted to Christians through the Essenians, who influenced Jesus — a very iconoclastic approach indeed.

The evaluation of the impact of anti-satanic fears is not an exact science, and I am conscious that my affirmation that it is weak is based on my personal judgement, cannot be demonstrated, and may be considered wrong by other scholars. My opinion that — by and large — the French public remains untouched by anti-satanic fears is, however, strengthened by the great ignorance of the general public on these matters.

In my descriptions of the activities of satanists I shall draw mainly on American and British sources, corresponding to countries where those fears are widespread.

Main features of the accusatory descriptions

Meetings of fundamentalist sects, police awareness-raising seminars, training sessions for convinced psychiatrists and therapists, all present a frightening picture of the satanists' activities, entirely oriented towards evil. It is 'a vast international, multigenerational, conspiracy, practising religious worship of satan through sex and death rituals involving torture, incest, perverted sex, animal and human sacrifice, cannibalism, and necrophilia'.[9] The worst is thus from the start given as possible, and even as certain. All the satanists' activities denote sacrilegious parody.

That satanism is essentially evil is conveyed symbolically in the inversions that fill descriptions of satanic rituals. Rather than preserving and protecting burial sites, satanists desecrate and loot them. Rather than expelling urine, satanists drink urine. Rather than giving blood to others to strengthen or save lives, satanist drink blood to enhance their own strength at the expense of others' lives... Rather than murder committed as a product of inflamed passion, satanists commit murders as a means of igniting their passions. Rather than nourishing, nurturing and fostering the unique selfhood of children, satanists consume, exploit, terrorise, brainwash and destroy children. Indeed they seek to absorb the unique life energy of sacrificial victims to enhance their own life energy, thereby making evil collectively stronger and good collectively weaker.[10]

Satanist are infanticides and cannibals, they 'subject human victims, preferably children, to obscene torments, then slash them to death, dismember them and drink their blood and eat their flesh and vital organs'.[11] The central theme of the descriptions concerns a Satanic or Black Mass of multiple forms.

Variations on this story include saying the Mass backwards over the naked body of a young girl (a virgin, parodying the Immaculate Conception) followed by copulating with her on the altar; desecration of the sacraments, fouling the chalice with human and animal excretory fluids, and sacrificing children for a cannibalistic Eucharist. These blasphemous acts may be performed in black-draped rooms lit with black candles, by persons in black robes and hoods.[12]

To answer the obvious objection — How is it possible that these large-scale sacrifices leave no evidence? — it is asserted that satanists know how to 'manufacture' their victims. Thus we have this declaration from a converted ex-satanist, introduced to the popular British newspaper, the *Daily Star*, by Maureen Davies, a Welsh ex-nurse and fundamentalist Christian, who founded the Reachout Trust and has multiplied sensationalist statements to the British Press.

There are temples all over the country where children are being bred solely for sacrificial purposes. Many of the babies don't get to full term before they are eaten by the satanists. Others are killed within a month or two without their births being registered. Women called 'brood mares' are kept for this purpose. They have sex with group members and the offspring are used for sacrificial purposes. It is not unusual to have MPs and police present at these ceremonies. The child is usually killed with a ceremonial dagger, then split open to have its organs removed and its blood drained off. The satanists then eat the organs and drink the blood, believing this will give them magical powers and bring them closer to Satan.[13]

One also finds descriptions of periodic nocturnal ceremonies, in which women — generally naked — dance in circles on the moors at the time of the full moon. These are performed not by satanists, but by witches, who complacently present themselves to the press and proclaim themselves the heiresses of 'a witch cult of en-lightened pagans, almost exclusively liberated women who worshipped a horned goatish figure, which had operated con-tinuously in Western-Europe since Druidic times'.[14] In the file of articles on the occult in the British popular press from 1980 to 1984 which was kindly sent to me by Gillian Bennett, this is the predominant type of description. One enters the realm of the 'picturesque' and the entertaining. These witches, however, give ominous warnings: they are good white magicians, but around them some wayward types practise aggressive black magic and human sacrifices.

Where do these accusatory descriptions come from?

Origins of the accusatory descriptions

The belief in diabolical witchcraft that prevailed in Europe from the fifteenth until the eighteenth century is the most elaborate example of the theme of a subversive religious group secretly perpetrating evil infanticide and cannibalistic rituals with the aim of subverting the very essence of society. Then this belief by and large dis-appeared. In the twentieth century, however, occultists, witches of the neopagan movements, and self-declared satanists have rebuilt the image of the evil satanists.

In the nineteenth century, Freemasons were frequently accused of subversion, and also of atrocious rituals, diabolical, infanticidal and cannibalistic. The Catholic Church supported and influenced these popular rumours, and also sustained a propaganda machine of accusations against Freemasons. It is this climate that explains the success of Léo Taxil's hoax.

In August 1891, a previously anti-clerical journalist, Léo Taxil, claimed to have been miraculously converted to Catholicism. In a series of sensational pamphlets, written under a variety of pseudonyms, he claimed that many Masonic lodges actively worshipped Satan and were linked by an international conspiracy. This plot was centred in London and Charleston, South Carolina, but involved sinister underground cadres in every major city of the world. Alleged ceremonies involved animal and human sacrifices, bisexual orgies and physical apparitions of the devil. [...] In 1897 the whole affair was exposed as a hoax perpetrated by Taxil.[15]

The activities of French occultists, notably Eliphas Lévi and, later, Joris Karl Huysman with his successful *La Bas* (1891), popularized the theme of the Black Mass, and found an echo in Great Britain, where the occultist Alister Crowley became notorious for his shocking declaration that he was 'genuinely involved in devil-worship', even implying that he had 'taken part in some kind of baby-killing ceremony'.[16] The press called him 'the wickedest man in England'. From the 1930s onwards, the popular novels of Charles Williams, and, more especially of Dennis Wheatley, exploited the theme of the dangers brought by satanists in widely read fantasy tales, whose climax was generally the Black Mass, celebrated during a huge Sabbat. The heroes of Wheatley's strongly reactionary novels are members of the upper-middle class — Anglo-Jewish, English or American — but mainly aristocrats; the main character is a Frenchman, the Duc de Richleau (Richelieu for English ears), who defends society and the establishment against subversive satanists. These evil characters (Wheatley wrote from the 1930s until the 1970s), are Orientals, Nazis, Communists, and leading Black Activists. During the 1960s, horror movies also started to exploit satanic themes, from *The Devil Rides Out* (a 1967 adaption of the Wheatley novel first published in 1934, but still in print in the 1980s), to the series of *The Exorcist*, through to *Rosemary's Baby*.

The renewal of witchcraft in the twentieth century is linked to the influence of Margaret Murray,[17] who elaborated on Michelet's[18] romantic theories, and considered the victims of witchcraft trials to have been the followers of a pagan religion secretly maintained since antiquity. Quickly discredited among historians and the intelligentsia, these theories have been well received by the general public, and have been picked up in many popular histories and works of fiction about witchcraft in the past. These theories have also been influential in the creation of several neopagan groups. In Great Britain, the most influential character of the 1940s and 1950s was Gerald Gardner, organizer of spooky ceremonials, the preface to whose book, *Witchcraft Today* (1954), was prefaced by Margaret Murray. Vaguely defending pantheistic beliefs, the groups of sorcerers gave expression to minor sexual deviations: 'Gardner seems likely to have been a flagellant sado-masochist for whom witchcraft served as an element of sexual theatre'. Since the 1960s, many of these neopagan groups have been influenced by the feminist movement: 'other witch groups have been explicitly based on the idea of witchcraft as a feminine religion worshipping a mother goddess and preserving the memory of sixteenth and seventeenth century women victims of male inquisition'.[19] Eager for publicity, and making frequent statements about their beliefs and practices to the popular media since the 1950s, these groups have become more visible as they were less persecuted, less liable to be treated as dangerous. They have accustomed the general public to the idea of an active presence of witchcraft in contemporary society.

Given the multiform religious experimentations of the 1960s, the appearance of sects openly declaring their devotion to Satan is not surprising. The new ethic of choice, an ethic that leads to the adoption of successive faiths, logically leads to an exploration both of the powers of darkness and of the powers of light, and hence the self-proclaimed American satanic Churches of Anton La Vey (Church of Satan), and then of Michael Aquino (Temple of Seth). Serious studies have been made of contemporary groups that have inherited the tradition of the occultists but turned them towards a power-oriented approach to magic, and they draw a picture that strongly differs from the misrepresentation given by their accusers of the popular media.[20] It is this misrepresentation that counts, however, for it builds the image accepted by the general public and influences the way these groups are perceived. A study by Rowe and Cavender[21] has shown a very different treatment in the American media of the 1980s: on the one hand, witchcraft was favourably treated, while on the other hand, satanism was loaded with iniquity.

Functions of the accusatory descriptions

It is legitimate to consider anti-satanic fears as unjustified panic. Though there is no convincing proof of their reality, and there is 'a complete absence of independent evidence corroborating the existence of such cults or their alleged activities such as human sacrifice, cannibalism, and sex and death orgies',[22] yet these extreme accusations have had a strong impact and entailed intense collective mobilization: 'It is precisely this combination of heightened anxiety, expanded activity and lack of corroborating evidence that characterizes a scare'.[23]

The anti-satanic panic is caused by new social factors that have brought a redefinition of elements already present in society, but seen as entertaining fiction, or touching only peripheral segments of the population. From the end of the 1970s, these redefined elements have seemed literally true and convincing to central segments of the American people.

Well adapted to our secular and sceptical age, these dangerous satanists are defined without reference to the supernatural. Except for the core of fundamentalist Christians, satanists are described in a manner suitable for atheists. The call to the Evil One and the submission to God's enemy which were at the root of the diabolical conception of witchcraft from the fifteenth to the eighteenth centuries are practically never there in contemporary descriptions. The fantastic trip to the Sabbat where the malevolent witches met their evil Master has been replaced by descriptions of atrocious acts that seem caused by a truly Nietzschean yearning for power and sadism and emptied of all supernatural dimensions.

The anti-satanist movement's success in attracting a broad audience has come through redefining the issue in non-religious terms. The movement's public claims focus on satanists as criminal, rather than spiritual or religious threats. This is a secular age, when a large proportion of the population doubts that demons and witches exist. However... satanism, when presented as a criminal problem, can become a frightening spectre. It is no accident, then, that anti-satanists concentrate on linking satanism to serial murders, teen suicides, child abductions, sexual abuse, and child pornography. These seem to be real-world threats... If satanism is somehow linked to these crimes, then this justifies concern about satanism. In particular, the anti-satanist movement emphasizes satanists' crimes against children. This theme links anti-satanism with other contemporary, broad-based, highly visible child-saving movements. [...] Because children can be seen as embodying the future, the image of the threatened child is particularly powerful in an era when many people lack confidence in their own futures.[24]

The movement took hold because of the diffuse anxieties present within society. This climate of anxiety is widely fed by the media and their systematically alarming treatment of information. A generalized violence seems to be at the heart of contemporary society through the media's descriptions, and society appears to be adrift in this uninterrupted and ever-growing succession of crises. Elaborating on facts that were, alas, all too real, new dangers presented as enormous have been denounced, since the end of the sixties, in several successive media scares.

Worries about the welfare of children have been central to our social concerns for three decades... These fears were exacerbated by public statistics about alcohol and other drug use, pregnancy, pornography, violence, suicide and declining academic performance among children. And consider the *general* social problems and concerns throughout this period: terrorism, drugs, sexual promiscuity, homosexuality, AIDS, secular humanism, economic deterioration, poverty and homelessness, political corruption and ineptitude, social unrest, racism, increased lawlessness, earthquakes, environmental disasters, radically changed weather patterns, constant warnings from all sort of 'experts'. This has been the breeding ground for the demonology of satanism.[25]

All problems are presented as urgent and major. Indeed, among the numerous items of information that reach them hourly, the media choose 'good stories'. To be real dramas, the 'good stories' upon which a social movement can be built must raise indignation, stimulate pity, or describe a danger potentially concerning each of us. Crime and violence, that seem forever on the rise, haunt us and reach us through a wealth of unpolished images and horror tales, without any analysis of their causes.

Resorting to the satanic scapegoat brings back social cohesion, since unity is found in the face of a common enemy. This also seems to account for the generalized crisis, as the satanist is then defined as essentially subversive and evil.

Satanists embody quintessential evil. Satanists are not simply child molesters or pedophiles. Such child abusers are defined as sick and usually social isolates. Satanists, by contrast, organise specifically to engage in abusive, destructive practices and even sacralise them through ritual. The existence of rituals is critical to counter-subversion ideology. Rituals demonstrate a high degree of organisation, patterned and repetitive activity, and endowment of antisocial, diabolical activity with an aura of the sacred.[26]

This vision is a demonology.

The allegations and their variants constitute a Christian form of a body of belief of a universally standing type, which we may call a demonology... an ideology of evil, an elaborate body of belief about an evil force that is inexorably undermining society's most cherished values and institutions. [...] Such beliefs invariably develop in times of intense, prolonged social anxiety, times when a significant proportion of people who share cultural values have come to feel that they are being let down or ignored by the social or government institutions that they have always supported and in which they have placed their trust. Something is very seriously wrong in society, and they are feeling increasingly helpless. The demonology provides an explanation for this state of affairs.[27]

The function of the extreme descriptions quoted earlier should now be clear. These are not, as it might seem at first, individual extravaganzas enunciated by pathological personalities. These descriptions are central to the processes of demonological elaboration of which contemporary anti-satanic fears are an example. Indeed, the themes of sacrilegious parody, of blood, of ritual human sacrifice, of cannibalism, are invariably present and associated in demonologies. 'At once symbolic, metaphorical and real',[28] these themes are present in accusations aimed at Christians in antiquity, at heretics, at lepers, at Jews and at witches. Their permanence has struck all observers.[29]

Thus is explained the place held in contemporary anti-satanic fears by the accusations of sacrilegious parody and of ritual cannibalistic infanticide: they are central to demonologies.

I heartily thank Gillian Bennett, Bill Ellis and Michael Goss who have generously shared their knowledge with me, and have sent me documents without which I could not have written this paper.

I also wish to express my gratitude to Caroline Oates for her linguistic help in the revision of this paper.

Notes

1. V. Campion-Vincent, 'Demonologies in contemporary legends and panics. Satanism and Babyparts stories', *Fabula*, 34, 3/4, 1993, pp. 238-51.

2. S. Mulhern, 'Think tank: investigation of ritual abuse allegations', Eighth National Conference on Child Abuse and Neglect, Salt Lake City, Utah, 1989; 'Satanism and psychotherapy: a rumour in search of an inquisition', in J. T. Richardson, J. Best and D. Bromley (eds), *The Satanism Scare*, New York: Aldine de Gruyter, 1991, pp. 145-72; 'Letter to the editor', *Child Abuse and Neglect*, 15, 1991, pp. 609-11; 'Ritual abuse. Defining a syndrome versus defending a belief', *Journal of Psychology and Theology*, 20, 1992, pp. 230-32.

3. R. D. Hicks, 'Police pursuit of satanic crime', *Skeptical Inquirer*, 14, 3, 1990, pp. 276-91, and 14, 4, 1990, pp. 378-89, but see p. 283.

4. L. Dégh, 'Satanic child abuse in a blue house', forthcoming.

5. M. Dash, 'The ease of the phantom social workers' *Fortean Times*, 57, Spring 1991, pp. 43-52.

6. J. S. La Fontaine, *The extent and nature of organised and ritual abuse*, London 1994, p. 6.

7. Dom Gabriel Amorth, *Un exorciste raconte*, Paris: Oeil F. X., 1993; Louis Costel, *Le diable et l'exorciste*, Rennes: Ouest-France, 1993; François Dunois-Canette, *Les prêtres exorcistes*, Paris: Robert Laffont, 1993; Isidore Froc, *Les exorcistes*, Paris: Droguet et Ardant, 1993; Georges Morand, *Sors de cet homme, Satan*, Paris: Fayard, 1993.

8. Gérald Messadié, *Histoire générale du diable*, Paris: Robert Laffont, 1993.

9. Frank W. Putnam, 'Commentary: The satanic ritual abuse controversy', *Child Abuse and Neglect*, 15, 1991, p. 175.

10. David G. Bromley, 'Satanism: The new cult scare', in James T. Richardson, Joel Best and David Bromley (eds), *The Satanism Scare*, New York: Aldine de Gruyter, 1991, p. 58.

11. Phillips Stevens Jr, 'The Demonology of Satanism: An Anthropological View', in Richardson, Best and Bromley (eds), *op. cit.*, p. 29.

12. Stevens, *op. cit.*, p. 31.

13. Bryan Rimmer, 'I was raped by cannibal gang says slave girl', *Daily Star*, 20 September 1990, p. 20.

14. Stevens, *op. cit.*, p. 32.

15. Bill Ellis, 'The Highgate Cemetery Vampire Hunt: The Anglo-American Connection in Satanic Cult Lore', *Folklore*, 104, 1993, pp. 13-39. See also the full account of the hoax in the article on 'Satanism' in *The Encyclopedia of Religion and Ethics*, E. S. Hartland, 1920, pp. 203-07.

16. Ellis, *op. cit.*

17. *The Witch-Cult in Western Europe. A Study in Anthroplogy*, Oxford: The Clarendon Press, 1921; *The God of the Witches*, London: Faber and Faber, 1931.

18. Jules Michelet, *La sorcière*, Paris: E. Dentu, 1862.

19. Roger Sandell, 'From evidence of abuse to abuse of evidence', *Magonia*, 38, January 1991, p. 6.

20. William Bainbridge, 'Social Construction from Within: Satan's Process', in Richardson, Best and Bromley (eds), , *op, cit.*, pp. 297-311; Tania M. Luhrmann, *Persuasions of the Witch's Craft: Ritual Magic in Contemporary England*, Cambridge, Mass.: Harvard University Press, 1989.

21. Laurel Rowe and Gray Cavender, 'Caldrons Bubble, Satan's Trouble, but Witches are Okay: Media Constructions of Satanism and Witchcraft', in Richardson, Best and Bromley (eds), *op. cit.*, pp. 263-75.

22. Putnam, *op. cit.*, p. 175.

23. Bromley, *op. cit.*, p. 61.

24. Joel Best, 'Endangered Children in Antisatanist Rhetoric', in Richardson, Best and Bromley, *op. cit.*, pp. 95-96.

25. Stevens, *op. cit.*, p. 30.

26. Bromley, *op. cit.*, p. 58.

27. Stevens, *op. cit.*, p. 21.

28. Stevens, *op. cit.* p. 24.

29. Campion-Vincent, *op. cit.*

PART THREE

SOME NEW RELIGIOUS MOVEMENTS

CHAPTER 11

Growth Patterns of New Religions: The Case of Baha'i

Margit Warburg[1]

Introduction and historical background

Baha'i communities have existed in Europe since 1900, and Baha'i is therefore one of the old, new religions in Europe. Baha'i is not indigeneous to Europe but originates from a heterodox Shi'ite movement in Iran in the middle of the nineteenth century. During the time of its leading prophet, called Baha'u'llah (1817-1893), it broke away from Islam and was proclaimed as a separate religion which would ultimately unify all religions and all mankind into one. The leadership of Baha'i resides in the Baha'i World Centre, which for historical reasons is situated in Haifa, Israel, and the active mission work is planned and coordinated here. Today, there are about 25,000 Baha'is in Europe and 5 million around the world, which makes the religion comparable in size to the Seventh Day Adventists and the Quakers. In spite of this, Baha'i has so far been relatively little studied from a sociological point of view.

In the West, Baha'i was first introduced to the USA in 1894, and shortly after, to Europe, on the initiative of the Baha'i leader, Abdu'l-Baha. From 1898, American missionaries were sent to England, France, Italy, and Germany, but their initial success was limited. In Britain, for example, there were no more than fifty active Baha'is in the period up to 1920.[2]

The real expansion in Europe began after World War II, when systematic mission was initiated, again following directives from the Baha'i World Centre, but under the practical leadership of the American Baha'i Community which had the necessary resources.[3] A European Teaching Committee, which was responsible to the

American Baha'i Community, was set up in Geneva in 1946 with the task of coordinating the mission activities in ten European 'goal' countries during the so-called North America's Second Seven Year Plan.[4] Around 1950, viable Baha'i communities had been established in all goal countries; thus, in Denmark the number of adherents grew to around 40 in the late 1940s as the result of the work of two leading American Baha'i missionaries.[5]

This paper is concerned with an analysis of the growth patterns of Baha'i in Europe. In this analysis I shall operate with three levels, a *local* level which is the individual country, a *regional* level, such as the Nordic countries, and an *international* level, which is the entire world. Historically, the influence of the Baha'i World Centre on the local Baha'i communities has been strong, and the various Baha'i mission plans mentioned above are but one example of the influence of the international level. The analyses in this study are based on statistical material which I have compiled on the growth and development of Baha'i in a number of European countries. The material has not only yielded figures on the overall growth of Baha'i in Europe, but has also allowed me to demonstrate the prominent role of migration for the growth rate of European Baha'i communities. This latter finding has general implications for the study of new religions.

Sources for the demographic analyses of Baha'i in Europe

In the light of the well-known problem of obtaining reliable demographic data on new religions, I shall briefly comment on the reliability of the data I have used.

Baha'i has a well-developed bureaucracy and detailed data on the number of Baha'is, on the enrolment of new members, on the transfer of missionaries, and the translation of Baha'i literature, the meeting activities of the local Baha'i groups, etc. are reported regularly on special forms by the national Baha'i communities all over the world to the Statistical Department in the Baha'i World Centre.[6] I have had personal access to these completed forms in Denmark, covering a period of nearly thirty years, which has made it possible to check the information through the use of other sources, such as the membership file, as well as to add to the material.[7] During a field work in Haifa, in 1988-89, I studied the processing of the statistical report forms, and I interviewed the responsible statistician on the various sources of error involved in the statistics. After closely investigating the whole procedure for the procurement of the demographic data, I am satisfied that it is unlikely that the data have been subjected to any systematic distortion during this process.

An alternative source might have been the *World Christian Encyclopedia* edited by David B. Barrett which is the standard source of information on membership of religious communities throughout the world.[8] Unfortunately, the figures given by Barrett for Baha'i in a number of European countries are between 2 and 9 times larger (typically 3-4 times larger) than the figures obtained from the Baha'is themselves. For example, according to Barrett's calculations there should be 1400 Baha'is in Denmark in the mid 1980s, when in fact there were only about 200 registred members of the Danish Baha'i Community at the time.[9] For the whole of Europe, Barrett gives a figure of 70,000 Baha'is, almost three times the 24,000 given by Smith and Momen (1989) — a figure also based on official Baha'i statistics.[10] The reason for these discrepancies is not evident, but it is obvious from the above that the data given by Barrett in this case are unreliable.

Comparative Baha'i demography in Europe

After the first successful phase in the late 1940s, Baha'i entered a period during the 1950s when the number of adherents grew only slowly. The mission strategy of that time was formulated in the so-called Ten Year International Baha'i Teaching and Consolidation Plan from 1953 to 1963;[11] the plan was ambitious and the leadership in Haifa urged Baha'is from non-European countries, in particular from Iran, the home country of Baha'i, to engage in mission work in Europe.[12] Consequently, a considerable number of Iranian Baha'is moved to Europe, and this meant that around 1960 the Danish Baha'i Community changed from an ethnically homogeneous group to an ethnically heterogeneous group. The immigration of Iranian Baha'is took another surge in the 1980s when Baha'is were severely persecuted in Iran after the revolution of 1979. Many fled to Europe

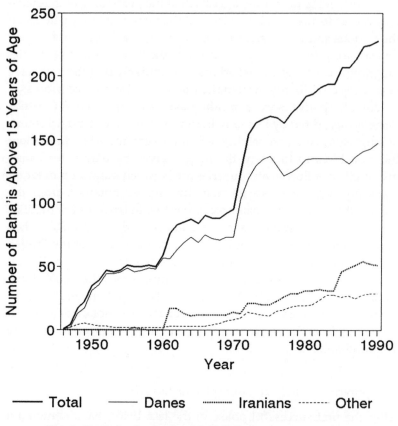

Fig. 1. Statistics for the Danish Baha'i Community, 1946-90.

and North America, as did thousands of other Iranians who were threatened by the Khomeini regime.

Taking Denmark as an example of the local level of the analysis, it is a noteworthy consequence of these international events that 35% of the members of the Danish Baha'i Community are today Baha'is of non-Danish, mainly Iranian, origin. Figure 1 presents the number and the ethnic composition of the members of the Danish Baha'i Community from 1946 to 1990.[13]

This figure, and in particular the curves for Iranians and other nationalities, shows that the development has indeed been influenced significantly by forces from outside Europe: firstly by the calls for missionaries from abroad issued several times since the execution of the Ten Year Plan in the 1950s and, secondly, by the rise of the Khomeini regime in Iran.

The figure also shows a jump in the number of Baha'is of Danish origin in the beginning of the 1970s. This jump is to be expected and is general for new religions in the Western world of the time. It is not surprising, therefore, that it is also the case with Baha'i.

Data from 1959 to 1991 on five northwestern European countries are presented in Figure 2. In order to make a meaningful comparison between countries of different population size the number of Baha'is are in this case expressed as the number of Baha'is per million inhabitants.[14] As appears from this figure, the development of the Danish Baha'i Community is strikingly parallel to three of the other four countries in northern Europe, namely the Netherlands, the Federal Republic of Germany (West Germany), and Sweden, because the curves coincide remarkably at this regional level. All show the same doubling in numbers in the beginning of the 1970s — and, as stated above, this jump is to be expected - and in all four countries there is a slow although steady real growth from 1975.

In contrast to this general pattern, the development in England (including Wales, but not Scotland and Northern Ireland) is quite different. In all the years up to the late 1970s the number of Baha'is per million inhabitants in England has been approximately double that of the other four countries, while displaying the same relative growth rate over the years. However, from the late 1970s Baha'i in England reached a standstill at a level of about 70 Baha'is per million inhabitants, and the gap between England and the other countries seemed to disappear. The special development in England may be related to a high proportion of Iranian Baha'is in the English community, because the English educational system attracted many Iranians, and today the Iranians make up about 45% of the community.[15] I cannot verify the figure, but it indicates that there is a large proportion of immigrant Iranian Baha'is in England. This means that the demographic changes in the English Baha'i Community have been profoundly influenced by migration, an issue to which I shall return below.

The great similarity between the population curves of Denmark,

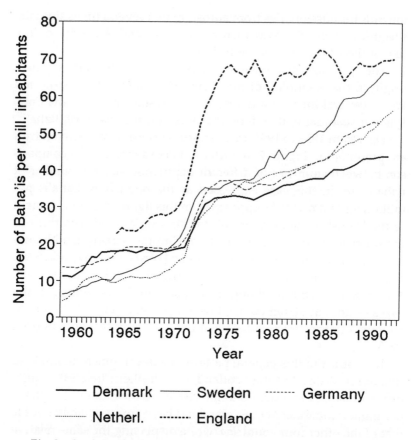

Fig. 2. Statistics for five Northwestern European Countries, 1959-91.

the Netherlands, the Federal Republic of Germany (West Germany), and Sweden indicates that from a sociological point of view the populations of these countries are comparable with respect to their acceptance of the coordinated Baha'i mission. This means, among other things, that in an analysis of Baha'i in Europe we may generalize with more confidence from the local level to the particular regional level in question. It would also be interesting to compare the Baha'i data with data on other new religions at the same regional level to see if the apparent similarity between these four northwestern European countries with respect to the growth of Baha'i can be generalized to a similar degree of responsiveness towards *all* new religions among their populations.

The Nordic countries are perceived as culturally very similar to each other, and it generally makes sense to consider them together at a regional level, but there are subtle differences between the Nordic countries too. Recent comparative studies of religion and religious change in the Nordic countries have unearthed some of the similarities and differences between the Nordic populations, the position of the national Churches, and the significance of religious communities outside the national Churches.[16] These studies were general sociological surveys of the majority population, and the theoretically interesting question is, of course, whether or not it is possible to infer anything about the relative success of new religions — which are expressions of minority behaviour - from such majority studies. However, with respect to the growth of Baha'i I did find differences among the Nordic countries in the period from 1979 to 1991; Baha'i in Norway appears to have been considerably more successful than in Denmark, Finland and Sweden, as appears from Figure 3.

In Figure 4, the fifth Nordic country, Iceland, is included for comparison, showing a remarkable influence of the local level.

Iceland has a population of 250,000, only one twentieth of that of Denmark, but there are nearly the same total number of Baha'is in the two countries, about 200. Multiplying both 250,000 and 200 by a factor of 4 gives the figure of about 800 Baha'is per million for Iceland. This is an unusually high figure for a European country and more in line with the figures for the USA (400-450 Baha'is per million during the last ten years). The number of 200 Icelandic Baha'is means, in fact, that one out of every thousand Icelander above the age of 15 is a Baha'i.

The relative success of Baha'i in Iceland compared with the other Nordic countries adds to the impression of Iceland's particular position with respect to religious climate. Thus, Petursson (1988) has shown that Icelanders differ on a number of points in their religious beliefs (e.g. belief in a personal god, belief in spiritual phenomena) from the rest of the Nordic populations.[17] It is also noteworthy that Baha'i seems to have considerable success in several other small island states around the world. For example, a number of nations

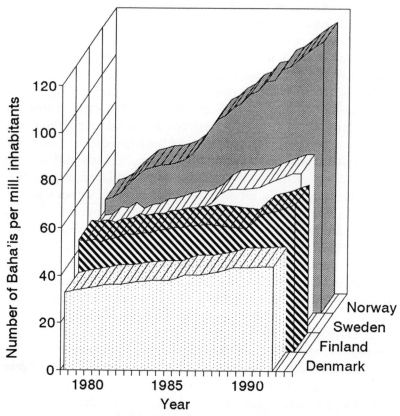

Figure 3. Statistics for Four Nordic Countries, 1979-91.

in the Caribbean and in Oceania claim to have from one per cent up to more than ten per cent Baha'is out of the total population.[18]

With respect to the relative success of Baha'i mission in Europe, Italy and especially France represent the opposite tendency, i.e. a rather low number of Baha'is per million inhabitants. Thus, by January 1992 there were 24 Baha'is per million inhabitants in France and 32 Baha'is per million in Italy. I shall not go further into this except to suggest that it reflects local rather than regional influences. For example, although Italy and France are predominantly Catholic, I see no obvious explanation in this, because Baha'i is quite successful in several other Catholic countries. In Spain there

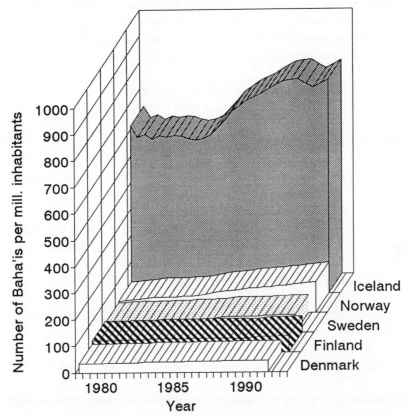

Figure 4. Statistics for Five Nordic Countries, 1979-91.

were 44 Baha'is per million inhabitants in 1992, which is the same as in Denmark, and outside Europe we may note that in Bolivia, Honduras and Panama more than one per cent of the population, or ten thousand per million inhabitants, are reported as Baha'is.[19]

Analysis of demographic changes

The overall growth rate of a particular Baha'i community is the net result of the demographic movements which are often considerable. The communities gain members not only through recruitment of new believers, but also through immigration of Baha'is from other countries. Conversely, the communities lose members through resignations, deaths, and emigration. All these demographic changes are therefore related through the below equation which can be seen as a modification of the basic demographic equation:[20]

> Growth (Gr) = Enrolments (Enr) + Immigration (Im)
> - Resignations (Rs) - Deaths (De) - Emigration (Em)

or in abbreviated form:

$$Gr = Enr + Im - Rs - De - Em \qquad \text{(Equation 1)}$$

Gr is the difference between the number of Baha'is at the end of a particular period and the number at the beginning of the same period. The other entities are simply the number of Baha'is who have enrolled, immigrated, resigned, died or emigrated, respectively, during that period.

The result of immigration minus emigration is called (net) migration (Mg):

$$Mg = Im - Em \qquad \text{(Equation 2)}$$

Consequently, if Mg is positive, immigration is larger than emigration, and conversely, if Mg is negative. We can thereby simplify Equation 1 to:

$$Gr = Enr + Mg - Rs - De \qquad \text{(Equation 3)}$$

The demographic entities in Equations 1, 2, and 3 are whole numbers. However, if we divide each entity in Equation 1 by the same number, the equation will still be valid. Thus, we may divide by the total average number of Baha'is during the period under study, whereby we obtain the *rates*. Rates are usually given as per cent; thus, if there is an immigration of 9 Baha'is, and the total number of Baha'is is 300, the immigration rate will be $9/300 = 0.03 = 3.0\%$.

In the following I shall demonstrate through a demographic analysis that the growth of Baha'i in Europe is as much the result of immigration as it is of recruitment of new believers. For the period 1987 to 1991 I have data on enrolments and deaths (no data on resignations and migration are available) among the Baha'is in all the European countries mentioned so far, which means that, both the growth rate and the enrolment and death rates can be calculated. By inserting these rates in Equation 3 it is possible to calculate the demografic change resulting from migration and resignation together, as is apparent when rearranging Equation 3:

$$Gr - Enr + De = Mg - Rs \qquad \text{(Equation 4)}$$

Western Baha'i communities, like other religious communities in modern Western society, will inevitably experience some resignations. This means that the combined result of migration and resignation will only be zero or positive if there is a considerable positive migration, i.e. if immigration is larger than emigration, cf. Equation 2. Table 1 shows that in Denmark, Sweden, Norway, Finland, and Germany there is definitely a positive migration, while the figures for Iceland, the Netherlands and England do not immediately lead to the same clear-cut conclusion.

Unfortunately, a resignation rate is available only for Denmark, and one can make only a crude guess as to its contribution to the demographic changes in the other countries. My data for Denmark show that over the period 1975 to 1990 the resignation rate was about 2% on average. This rate was a little more than half of the enrolment rate in the same period. A constant resignation rate of 2%, or a resignation rate which is half the enrolment rate, expresses two different interpretations of the same data. Since we have no other information on resignation rates among other European countries, the situation in Denmark will be taken as typical. Whichever of the two interpretations is chosen as the more representative for the European countries, however, the small negative numbers for the Netherlands and England in the bottom line in Table 1 can be explained by the effect of resignation alone, which indicates that migration is also positive for these two countries. The situation in Iceland, however, is different, because there are virtually no immi-

Table 1: Summary of Demographic Movements, 1987-91

	DK	S	N	SF	ICL	D	NL	Engl.
Growth rate	2.3%	3.7%	5.6%	3.6%	2.6%	5.2%	4.0%	1.4%
− Enrolm. rate	3.0%	2.5%	3.6%	1.9%	5.3%	2.0%	5.2%	2.6%
+ Death rate	0.7%	0.3%	0.2%	0.2%	0.2%	0.3%	0.3%	0.5%
= Net migra-tion minus resignations	0.0%	1.6%	2.3%	1.9%	-2.5%	3.4%	-1.0%	-0.7%

Note that the percentages in the bottom row may not always add up due to rounding.

grant Baha'is in Iceland.[21] Thus, except for Iceland, the growth of the Baha'i communities in all the European countries is sustained by an often considerable immigration of people who are already Baha'is. As will be shown below, it is probable that Iranian Baha'is constitute the largest contingent of immigrants.

Table 1 also shows that apart from England also Sweden, Finland and Germany have low enrolment rates, and the relatively high growth rates in the last-mentioned three countries, compared with England must to a large extent be caused by immigration. The standstill in the English Baha'i Community during the 1980s is therefore mainly a result of less immigration than of unsuccessful recruitment, compared with the other European countries. (The standstill might, of course, also be the result of an extraordinary high resignation rate in England, but there is no evidence to support that assumption).

Taking a closer view of the migration in and out of the Danish Baha'i Community in the period from 1975 to 1990, the migration pattern of the various ethnic groups shows some interesting features, demonstrated by the numbers in Table 2.

Whereas there is an overall immigration of foreign Baha'is, there is an overall emigration of native Danish Baha'is. The emigration of native Danish Baha'is and the immigration of non-Danish Baha'is have changed the ethnic composition of the Danish Baha'i Commu-

Table 2: *Migration in the Danish Baha'i Community, 1975-90*

	Immigration	Emigration	Net migration
Danes	4	17	–13
Iranians	49	17	32
Other	46	29	17
Total	99	63	36

nity profoundly during the last twenty years.[22] The large number of migrants is a direct consequence of the Baha'i World Centre's calls for mission abroad, and this again stresses the importance of analysing the new religions not only in their local but also in their regional and global context.

The above analysis of the migration data also leads to the general conclusion that growth figures for new religions in Europe should be treated with the utmost caution when interpreted as indicative of how successful the religions are recruiting new adherents. If migration is not considered we may well grossly misinterpret the growth rates of these new religions. This seems often to be the case; a recent example is Duke et al. (1993) who calculated conversion rates (using data from Barrett) between all religions worldwide without considering the effect of migration.[23]

Conclusion

In the present study, demographic data have been interpreted at three levels of analysis with the aim of understanding the growth patterns of Baha'i in Europe, and possibly also some of the other new religions. Starting with the international level, it is evident from the analyses that the Baha'i Year Plans are not just pieces of deskwork, for they have substantially shaped the Baha'i communities throughout Europe by emphasizing systematic mission outside one's own country. In fact, the influence from Baha'i World Centre is pervasive and cannot be neglected in any study of Baha'i.

The growth of Baha'i in Europe has, however, also been influenced by factors at the regional and local levels. The synchronous growth in Denmark, Sweden, the Federal Republic of Germany and the Netherlands corroborates our general impression of the similarities between the continental northern European populations. The remarkable success of Baha'i in Iceland, on the other hand, stresses that sometimes the local level is the most meaningful level of analysis.

It has not been reported previously that immigration accounts for a substantial part of the growth of the European Baha'i communities. The observation questions conversion data on new religions in general, and actual conversion rates may be considerably lower than anticipated.

The statistical analyses of Baha'i in Europe are thus important for understanding Baha'i, but, as I have indicated, they may also contribute to a better understanding of the growth pattern of other new religions in Europe. Because Baha'i has been recruiting adherents in Europe for many years, a historical approach becomes meaningful, and because of the centralized and systematic Baha'i mission policy, it might be argued that the similarities and differences between the Western European countries reflect distinct cultural similarities and variations across Europe, rather than just arbitrary differences among the various Baha'i communities which are responsible for the mission work.

Notes

1. This paper was written during a stay in 1992-93 at the Committee for the Study of Religion, Harvard University, Cambridge, Mass. Peter B. Andersen and Morten L. Warmind, both from University of Copenhagen, are thanked for valuable comments on the presentation of the demographic analyses.

2. P.R. Smith, 'What Was a Baha'i? Concerns of British Baha'is, 1900-1920', in M. Momen (ed.), 'Studies in Honor of the Late Hasan M. Balyuzi', *Studies in the Babi and Baha'i Religions*, 5, Los Angeles: Kalimát Press, 1988, pp. 219-51.

3. Shoghi Effendi, 'Inauguration of Second Seven Year Plan. Message to 1946 Convention', in Shoghi Effendi, *Messages to America. Selected Letters and Cablegrams Addressed to the Baha'is of North America 1932-1946*, Wilmette, Ill.: Baha'i Publishing Committee, 1947, pp. 87-89.

4. *Annual Baha'i Reports Presented to the Baha'is of the United States and Canada for the Year 1946-1947*, National Spiritual Assembly of the Baha'is of the United States and Canada, Wilmette, Ill., 1947, pp. 21-23.

5. M. Warburg, 'The Circle, the Brotherhood, and the Ecclesiatical Body: Baha'i in Denmark, 1925-1987', in A.W. Geertz and J.S. Jensen (eds.), *Religion: Tradition and Renewal*, Aarhus: Aarhus University Press, 1991, pp. 201-21.

6. The Baha'i community of each country submits a yearly report to the Baha'i World Centre (until 1990 the reports were sent twice a year). The annual report consists of a written progress report with attached forms containing statistical information on: The number of Baha'i groups and localities in the country, the number of members distributed according to county, sex, and age group, the number of groups which regularly held certain specified feasts and activities, names of foreign missionaries who have arrived to or departed from the country in question, and a list of new publications issued by the community. These data are transferred to a computerized data base in the Baha'i World Centre and used for internal reporting at the centre.

    I have received membership data from the following countries and periods from the Baha'i World Centre: Denmark 1959-91, Sweden 1959- 91, Norway 1979-92, Finland 1979-92, Iceland 1979-92, Germany (West) 1959-90, the Netherlands 1958-92, England (incl. Wales) 1965-92, France 1958-60 and 1964-92, Italy 1979-92, Spain 1979-92 and the USA 1959-92. Furthermore, I have received data on the total number of Baha'is on each continent: Africa, the Americas, Asia, Australasia, and Europe for the period 1963-1986. These data have been used in the internal Baha'i World Centre report, *The Seven Year Plan 1979- 1986. Statistical Report* which contains a wealth of useful statistical material on Baha'i worldwide.

7. I have compiled demographic data on the Danish Baha'i Community through the courtesy of the National Spiritual Assembly of the Baha'is of Denmark which has granted me access to the following material in their archive,
    - A card index of all members of the Danish Baha'i Community for the period 1980-81, except for 10 members who requested anonymity. The total number of registred members at that time was 184.
    - *Baha'i Nyhedsbrev* (Baha'i Newsletter) which has been issued 19 times a year by the National Spiritual Assembly to all Danish Baha'is since 1968.
    - Annual reports of the National Spiritual Assembly, issued since 1962.
    - *Annual (semi-annual) statistical reports* to the Universal House of

Justice, issued since 1962.
- Correspondence to and from the National Spiritual Assembly, except for correspondence classified as 'personal'.
The material only covers the period from 1962, when the National Spiritual Assembly was formed, to 1992. Furthermore, the periodical material is far from complete.

In 1981 a Danish Baha'i, Ms. Kaya Holck — for many years the secretary of the Local Spiritual Assembly of Copenhagen — prepared a list of all members of the Danish Baha'i Community with dates of their conversion, resignations, deaths, and migration. This list, excluding the names of the members, was made available to me and enabled me to reconstruct the development in membership from 1925 to 1962 when the official statistics started.

The data from the Danish Baha'i Community has allowed me to make a complete census of all the members of the community from its very start. The census includes the total number of members for each year distributed according to ethnicity (native Danes, Iranians, and Other) and figures on immigration, emigration, enrolments, resignations and deaths for each year. The census, which is derived from sources independent of the Baha'i World Centre, fits the statistical data from the Baha'i World Centre data base (*cf.* note 6) accurately and without systematic bias.

8. D.B. Barrett (ed.), *World Christian Encyclopedia*, Nairobi: Oxford University Press, 1982.

9. *Op. cit.*, p. 263.

10. P. Smith and M. Momen, 'The Baha'i Faith 1957-1986: A Survey of Contemporary Developments', *Religion*, 19, 1989, pp. 63-91.

11. [Shoghi Effendi], 'Ten-Year International Baha'i Teaching and Consolidation Plan 1953-1963', in [Shoghi Effendi], *The Baha'i World. A Biennial International Record*, 12, Wilmette, Ill.: Baha'i Publishing Trust, 1956, pp. 256-57.

12. Shoghi Effendi, 'The Summons of the Lord of Hosts', in Shoghi Effendi, *Messages to the Baha'i World 1950-1957*, Wilmette Ill.: Baha'i Publishing Trust, 1958 (reprinted 1971), pp. 30-39.

13. This figure is based on the census of the Danish Baha'i Community, *cf.* note 7.

14. Statistical information on the population size of the relevant countries for different years is derived from the following sources:
    - *Department of International Economic and Social Affairs, Statistical Office, 1990 Demographic Yearbook*, 42nd ed., New York: United Nations, 1992.
    - B.R. Mitchell, *International Historical Statistics Europe 1750-1988*, 3rd ed., New York: Stockton Press, 1992.

– *Statistical yearbook 1991*, Paris: Unesco Nations Educational, Scientific and Cultural Organization, 1991.

– U.S. Bureau of the Census, *Statistical Abstract of the United States 1992. The National Data Book*, 112nd ed. Washington DC, 1992.

15. Interview with Baha'i officials in London, 22nd and 23rd of March, 1993.

16. G. Gustafsson, *Religiös förändring i Norden 1930-1980*, Malmö: Liber Förlag, 1985.

17. P. Petursson, 'The Relevance of Secularization in Iceland', *Social Compass*, 25, 1988, pp. 107-24.

18. *The Seven Year Plan 1979-1986. Statistical Report*, Haifa: Universal House of Justice, 1986, p. 51.

19. *Ibid.*

20. C. Newell, *Methods and Models in Demography*, London: Belhaven Press, 1988.

21. Interview with Baha'i official in Reykjavik, 25th of August, 1992.

22. *Cf.* Figure 1.

23. J.T. Duke, B.L. Johnson and J.B. Duke, 'Rates of Religious Conversion: A Macrosociological Study', *Research in the Social Scientific Study of Religion*, 5, 1993, pp. 89-121. For reference to Barrett, see note 8.

CHAPTER 12

The Raëlian Movement International

Susan J. Palmer

What is the likely future of this futuristic new religion? Moving into the ecological niche created by the declining Catholic Church in Quebec, this 'UFO cult' is a synthesis of symbols from popular folk materials, myths from Golden Age science fiction, and therapeutic techniques borrowed from the Human Potential Movement. This study explores the appeal of this movement for youthful and upwardly-mobile Quebecois from the working class, and examines the various strategies whereby this small society defines, defends and expands its boundaries.

The History

The Raëlian Movement International was founded by a French racing car driver and journalist, 'Raël' (born Claude Vorilhon in 1946), in 1973, as a result of his alleged encounter with space aliens during a walking tour of the Clermont-Ferrand volcanic mountain range in France. These beings, whom Raël describes as small human-shaped beings with pale green skin and almond eyes, entrusted him with the 'message'. This message concerns our true identity: we were 'implanted' on earth by superior extra-terrestrial scientists, the 'Elohim', who created humanity from DNA in their laboratories. Raël's mission, as 'the last of forty prophets', crossbred between Elohim and mortal women, is to warn humankind that, since 1945 and Hiroshima, we have entered the 'Age of Apocalypse' in which we have the choice of destroying ourselves with nuclear weapons or making the leap into planetary consciousness which will qualify us to inherit the scientific knowledge of our space forefathers. Science will enable four percent of our species in the future to clone themselves and travel through space populating virgin planets 'in our image'.[1] Raëlians wear large medallions of the swastika inside the Star of David, which they believe is an ancient symbol of the integrity of time and space.

Membership

The movement claims between 20,000 and 30,000 members world-wide, distributed mainly throughout French-speaking Europe, Japan and Quebec, and endeavours through its books and lectures to unite Christians, Jews and Muslims in a 'de-mythologized' interpretation of scripture as the true history of a space colonization. Four thousand is the figure generally quoted for membership in Quebec and in Japan. According to the British National Guide, Dr Marcus Wenner, there are around 10,000 members in Europe, and the 'Raëlian Movement exists in 67 countries'. No figures are kept for Britain but he estimates that 60% of British members are female. He states, 'I can tell you right now that in England we do not keep on record any data concerning marital status, number of children...' and Quebec has a similar policy (or lack of interest).[2]

There are two levels of commitment in the membership. 'Raëlians' are those who have acknowledged the Elohim as their fathers by taking the two steps of undergoing initiation and making funeral arrangements; the 'Structure' are those who actively serve the organization and are committed to the two goals of the movement, i.e. spreading the message to mankind and building an embassy in Jerusalem by the year 2025 to receive the Elohim.

While members of the Structure dedicate much of their energy towards fulfilling Raël's goals, and tend to be disciplined in their diet and pay their tithes, the outer circle of Raëlians might be described as 'world affirming' in their orientation towards society.[3] Members are encouraged through summer courses to achieve success in their careers, to have better health through avoiding all recreational drugs and stimulants, and to enlarge their capacity to experience pleasure, which, Raël claims, will strengthen their immune system and enhance their intelligence and telepathic abilities. Those who find total self-fulfilment will be immortalized through cloning. Meanwhile, Raël advises Raëlians not to marry or to exacerbate the planetary over-population problem, but to commune with the wonder of the universe by exploring their sexuality with the opposite sex, the same sex and any other life forms — even ETI.

Our 1991 study of sex ratios in Quebec revealed that twice as many men join as women, and that there is a larger proportion of women in the Structure than among the inactive 'Raëlians'. The sex ratios of members in the Structure, from the beginner level to Raël in level 6, are as follows:

Sex ratios in the Raelian structure in Canada

Level	Title	Female	Male
0	Probationer	15	23
1	Assistant animator	48	52
2	Animator	45	77
3	Assistant guide	25	34
4	Priest guide	4	14
5	Bishop guide	–	3
6	Planetary guide	–	1

The UK leader, Dr Wenner, reports that in Europe, 'only 15% of Priests and Bishops are women'. There appears to be a recent trend towards promoting women leaders, and Raël has appointed female Bishop Guides in Korea and in France, and sent a woman Priest Guide to direct the movement in the United States.

The average age of members in Quebec, according to the 1988 Raëlian Conseil Decisionel Survey on 399 respondents, was 35, and the median age was 33.9 for those in the Structure and 32.3 for 'Raëlians'. Our 1991 Dawson survey (30 respondents) came up with 28 as the average age for women and 33 for men. The figures for Europe are not known or unavailable.

Of the thirty respondents in the Dawson Survey, all but one came from a Catholic background. Their parents (or rather their fathers) were described as fruit vendors, farmers, clerks, janitors, etc., and the respondents themselves tended to hold jobs in technological or in para-scientific professions, such as laboratory technician, industrial technician, dental assistant, paramedic or male nurse, and security guard for a psychiatric ward. Also, a surprising number of strippers, both female and male, were encountered by this researcher and her students in the meetings. At one meeting we noted four male strippers present (fully clothed: they had mentioned their profession in the course of our conversations). It would be interesting to conduct a similar survey on members in Europe.

Rituals

Denying the existence of God or the soul, Raël presents, as the only hope of immortality, a regeneration through science, and to this end members participate in four annual festivals so that the Elohim can fly overhead and register the Raëlians' DNA codes on their machines. This initiation ritual, called the *Transmission of the Cellular Plan*, promises a kind of immortality through cloning. New initiates sign a contract which permits a mortician to cut out a piece of bone in their forehead (the 'third eye') which is stored in ice awaiting the descent of the Elohim. New initiates are also required to send a letter of apostasy to the Church in which they were baptized.

During the monthly meetings members participate in a guided meditation called *Oxygenation* which involves deep breathing and concentrating on a mental anatomical dissection of the body, arriving at the brain which engages in a visualization exercise of the planet of the Elohim, to the accompaniment of New Age music. Many Raëlians perform the *Sensual Meditation* daily with a cassette tape which involves sensual and body awareness techniques and a guided meditation into the infinity of space and time envisioned as inside the body. Raëlians participate annually in a Sensual Meditation seminar, in a rural setting, which features fasting, nudity and sensory awareness exercises and sexual experimentation, the ultimate goal being to experience the 'cosmic orgasm'. The movement owns a camp-site in Quebec for North Americans, and one in the South of France, near Alby, for Europeans.

Millenarian Goals and Evangelism

The Raëlians have a strong millenarian focus in preparing for the descent of the UFOs bearing the Elohim and the 39 immortal prophets (Jesus, Buddha, Mohammed, Joseph Smith, etc.), who, according to Raël's revelation, were born from the union of a mortal woman and an Elohim. The movement has two goals: to 'inform the public', and to build an intergalactic space embassy in Jerusalem.

While members of the Structure are committed to making the message available to those who are 'already Raëlian but haven't realized it yet', they are instructed to avoid pressure tactics and evangelizing. Members who attempt to force their ideas, or unwelcome sexual attentions, on others are excommunicated from the movement for seven years, being the time it takes to replace all their body cells. While it is their mission to 'inform the public', Raël was told by extra-terrestrials that only 4% of humanity is sufficiently intelligent to understand the Message, so Raëlians are not disappointed by the overwhelming scepticism of their audiences. Since it is essential to have the cooperation of the Israeli government to prepare for the descent of the Elohim, however, Raëlian guides pursue more energetic evangelical strategies regarding the Jewish people.

Sexual Experimentation

Raël's vision of a perfect society in the future, ruled by the 'geniocracy' of intelligent scientists, is based on revelation and reflects the sexual customs of those extra-terrestrials whom he (allegedly) observed when they (allegedly) took him to their planet in 1975. As he described it, Elohim society is composed of two planets: the Planet of the Immortals houses ninety thousand quasi-immortal men and women who 'can unite themselves freely as they wish, and any form of jealousy is eliminated'; and the other planet where citizens must go before a review board for cloning privileges, and are limited to two children per couple. This mirrors Raëlian society in which members of the Hierarchy tend to avoid marriage and procreation, whereas simple 'Raëlians' lead a less committed lifestyle. Raël[4] describes his own encounter with alien sexual mores and recommends experimenting with both sexes and different races in order to discover one's natural tastes, and advises women to postpone reproducing until they have completed 'the fulfilment of your body' and 'the blossoming of your mind'. Contrary to recent accusations in the French Press, there is no evidence whatsoever that Raël or Raëlians advocate, or are inclined towards, sexually abusing children. This researcher's impression is that children are not regarded as objects of lust, but rather as boring nuisances who who must be prevented from intruding upon the adults' fun.

Charisma and Religious Experience

How does charisma operate in the Raëlian movement, and how does the authority of the Elohim, invested in Raël, percolate down through the Structure? Is the ET connection a strong appeal, or is it Raël's charisma that first impresses the 'seeker'? Our Dawson College survey, conducted at the November 1992 meeting, attempted to address some of these questions. Nine Dawson students passed out 50 questionnaire forms and managed to receive 33 responses. Question 6 asked: ' a) Had you read science fiction books before joining? b) were you already interested in UFO sightings and contactees? c) Had you ever seen a UFO or felt the presence of extra-terrestrials before?' As the results below indicate, it appears the majority of members were interested in aliens and UFO lore before encountering the movement, but had not realized the personal, emotional or religious implications of this interest until meeting Raël himself.

Dawson College 'Raëliens and Charisma' Survey

Previous Interest	Negative	Positive
Read Science fiction	11	22
Aware UFOs, contactees	8	25
See UFO, felt ETs	20	13

There is no evidence that 'joiners' were necessarily more deeply versed in science fiction than were their contemporaries. Although twenty-two respondents claimed they had read science fiction, the responses to Question 9 indicated they had apparently not read very much; most were familiar with only the most popular 'golden age' writers such as Asimov, but had watched a lot of Star Trek and seen science fiction movies. In contrast, their interest in UFO sightings and contactee reports was deeper; they had read widely and kept clippings. Whereas only eight had felt the presence of extra-terrestrials before encountering the movement, five claimed to have actually seen UFOs.

The Raëlians' attitude to other UFO cults and contactees is ambiguous. While they are quick to point to reports of UFO sightings in the news as corroborating Rael's story, they are inclined to dismiss the claims of career contactees as erroneous. Thus, while many members were interested in the possibility of communication with extra-terrestrials before they encountered the Message, they now disassociate themselves from ufologists, and play down the numinous quality of encounters of the third kind. One Priest Guide declared it had always been obvious to him there was intelligent life outside this planet, but only when he met Raël, 'I found something... and it fitted!' He outlined the movement's position on UFOs as follows:

We often encounter ufologists or UFO addicts similar to 'trekkies', who are interested in nothing but UFOs, but we're not interested in UFOs *per se*, just the Message and those people who might be *inside* the UFOs.

A key to understanding how charisma operates in the movement was found in the responses to Question 10. Questions 10 was worded as follows:

When (if ever) do you feel in mental communication with extra-terrestrials?
   a)   During sensual meditation?
   b)   In the presence of Raël?
   c)   Through the guides?
   d)   Other occasions?

The majority of respondents (17) claimed they felt in touch with the Elohim in the Sensual Meditation, whereas only six felt in contact through Raël's presence, and only one respondent felt in contact through a guide. In response to Question 11, regarding the initiation ritual ('Describe how you felt during the Transmission of the Cellular Plan'), only four initiates felt a sense of communication with the Elohim. Three respondents reported feeling 'nothing', two felt joy in belonging to 'la belle famille Raëlien', nine expressed feelings of happiness and satisfaction, two were 'set free', and four reported intense or dramatic experiences ('I felt filled up to the brim, enlightened'; 'My emotions were so strong, I wept'; 'I felt waves of electricity from Raël's hands'; 'Nothing at the time, but then all night I was having visions of criss-cross hexagonal forms').

Members are encouraged to practise a guided meditation/visualization technique daily, the aim being to transmit love to, and establish telepathic links with, the Elohim, and to achieve harmony with infinity. This technique involves relaxation, situating the self in relation to the surrounding world, and expanding one's frame of reference until the self becomes a tiny atom in the galaxy. Next, through body consciousness, sensitivity and sensual stimulation, the bones and organs are visualized and finally, the atoms of the body. Through making this mental leap from microcosm to macrocosm, Raëlians seek to achieve harmony with the infinite and with their Creators. Responses to the questionnaire revealed that experiences as varied as sensations of physical well-being, psychic abilities, enjoying the beauty of nature, and sexual arousal were all interpreted as signs of establishing telepathic communication with the Elohim. The responses to Questions 10 and 11, therefore, suggest that Raëlians undergo an educational process whereby they learn to contact and recognize the charisma of aliens through practising this meditation ritual, in which Raël himself was (allegedly) instructed when he visited the planet of the Elohim.

Raël creates the impression of being a gentle, unpretentious and reasonable man. He usually underplays his prophetic role ('Do not look at my finger, look at what it's pointing to'), but at other times seems to employ charisma-building strategies. He tends to drop into meetings as if he just fell to earth. In his last appearance in Montreal, for example, he crept in during the *Oxygenation* ritual while peoples' eyes were shut, and took over the microphone. Hearing his voice, the Raëlians opened their eyes and cheered, and he stood smiling in his heavily padded white 'space suit', his long hair and beard dishevelled as if he had just removed a space helmet. A guide who had been lying on the ground oxygenating then stood up and declared, 'I had my eyes shut, but suddenly I felt a violent storm of serenity and peace, and I knew Raël must be near!'.

Only Raël's own communications with the Elohim are recognized as authentic. The former national guide of Canada, Victor Legendre, resigned his position and left the movement in August 1992 because his girlfriend was a 'mystic' and claimed she had received a message from aliens and that Raël was not the only prophet of our time. She was in level 3 of the Structure, but began to challenge Raël's scientific materialism by announcing she was a reincarnation of a seventeenth century French prophetess, and by exhibiting telekinetic powers in lifting tables — and Legendre supported her claims. He was confronted by Raël at the summer Sensual Meditation Camp and asked to choose between the movement and his girlfriend. At first he renounced her, but later admitted he was too much in love and chose to resign instead. The Raëlians appeared to enjoy this drama, and the National Guide exited, not as one in disgrace, but rather as a romantic hero. 'He was torn between the movement and his love for a woman... His love was stronger than the message', one female assistant guide commented approvingly.[5]

In spite of Raël's insistence on orthodoxy and his extravagant claim to be an alien half-breed and the 'Last Prophet of our Time', he conforms more closely to Weber's model of an exemplary prophet than to the more powerful and demanding ethical type of prophet.[6] Members interviewed tended to stress the appeal of the Message and of the Raëlian community rather than the lure of Raël's charisma in describing how they joined. It appears that discipline over the outer circle of members is weak, for many Raëlians interviewed confessed to not paying their tithes, and to indulging in wine and cigarettes. Only 15% of members pay the ten per cent of their net income, of which three per cent goes to their national movement and seven per cent to the international movement. Members of the core group, or Structure, on the other hand, pay their tithes and refrain from reproducing and from recreational drugs — and they are more likely to view Raël as an ethical prophet. Raël's speeches constantly emphasise the importance of choice, of individuality and of freedom. Within the context of Bird's theory of charisma and ritual, Raëlians can be seen to tune in to their inner voices of authority through the ritual catharsis of breaking taboos, and seem to emerge with a clearer sense of identity and direction. When they look to Raël, it is not to tell them how to live their lives, but rather for inspiration — as a living example of the self-made, self-realized man of the future.

Raelian Controversies and Activist Responses

Some of the Raëlian actions seem calculated to provoke or to shock society, and others appear designed to appease. The Raëlians plan a series of domonstrations and a publicity campaign for their annual Planetary Week, and their activities seem designed to 'gross out' the Catholic Church and to court the approval of secular-minded upper middle class liberals.

The barbs directed at Catholicism are numerous. As mentioned above, all initiates send a 'Letter of Apostasy' to the church into which they were baptized, and this means that the Catholic Church in Quebec has received over four thousand such letters. In a fool-hardy gesture inviting the attention of the anti-satanic movement, one Guide announced at the September 1991 meeting that the 'theme' for the year would be, 'Lucifer, Je T'Aime!', and urged members to scribble this logo on walls throughout the city. He went on to explain that 'Lucifer' was actually a team of renegade scientists who gave homo sapiens his first science lessons, whereas 'Satan' was the opposing team on the home planet.[7]

Operation Condom was a well-publicised protest against the Montreal Catholic School Commission's decision to veto the proposal to install condom machines in their high schools. Late in 1992, a 'condom-mobile', financed and staffed by the Raëlians, toured the provinces of Quebec and Ontario and parked outside Catholic high schools where they distributed 10,000 condoms to the students during their recess, as well as large pink buttons which read, 'Oui aux condoms à l'Ecole'. The driving force behind this campaign appeared to be the Guide, Marie Marcelle Godbout, a nurse and long-time volunteer counsellor for women with AIDS. She explained to the press that she was protesting about the 'ostrich-like stance' of the MCSC and quoted daunting statistics concerning teenage pregnancies and STD in Quebec. Another Guide claimed it was a goal of the movement to teach people to live by pleasure for pleasure's sake, and that being handed a condom conveys to teenagers a positive attitude to sex. The Montreal anti-cult organization, *Infosect*, reacted to the Raëlians' favourable publicity in twenty-two newpapers by publishing an exposé of Raël's 'fascist' ideas on government. Raël's *Geniocracy*, a utopian fantasy proposing a meritocracy along the lines of the Confucian mandarins or Plato's Guardians, is presented as a serious threat to democracy.[8]

Certain actions, on the other hand, seem designed to accommodate society. The transformation of the angular swastika symbol into the curving petals of a flower was explained as an effort to placate the Jews, who were reacting negatively to the swastika.[9] It has been a long-term Raëlian policy not to admit children to the Sensual Meditation rooms or camp areas, so as to avoid allegations of indecent exposure or child molestation. Raël consistently urges members to obey the local laws concerning sex of the country they live in, while adding, 'but we must strive to *change* the law!' Raëlians are conspicuously 'politically correct'. They denounce racism and sexism, and joined in the Montreal Gay Parade in March 1993 to protest against sexual discrimination.

A comparison of their early and recent literature reveals a developing sophistication or 'slickness'. Their magazine, *Apocalypse*, no longer features the incongruous mixture of homo-erotic and Playboy-style photographs it sported in the eighties. There has also been a recent trend to demote some of the early Guides who joined in the late seventies and who hold blue-collar jobs, and to promote the more recent, but highly-educated, members with prestigious professions, to the fourth or fifth level. The movement as a whole appears to be achieving upward social mobility.

Media attention in Quebec has been favourable or tongue-in-cheek, until a television and radio documentary were broadcast in the Spring of 1991, which portrayed the Sensual Meditation Camp as an unbridled sex orgy where perversions were encouraged. Local rabbis interviewed on the show failed to be amused by Raël's racial theory, or by his Guides' evangelical efforts outside the synagogue. Since then, the parents of several youthful members have reacted with alarm. One 19 year-old complained that her mother, on finding her listening to the Sensual Meditation tape, insisted she see a psychiatrist. Raël appeared on the Geraldo Show in late 1991 and seemed to be oblivious to the host's habitually aggressive and derisive manner.

Journalists seem to have absorbed the anti-cult perspective. In October 1992, Raël was interviewed on a French weekly television programme called *Ciel Mon Mardi*. When it was aired on a Tuesday evening, Raëlians were upset to find that, 'the interviewer, the producer, the cameraman had all collaborated in destroying Rael's reputation'. Scenes from *The Triumph of the Will*, a film about the Jonestown suicide, shots of Charles Manson and of battered children were interspersed throughout what Raël had thought was an innocuous interview. The unfortunate death of a child at the Sensual Meditation camp-site outside Paris, the year before, was made out to be 'mysterious', and reeking of foul play. (Raël explained that the child was riding a bicycle and accidently fell into an empty swimming pool.) A disgruntled apostate was brought on, who accused Raël and his followers of brainwashing his wife, separating him from his children, practising satanic rituals, and sexually abusing children during the Sensual Meditation seminars.

The history of this apostate was explained by three members of the Structure. He is a French citizen who owned a car repair shop and used to smuggle cars and drugs between France and Algiers to sell on the black market. Soon after he and his wife became Raëlians, he was arrested for drug peddling in Algiers and jailed. Raël raised money and hired a lawyer to have him transferred to a more comfortable prison in France. After six years he was released, but was enraged to find his wife and two children had lived with a Raëlian Guide for two years. He made an assault on the Guide during a Raëlian conference, but was restrained. In August 1992, he claimed his wife and children were being held prisoner in the camp-site where the two-week Sensual Meditation seminar was held in the south of France, and attempted to enter the camp gate to kill Raël, but his way was barred by the guards. Raëlians were outraged that this man was presented as a respectable citizen and concerned father on the television show, and that his drug dealing, jail record and alleged murder attempts were not mentioned.

An unofficial story persists among Raëlians that Raël was kidnapped in France in the early eighties by three men disguised as terrorists, and was held for three weeks and forced to fast. On being released, he gave up lecturing for a whole year to recuperate from the ordeal. The identity of the kidnappers was never established. This enigmatic rumour of persecution enhances Raël's charisma, but also reveals interesting parallels with UFO abduction accounts.

In 1992, the last will and testament of a former nun who became a Raëlian and then died, leaving her property to the movement, was disputed in court by her brother. A struggling farmer with a large family to feed, he claimed she had been the dupe of brainwashing techniques and the seductive attentions of one of the Guides.

Dr. Daniel Chabot, Bishop and Continental Guide of the Americas, has become a controversial figure since his participation in the July 1993 conference on masturbation, organized by the Raëlians. The 'Corporation professionelle des psychologues du Quebec' held an inquiry during the first week of July to determine whether Chabot was using his professional status to attract converts to his sect, and whether his speech on the therapeutic benefits of masturbation and his involvement in an 'erotique-esoterique' religion conflicted with the scientific principles generally recognized by members of his profession.[10]

Raël and his Guides have responded to the increasing external pressure by pursuing a self-defensive course of activism. At the November 1992 meeting in Montreal, Raël requested donations for the widow of Jean Migueres, the late author of books on extraterrestrials, who had been 'assassinated' by his father-in-law, a member of an anti-cult organization. Raël insisted that, although Migueres was wrong in claiming he had been abducted by aliens, he had the right to be heard, and to receive protection for his freedom of speech from the Charter of Rights. Raël then read out a long letter he had writtent to Migueres' widow, and urged his followers to sign a form protesting against the French government's granting of financial support to anti-cult agencies who promote hatred towards religous minorities. Raël proceeded to publish a book denouncing the French government's support of anti-cult organizations, *Le Racisme Religieux Financé par le Gouvernement Socialiste*. He also founded FIREPHIM, an organization dedicated to protecting the rights of religious, philosophical and racial minorities.

Dr Marcus Wenner, the National Guide in Britain, explained the origin and purpose of FIREPHIM as follows:

In France the media... under more government... along with the Catholic Church has mounted a smear campaign against the French Raëlian Movement, resulting in many job losses and much violence directed against French Raëlians. The French Raëlian Movement took some of the perpetrators to court, but the judge 'mysteriously' lost all the documents. Raël responded with the creation of FIREPHIM, the International Federation of Minority Religions and Philosophies, in order to protect the right to believe in what one wishes. FIREPHIM is also creating an independent Ethical Committee to expose, control and prevent any organization from joining it who might use FIREPHIM as a cover under which they abuse these basic human rights.[11]

When a journalist, Jean-Luc Mongrain, attacked the Raelians on his programme on Tele-Metropole in early December 1993, the station was visited the next day by seventy Raëlians who marched in to stage a protest demonstration.[12]

The Appeal of the Raëlian Movement

Having studied the movement and its members in its social context in Quebec, I would propose three main reasons for its appeal. First, in Quebec, the Raëlian movement replaces and replicates the Roman Catholic Church. The Guides refer to it as 'the first atheistic religion'. It provides answers to moral ambiguity, guidelines for relating to others, and clear answers concerning our origins and destiny. Rejecting traditional, archaic religious language, it adopts the language of science for its discourse.

Secondly, like other new religions, the theology rejects the distant, judgmental God of the Old Testament, and replaces Him with a symbol closer to the human being, and emphasizes man's divinity. Raëlian theology 'spiritualizes matter' by emphasizing the infinity of matter and the eternity of time. Raëlians strive to expand the limits of their consciousness through meditation techniques, and cultivate a 'platonic sense of wonder at the whole of being'.

Thirdly, the movement provides a forum for sexual experimentation and for the redefinition of gender within an experience of *communitas*. This process is supervised by Raël and his Guides, who might be compared to the shamans or ritual elders in primitive tribes. Men and women apparently seek out a 'liminal period' in which to engage in intense therapeutic work and ritual activities, and appear to emerge better equipped to deal with the problems of adult life and the ambiguity surrounding gender issues in the larger society.

These attractions, and the effective resource mobilization demonstrated by the leaders,[13] suggest that this new religion has potential for survival into the future, although if the extra-terrestrials fail to materialize, the Message might require some creative revisions.

Future Missionary/Millenarian Activity

Raël is planning a trip to Moscow in March 1993 to meet a group of Russians who are receptive to the Message. His book was smuggled into Moscow by sending a series of hand-written letters in French, which were then translated, and is currently being printed. There is — to date — no Raëlian Movement in Eastern Europe according to local Guides.

As the year 2025 approaches, Raëlians plan to intensify their missionary and millenarian activity in Israel. A team of eighteen Quebecois and thirty European Guides are planning a two-week tour of Israel. Their agenda includes a visit to the Wailing Wall to announce the advent of the Messiah, a lecture tour of six cities, a meeting with the 'Great Rabbi' to request the assembly of all rabbis and Jewish leaders in a *Knessed* and a *sanhedrin* in order to announce the Messiah and his Message. The last event in their itinary will be a transmission of the cellular plan (baptism ceremony) performed at the very site where Jesus was baptized. Every Israeli embassy in the world will shortly receive a letter requesting that the Israeli government donate a piece of land (347 hectares) where the Raëlian Movement can 'establish the Embassy of the Elohim, the Third Temple, where the Messiah will welcome our Creators, the Elohim'.

Predicting a successful future for the movement, Dr Marcus Wenner, National Guide of Britain, also conveys insights into the appeal of the Message for contemporary youth, when he writes:

As the public begins to go beyond the initial surprise of the 'ET' aspect and understand how profound is our de-mystification of religion and spiritualization of science, a new phase of respect for the human values we stand for and what we are achieving is appearing. People are just beginning to understand that we represent a lifestyle of fulfilment and freedom open to the future rather than fearfully clinging to the past.

Notes

1. A. Bouchard, 'Movement Raelien', *Nouvel Age... Nouvelles Croyances* (sous la direction du Centre d'Information sur les Nouvelles Religions), Montreal: Editions Pailines et Mediaspaul, 1989; C. Vorilhon, *Space Aliens Took me to Their Planet*, 1978.
2. This statement was in a letter Wenner sent me on March 3 1993 (47 years after Hiroshima). I received no reply from letters and faxes requesting data on membership sent to the other National Guides in Europe.
3. R. Wallis, *Salvation and Protest*, London: Frances Pinter, 1979.
4. *Op. cit.*, pp. 210-13.
5. An account of this crisis in leadership was related to me by three animators on different occasions, and their stories 'jived'. They explained in a down-to-earth fashion that rival contactee claims could not be tolerated, as they would give rise to schism.
6. Max Weber, *Essays in Sociology* (ed. H. Gerth and C. Wright Mills), New York: Schocken Books, 1946.
7. This action occurred at a time when the 'great satanic cult scare' was at its peak.
8. *Le Devoir*, Friday 4 December 1992.
9. This was announced in the October, November and December meetings in Montreal.
10. *La Presse*, Friday 9 July, 1993.

11.   This passage is from a letter he wrote to me dated 3 March, '47 after Hiroshima' (1993).

12.   *Journal Vedettes*, 9, 1993, p. 1.

13.   Rodney Stark, 'How New Religions Succeed: A Theoretical Model', in D. G. Bromley and P. E. Hammond (eds), *The Future of New Religious Movements*, Macon: Mercer University Press, 1987.

CHAPTER 13

Dread in Babylon: An Explorative Field Study of the Twelve Tribes of Israel

Sarah Bracke and Stef Jansen

Greetings in the divine and most high name of our Lord and Saviour Jesus Christ who has revealed himself in the personality of His Imperial Majesty Haile Selassie-I, King of Kings, Lord of Lords, Conquering Lion of the Tribe of Judah.

Greetings through the Orthodox faith, which is not a faith of writs nor rites, but a function of the heart: true liberation through our Lord Jesus Christ, mystically incorporated into our hearts.

Greetings in the name of the Twelve Tribes of Israel, who were once lost and scattered abroad but now regathered on the sweet little island of Jamaica by our beloved prophet Gad.[1]

In researching their graduate thesis, the authors conducted two months of field work in London among members of the Twelve Tribes of Israel. The research method applied was covert participant observation. The study involved taking part in meetings and ceremonies, but also — more importantly — in the everyday life of the members.

This graduate thesis consists of two main parts: on the one hand an explorative field study, and on the other hand an intensive study of the literature on the subject. This led us to believe that the description of Rastafari as merely a sect or a cult is too narrow a concept. Instead, we would argue that the movement's importance is generated mainly by its significance at the level of subcultural style.

Knowing the limitations of our field work and the scope of a graduate thesis in general, we have no intention of dwelling upon the general features of Rastafari. After a very brief outline of organizational aspects of the Twelve Tribes, we will develop a set of selected topics, which we consider to be particularly interesting. Special attention will be paid to the role of style aspects and their relationship to religious beliefs and ethical patterns.

The Twelve Tribes of Israel within Rastafari

The Twelve Tribes of Israel were founded in 1968 in Jamaica by a man named Vernon Carrington, known to members as Prophet Gad or Gadman. The message of the prophet was straightforward: read the Bible a chapter a day. The particular cultural characteristics of the sixties in Jamaica had a tremendous impact on the structure and the ideas of the organization. After a period in which rasta was associated with violence and drugs, the Twelve Tribes of Israel, among others, attempted to stop this moral panic. The objective was to gain respectability and appreciation for their beliefs and their ethics; they even strived for recognition as an official religion by the Jamaican government.

This implies that the Twelve Tribes' position within the Rastafari movement is looked upon with mixed feelings by other rastafarians. The Tribes are the largest rasta organization outside Jamaica. Most rastas do not want to join an organization at all, however, preferring to *live* their rasta philosophy on their own. Traditionally, Rastafari leaves a lot of room for subjective interpretations, and therefore, even in the Twelve Tribes of Israel, the degree of individual freedom and personal interpretation is very high. Members consider their relationship with God to be an individual one.

Many rastas criticize the Twelve Tribes for what are considered to be compromises with Babylon, i.e. the evil 'Western, Catholic, capitalistic world'. As far as we know, the Twelve Tribes is one of the few rasta organizations which allows whites to be members. Women play a rather important role in the organization, which is also uncommon in Rastafari. The Twelve Tribes meetings may be considered sacred ceremonies, with a high degree of ritualization. Moreover, funds are collected for repatriation, instead of waiting for Babylon to fall by the hand of Jah (Jehovah). The combination of all these factors makes the organization a thorn in the side of many rastas.

Nevertheless, we regard the Twelve Tribes of Israel as an interesting object of sociological study, precisely because of the ever-present confrontation with Babylon. As we shall argue in this paper, we think this situation has contributed to the phase of transition in which the organization currently finds itself.

Children of Jah in London

The twelve sons of Jacob

Rastas define themselves as the chosen people of Jah, the true Israelites, the 'Black Jews'. Referring to the book of Genesis, which tells of the origin of the People of Israel, the members of the Twelve Tribes consider themselves to be the descendants of the twelve sons of Jacob.

Each of the twelve sons of Jacob was the founder of a tribe named after the ancestor: Rueben, Simeon, Levi, Judah, Issachar, Zebulon, Dan, Gad, Asher, Naphtali, Joseph and Benjamin. These original twelve tribes were the chosen people with whom God established a covenant. The members of the Twelve Tribes of Israel look upon the Bible as the book which contains their history: their past as well as their future.

The book of Revelation prophesies that only 144,000 will be saved: 12,000 of each tribe. The most quoted verse within the organization is, 'Many are called, but few are chosen'. The central feature of the teachings of the Twelve Tribes is the emphasis on reading the Bible the 'right way': a chapter a day from Genesis to Revelation reveals the Truth.

The concept of the twelve Biblical tribes is reflected in the structure of the organization, as we will explain below. The members address each other with their tribe names. These names correspond more or less with the twelve months; depending on the month one was born in, one belongs to a specific tribe. Many members were known only by their tribe name. Others had their own name followed by the name of their tribe, such as Ruth Asher and Kwesi Naphtali. To each tribe is attributed a tendency, a body part, an apostle, a faculty and a colour.

The House of the Lord has many rooms

Soon after the foundation of the organization in Jamaica, several branches were established throughout the rest of the world. These local branches are referred to as 'houses'. To set up a 'house', it is considered crucial to contact prophet Gad in Jamaica. Gadman will explain the structure of a house, and his instructions are to be obeyed.

In order to set up a house, twelve men and twelve women are required, one from every tribe. They are the executives of the house, referred to as the 'firsts'. All 24 members of the first 'benches' need to have a 'second', someone of the same gender and of the same tribe. Thus at least 48 people are required to set up a house.[2] The Twelve Tribes of Israel have two official branches in the UK, one in London and one in Manchester. Membership is formal; the official membership card is called the 'Jewcard'.

Members can gather in 'bodies' in which they can practise several activities: football, cricket, music, art, etc. These bodies have an important social function, since they create the opportunities for members to establish social contacts and to meet people who share the same ideals and beliefs.

We had the impression that the organization has a high degree of internal democracy. The power of the executives is concentrated at the practical level. The executives conduct the public meetings, but every member and even every visitor is given the opportunity to share his reading of the Bible and his testimony. The members are also encouraged to be critical of what is told by others, including executives. It is emphasized that the reading of the Bible is open-ended: no normative or dogmatic order is imposed.

When an executive leaves in one way or another, the second will take his or her place. The person of the same tribe and gender who is registered next will be asked to take the place of the second. This system of seniority shows how succession is more or less guaranteed by a system of ascription.

Dread times: Bible readings and testimonies

A public meeting is held monthly, conducted by the first brother of the tribe identified with the month and the full bench of first sisters. We were told that two years before it was the reverse: the meetings were conducted by the first sister and the full bench of 'brethren'. Each month the headquarters are decorated with the colour of the tribe of that particular month. The members wear a cap, called a banner, in the Ethiopian colours of red, gold and green.

Meetings take place on Sunday afternoons and last for at least four or five hours. The ceremony consists of readings from the Bible, testimonies, individual and collective prayers, and hymns. Everyone attending the meeting, including the children, has an opportunity to address the gathering.

As a rule, the specific topic of the testimonies varies, but the underlying theme remains the same. The speaker would talk about evil on the earth such as war and famine, and, often referring to the book of Revelation, he or she would warn that times will only get worse. But redemption from those atrocities is at hand: follow the word of Jah. As one member put it, 'We warn people and we save souls, so we don't have any blood on our shoulders.' The Israelites, God's chosen people, will be saved and led to the promised land on Judgement Day.

After the religious part of the meeting, there is an open financial report by one of the executives and several announcements concerning gatherings of the bodies, letters from other houses, and so on. Then, afterwards, the headquarters functions as a clubhouse: people chat, food and drinks are available, video tapes are shown, games are played, and people smoke *ganja* (marijuana), although there is no smoking during the meeting. Similar informal meetings are held on Friday nights.

Selected Topics

The divinity of Haile Selassie: Jah live?

In 1930 Ras Tafari Makkonen was crowned Haile Selassie, Emperor of Ethiopia. Traditionally, rastas consider this event to be the historical fulfilment of the biblical Revelation. Haile Selassie is thought of as the second coming of Jah on Earth: not as the Lamb, like Jesus Christ, but as the Lion of Judah, in his guise of king. The death of Haile Selassie in 1975 did not turn out to be the end of this belief. Many rastas believe the Emperor's spirit still dwells on Earth to bring about the redemption of the Israelites.

In spite of the emphasis which most of the literature places on the divinity of the Emperor as one of the key tenets of Rastafari, there is evidence that this is not quite so. Throughout the history of the Rastafari movement, subtle differences have existed in the conception of Haile Selassie's divine status. Although Rastafari has always been loaded with many spiritual 'African' meanings, it cannot be considered merely a sect organized around the divinity of the Emperor.

Even the Twelve Tribes of Israel, who are known for their loyalty to the Ethiopian Royal Family, do not seem to adhere to this 'key tenet'. The traditional view, of course, reflected in the opening greetings, does affirm Haile Selassie as the living God. However, we witnessed one of the first 'sistren' express doubts about the divine status of the Emperor during one of the meetings. Haile Selassie, she said, was certainly a great king, but could someone who prays to God *be* God?

To many of the more traditional rastas this was an offence; someone shouted 'Selassie-I', and a murmur rose. No effort was made to stop the sister, however, which illustrates the high degree of tolerance and permissable deviance within the Tribes. Although not all of them agreed with the sister, all members stressed having *'nuff respec'* for her opinion. It was clear to us that not all members believe in the divinity of Haile Selassie, but as yet there seems to be no articulated alternative.

As we will argue below, this may lead the organization further away from the traditional rasta beliefs, and transform it into an African inspired Christian faith.

An important element in the debate is the fact that the Twelve Tribes of Israel have actual contacts with their (Ethiopian) Royal Family, who live in exile in New York. It was striking that invitations and posters of the organization are increasingly decorated with a photograph of Amha Selassie, the son of Haile

Selassie. This is justified by the biblical quote, 'I and the father are one'. In this way the Twelve Tribes of Israel try to forge a well-grounded link between the religious aspects of the movement on the one hand, and secular support to a royal house in exile on the other hand.

Movement of Jah people: repatriation to Shashamane

The most important source of positive self-identification for the rastas is the mythical Africa. Africa, and especially Ethiopia, is really considered heaven on earth. Africans are said to be humble and hospitable, crops are said to grow twice as fast as in Britain, and African nature is considered to be much closer to creation than ours. For that matter, the term 'creation' is laden with a strongly positive and energetic connotation. As we mentioned above, the Twelve Tribes of Israel collect money for an actual repatriation scheme. They run a small settlement in Shashamane, in the South of Ethiopia, given to the rastas by Haile Selassie. Only few members live there, but a great number of them have visited the place (e.g. all the firsts).

There is a constant reminder of how much work still needs to be done to make Shashamane a nice, beautiful spot to live. Again, in this matter the Twelve Tribes of Israel hold a special position within the Rasta movement. Instead of waiting for a supernatural repatriation realized by Jah, the Tribes look for self-repatriation.

However, members do not seem to want to pack their belongings and leave straight away. They stress the importance of getting prepared and organized beforehand. Only in this way, and by living the word of Jah, do they believe they will reach the Promised Land.

There appears to be a discrepancy between the stress on repatriation and the situation of the Twelve Tribes in London. Although most members live in the poorer sections of the city, the headquarters is situated in a brand new, rather luxurious house in one of the better areas of London. It seems contradictory that an organization should claim to want to leave Babylon as soon as possible, and yet nestle so easily in the very same Babylon.

218 Sarah Bracke and Stef Jansen

Of kings and queens: traditional gender roles undermined?

Traditional rasta ethics regarding the roles of men and women are strongly rooted in the Bible. By selective reading and emphasis, rastas conclude that men and women are equal, *but* they have different tasks to fulfill. Kings (men) have to play a leading role in the unity they form with their queens (wives). The characteristics most appreciated in women are humility and domesticity. Rastas stress the fact that a real 'rasta queen' should be approached with great respect.

Several biblical verses concerning women are interpreted in a literal way by more traditional rastas. For instance, women should cover their hair when they pray, but some rastamen argue that everything you do should be dedicated to Jah like a prayer; so they want their women always to cover their hair. Women also have to wear long skirts. The Old Testament, especially, contains several proscriptions for women: a women who menstruates is forbidden to enter the kitchen, nor can she make a meal for her husband. Moreover preservatives are rejected.

However, we perceived a transformation of those traditional gender roles among certain members of the Twelve Tribes. While they persist, new roles and values are being negotiated. Presently, a group of young women refuse to attend meetings unless they are allowed to wear trousers in the headquarters. There is a change in the meaning of the menstruation; instead of seeing it as a period of 'impurity', some women use it as a time off duty. Then, men will for instance cook dinner for them. Some women go as far as considering the pill, looking at the matter as a personal decision, for which Jah is the only authority to whom they need give account. These changes are connected with a gradual shift to a more metaphorical reading of the Bible.

Black/White in the Twelve Tribes: One Love

One of the most unusual characteristics of the Twelve Tribes of Israel is the fact the organization allows whites as members. Having the basic ideas of Rastafari in mind, it is normal that the majority of people attracted by rasta philosophy should be from an Afro-

Caribbean background. Of those attending the meetings, about five to ten per cent are whites. This distribution is reflected in the executive structure: both benches (male and female) number one white executive.

Most white male members distinguished themselves from their female counterparts by the interest they take in the typical rasta style. Besides the long plaited dreadlocks, they wore tams, lockets and other attributes. Moreover, most of these men turned out to be also seriously into reggae music and ganja smoking.

This marks a striking difference with the white female members. Although most of them wore long skirts like their black sisters, they were much less interested in rasta style. We should mention that this was also the case for black women, but nevertheless we had the impression that white female members were more engaged in the general Christian aspects of rasta. They consider rasta as a return to real Christianity, using the Bible as the source of their belief.

All of these white rasta women, however, were convinced of the importance and the necessity of repatriation to Ethiopia. They hope for a better future in Africa, living in a peaceful and Christian community and reaching a balance between material and spiritual matters. In this context we think that the construct, Africa or Zion, can be read as, 'a place closer to God'.

Strictly roots and culture: subcultural identity and style

As we mentioned before, Rastafari experienced a boom in Britain in the 1970s. Crucial to this success, the widespread reggae music among black youth was an important vehicle for rasta concepts and philosophy. The *ridims* and the lyrics of singers like Bob Marley, himself a member of the Twelve Tribes, delivered the message of Rastafari to black youth in English cities. They gathered round their sound systems and soon developed their own versions of the thick dread talk, the dreadlocks, the tams and the symbols, the ganja smoking and even the walking style.

Style has always been one of the most important aspects of the rasta movement. The literature on the subject suggests that Haile Selassie and repatriation form the core of rasta, but we would argue that aspects of style have been more constitutive for the development of Rastafari in England, which makes sense when one bears in mind that rasta has been particularly attractive to black adolescents, i.e. in a phase of life characterized by active identity-construction.

Their metropolitan life-world bore the features of the late modern experience: an increasingly individualized world where no fixed 'selves' are to hand. In late modernity, people engage in processes of identity-construction best described by the notion of *bricolage*. Identity bricolage involves a permanent redefinition and reinvention of one's identity, drawing on raw material from an (often limited) reservoir. Moreover, the 'bricoleur' has a wide range of building materials at his or her disposal, without being hindered by too rigid a framework.

An interest in rasta does not inevitably lead to one sort of 'religious rasta', as is sometimes suggested, but leaves many ways open to the 'bricoleur'. Our opinion is that this open-ended, free and individualized character of rasta, far from being a weakness, has been a major attraction. In a highly individualized atmosphere, reggae served as an effective medium for rasta concepts, style and ideas. Everyone could develop his own version of rasta *livity*, without having to fit into one of the existing structures or organizations. Style signalled a significant difference from the outside world and affirmed the group identity.

The bricolage of rasta identity led many rasta to become interested in Rastafari spirituality, but we see no core tenets which one has to adhere to in order to be a 'true rasta'. Rastafari has always been more a form of spirituality and *African-ness* than a religion. We believe that this spiritual aspect distinguishes rasta from youth subcultures, and this explains partly its enduring impact on Afro-Caribbean culture in England. In the light of these findings, it is easy to understand why rasta organizations have never succeeded in attracting a great number of rastamen and rastawomen. As a socio-religious subculture, rasta attracted mainly young people who were not eager to step into any organization. As many rastas consider organized parts of the movement to be wrong, we believe that the Twelve Tribes of Israel must have attracted a particular kind of rasta, i.e. religious individuals who believed in the advantages of organization and structure. Given their socio-economic situation and the reputation of rastas in general, the headquarters offers a respectability not easily gained elsewhere. Further, the Twelve Tribes appealed to white rastas, as it was the only organization would admit them as members and even executives.

However, style still plays an important role for the members of the Twelve Tribes of Israel. They construct a particular identity through wearing locks, through banners and craftwork, listening to reggae music and smoking the *holy herb*.

During our two months of field work in South London, we gained the impression that Rastafari had lost its appeal for black youth. The Twelve Tribes of Israel count very few members between twelve and twenty years old. It seems that black youth now has at its disposal new (though not completely new) sources of identification. In their 'bricolage' of an identity, many draw upon other subcultures, as for instance *hip hop*, which again is related very closely to a particular sort of music, *rap*.

Hip hop originated in the black ghettoes of the United States; rhythms and lyrics are often of a militant blacknationalist nature. It is not surprising, then, that Malcolm X caps and T-shirts are extremely popular in Brooklyn and in Brixton. As with rasta, identity is communicated through style: baseball caps, football jackets, large trainers and gold jewelry. We noticed that some rasta icons have been incorporated in this style, most notably the identification with Africa displayed in badges and lockets, and the black pride discourse. It would be interesting to analyze the degree to which the hip hop subculture is reflected in a political shift towards Black Power ideas.

Conclusions and hypotheses

The high degree of permitted deviance and individual freedom of interpretation is no longer a strength when taken over in an organization. Since the interests of the organization and individual members may clash, this may weaken unity. We observed at least two tendencies which may turn out to be incompatible in the near future.

On the one hand we distinguished traditional members who are mainly concerned with Rastafari as a socio-religious subculture. They stick to the *rasta livity* as developed in the early years of the Twelve Tribes. These members are firmly integrated in the subcultural setting. Their rather conservative attitude is reflected at the level of religion and ethics; they believe in the absolute divinity of Haile Selassie and traditional gender roles. On the other hand, we observed members who are interested in the Twelve Tribes mainly because of its organizational character. They strive for adjustments that they believe can guarantee the survival of the organization. Step by step, they want to adapt certain aspects to present circumstances: the divinity of Haile Selassie is questioned, gender roles are modernized, etc. In general the Bible is interpreted less literally, and in a more metaphorical way.

If our observations reflect real tendencies, and if they continue to develop, the state of transition may result in one of a number of outcomes. The Twelve Tribes could hold on to traditional rasta livity. In this case we think that survival would be extremely difficult for the organization. At present there are a number of members who question the traditional ways and who might leave. Moreover, as we already argued, rasta subculture does not seem to have sufficient appeal for the new generation.

Another, more probable, development would be an evolution towards a Christian New Religious Movement, with the claim of a specific 'African' spirituality. Rasta style may then lose some of its importance within the organization. Although less charged with religious connotations, style may continue to be the 'raw material' for the creation of an identity. In this case, the relationship with the Ethiopian Royal Family will undergo an evolution, too. It seems likely that the Twelve Tribes would continue to support the Royal Family in a secular way. The royal connection would be a source of respectability for the organization and ensure the chance of repatriation.

What will continue to distinguish the Twelve Tribes of Israel in the market of Christian New Religious Movements will be its continued reliance on its 'African' spirituality.

Notes

1. Official greeting of the Twelve Tribes of Israel.
2. A local branch also needs a 'sister Dinah', who represents the only daughter of Jacob.

CHAPTER 14

African Independent Churches in Britain: An Introductory Survey

T. Jack Thompson

By far the greatest concentration of new religious movements exists not in USA, nor in Europe, but in Africa. The diverse group of movements generally known as *independent churches* numbers somewhere in the region of twelve thousand separate movements, and has been researched and documented to a considerable extent over the last forty years. Amongst a host of scholars in this field, perhaps the names of Bengt Sundkler and Harold Turner are pre-eminent, as two writers who took (and persuaded others to take) this phenomenon seriously.

The term *African independent churches* covers a vast theological and sociological spectrum, but, for the purposes of this paper, we might define them as religious movements started by and led by Africans, and containing in varying combinations elements of western Christianity and African traditional religion.

History in Britain

The wider phenomenon known as *black majority churches* (until fairly recently more commonly referred to as black-led churches) in Britain is made up of somewhere between two and three hundred movements. Between eighty and eighty-five per cent of these movements are of Caribbean origin, and will not be dealt with in this paper. The remaining fifteen to twenty per cent are movements of African origin, either in the sense that they are branches of existing movements in Africa, or, in a minority, but growing number of cases, in the sense that they have been founded by Africans in Britain.

In Britain, almost all of these movements are of West African origin, and predominantly from Nigeria and Ghana. They first began to appear in Britain as a result of the arrival of significant numbers of West African students coming to Britain to study in the 1960s.

The first organized churches in Britain were the *Church of the Lord, Aladura*, formed in 1964, the *Cherubim and Seraphim Society*, 1965, the *Celestial Church of Christ*, 1968, and the *Aladura International Church*, 1970. The last of the above-mentioned groups is particularly significant in that it was the first African independent church actually founded in Britain. Its founder (now Archbishop) Olu A. Abiola has made it clear that he founded his church in the first place because so many African Christians coming to Britain experienced a sense of rejection in the mainstream churches, and, more positively, because he wanted to offer pastoral support to African students in a cultural and religious milieu with which they would be familiar.

Whether or not it appears in their title, most of the African churches in Britain belong to a tradition known as Aladura (Yoruba for *praying people*). This tradition, which arose in the 1920s in West Africa (and is quite closely connected with the traumatic aftermath of the 1918-19 influenza epidemic, which killed more people than the First World War), might be described briefly as a mixture of high Anglican ceremonial and pentecostal enthusiasm.

Geographical Spread

Roswith Gerloff, who through her pioneering work — pioneering both in terms of academic research, and also of practical involvement — has done more than perhaps any other single individual to bring this phenomenon to the attention of the mainstream British churches, has estimated that the black majority churches are presently in twenty-nine out of forty-eight English counties. This figure is for both Afro-Caribbean and African movements, of course, but, nevertheless, it gives a surprising insight into the wide geographic spread of such movements in Britain.

Clearly, as with practically all types of new religious movements in the country, the greatest concentration of African movements is in London; but they are also to be found in Birmingham, Bristol, Liverpool, Manchester and Glasgow. The beginning of the *Church of Cherubim and Seraphim* in Birmingham is a typical example of how many of these movements spread. Most of the leadership of such movements is part-time and voluntary, fitting their religious duties in alongside their secular jobs. When they are transferred to other areas, they often take their churches with them, gathering a small group of followers in the new town, and gradually attracting new adherents. This is precisely what happened when A. A. Olatunji was transferred to Birmingham in the late 1960s, and founded the first African independent church there.

Issues Raised

It is now almost thirty years since the first of these movements was formed in Britain. In that time more than fifty separate movements have been started, although perhaps as many as 15% have become extinct for one reason or another. Nevertheless it seems clear that African independent churches are here to stay, at least for the foreseeable future, as a small but distinctive part of the British religious scene. This raises many issues for those involved in the study of new religious movements, a few of which I shall deal with below.

1. Relation to mainstream churches and to the ecumenical movement

The majority of British Christians know little or nothing about these movements. Indeed, G. P. Hunt, in the introduction to his 1973 M.Phil. thesis on 'Transmission of knowledge within a West African immigrant religious group', makes the point that:

In considering the literature on immigrant groups in England, and especially London, I was struck by the lack of information on Africans, and the plethora of material on West Indians and Asians.

Though this comment is made about academic papers, it would also apply more generally to public perceptions.

Yet the fact remains that, on the whole, these movements have had a very positive relationship with other mainstream churches in Britain. At first glance this is somewhat surprising, given the general attitude towards new religious movements in general, and more exotic Christian-based groups in particular.

It has to be remembered (and this is not meant to be a critical theological judgment in what is a very complicated area) that several of these groups are, from a doctrinal point of view, apparently more heterodox than some of the more controversial non-African Christian-based new religious movements such as the Central London Church of Christ or the Jesus Army. Take, for example, the opening words of the editorial of the first issue of the newsletter of the *Brotherhood of the Cross and Star*, published in June 1992:

A great and supernatural being has come into the world. His ways, His prophecies and the fulfilment of these prophecies, His teachings and the method of imparting the recondite wisdom of the Almighty Father, his life and testimonies about His deity confirm that a great being, the cosmic teacher and leader, a charismatic ruler, and incomparably powerful spiritual leader has come into the world. His name is Olumba Olumba Obu. He is the Word of God and the Holy Spirit personified.

While it needs to be said that the *Brotherhood of the Cross and Star* is, from a Christian perspective, considerably more heterodox than most of the African independent churches present in Britain, the fact remains that the movements as a whole have been well received. There are several reasons for this. In the first place, since, by and large, they attracted adherents predominantly from the African community, they were not seen as a threat by mainstream churches. In the second place, from very early days they attracted a small but important group of sympathizers in high places, including a few Anglican bishops, and several staff members from the British Council of Churches. In the third place, they began to be organized at precisely the time when de-colonization was taking place in Africa, and when European interest in and fascination with African independent churches was growing (witness the acceptance of the *Kimbanguist Church* from Zaire into membership of the World Council of Churches in 1969).

By the mid 1970s, when the *Cherubim and Seraphim* were showing an interest in joining the British Council of Churches, it was suggested that they might have a better chance of being accepted if the various small groups formed a council of churches. This they did, and the council was accepted as an associate member of the British Council of Churches in 1978.

2. Relation to each other and to Afro-Caribbean movements

The process of fission is very common in many of these groups in Africa. Often this is caused by internal rivalries and leaves a certain amount of friction in its wake. In Britain, perhaps because of a common feeling of marginalization and ethnic solidarity, there has been, on the whole, a large measure of co-operation between the African churches. This has led to the formation of several councils of churches, including the *Cherubim and Seraphim Council of Churches*, mentioned above, and the *Council of African and Allied Churches*, inaugurated in 1981.

In a wider sense, however, a consciousness of a common Afro-Caribbean identity in Britain has led to several developments. Among these should be mentioned the formation of the *Council of African and Afro-Caribbean Churches*, and the growing interest of many of these churches in social and racial issues through such bodies as the *Community and Race Relations Unit* of the British Council of Churches (now the Council of Churches in Britain and Ireland), and the *Zebra Project*.

Perhaps more important than any of these, however, was the *Centre for Black and White Christian Partnership*, established at Selly Oak in Birmingham in 1978, following a joint working party of black and white churches, inaugurated by the British Council of Churches in the previous year. This is not the time to speak of this development in any detail, but it has provided both black and white Christians with a chance to meet each other, to be educated together, and to understand one another's perspectives and problems. Perhaps more than anything else, it has provided many members of the black majority churches with the first formal theological education to which they have had access.

3. Ethnic composition and missiological understanding

The African Churches in Britain provide an excellent opportunity to study how such movements develop in *diaspora*. In Africa, it hardly needs to be said, such groups are almost entirely African in composition. An obvious starting point for a study of such movements in *diaspora* is to ask whether or not, in a much more pluralist society, they retain their essential ethnic character, or whether they attract members from across ethnic boundaries. Statistically, they remain predominantly African, as one might expect, but there are interesting variations. Some churches which in Africa are very geographically specific, in Britain attract members from other parts of the continent. A recently published history of the *Cherubim and Seraphim Church*, a predominantly Nigerian movement, has been written by a member who originates from Malawi, on the other side of the continent. Some churches attract a minority of Afro-Caribbean members, and a few even have a handful of white members, usually through marriage. The only Caucasians I am aware of in a position of leadership in one of the African churces are Bishop Jeremy Goring and his wife Deaconess Rosemary Goring of the Brotherhood of the Cross and star. Bishop Goring was personally chosen by Olumba Olumba Obu as his representative in Europe. Whether he will remain in that position following the recent death of Olumba Olumba Obu remains to be seen.

In a wider sense, however, some of these groups see themselves as having, in one way or another, a missiological role in Britain. Take, for example, the following quotation from Dr W. M. Chirwa's recent history of *Cherubim and Seraphim*, mentioned above:

It is of the utmost importance to every African to realise the significance of the establishment of the first African Church in Britain. This meant that, for the first time, Africans had brought religion to the home of their Missionaries. They too had become missionaries in the land of their teachers and benefactors. They came to proclaim the word of God even though, primarily, their aim was to study in Britain.

Many Africans (and indeed Afro-Caribbeans) coming to Britain for the first time are genuinely shocked by the secular nature of British society, and see themselves as having a role in recalling Britain to what they would see as a more moral way of life.

4. Cultural and liturgical change in diaspora

The earliest of the African independent churches have now been established in Britain for nearly thirty years, and many of them have been here for over twenty years. Though membership is to some extent transient, as some of the members are students in temporary residence in Britain, there is also an increasingly permanent element in the membership, and indeed a growing number of British-African membership. It would be surprising in these circumstances if the customs and liturgy of these curches remained static. Certainly, English is used in worship alongside Yoruba in many of these curches, and alongside more traditional melodies can now be found hymns picked up from the wider evangelical constituency.

Beyond the narrow area of liturgy, there remain many areas of research to be undertaken, on possible changes in world-view, on socio-political position, etc.

5. Self-Understanding

Many of the above areas raise the question of how these movements see themselves in terms of the British religious scene. While most of the very limited academic work in the area has until now be done by Europeans — notably Roswith Gerloff's massive two volume work, *A Plea for British Black Theologies* (which nevertheless deals predominantly with Afro-Caribbean movements) and Terry Booth's *We True Christians*, a study of the *Cherubim and Seraphim* in Birmingham — in recent years several of the movements have begun to produce their own histories. In addition, the Nigerian scholar, Dr Chris Oshun (himself a member of the *Christ Apostolic Church* in Nigeria), has spent a year in Britain researching the *Aladura* curches in *diaspora*.

It has already been noted above that some of these groups have, from an early stage, shown an interest in ecumenical relations with the mainstream curches. This tendency has been increased with the recent formation of the *Council of Churches for Britain and Ireland*, the major ecumenical body in the United Kingdom, which has actively encouraged the participation of the black majority churches, including the African independent curches. Several of these churches are now members, either in their own right or as members of wider councils of churches, and Archbishop Olu Abiola, the founder of the *Aladura International Church*, is a co-chairman.

It seems inevitable that, as these movements sink their roots more deeply into British soil, their own self-identity will begin to change.

6. Newer African Movements

Most of the movements discussed above belong to the *aladura* group of churches, which arose in West Africa in the 1920s and 30s. In Turner's terminology, these were were PRINERMS, being a mixture of mainstream Christianity and African traditional religion. In the last decade, a much wider range of movements has developed in West Africa, adding to the above mixture, pentecostal, eastern and New Age elements. There is some evidence that these more complex movements are beginning to make their way to Britain. To what extent these newer, and more exotic *mélanges* will have an impact on Africans in Britain, and on public attitudes to African movements in general, remains a matter for further research.

CHAPTER 15

Tocqueville's Lessons from the New World for Religion in the New Europe

Phillip E. Hammond

'The religious atmosphere of the country was the first thing that struck me on arrival in the United States.' So wrote Alexis de Tocqueville soon after his extended visit in 1831.[1] Expecting to find in America the situation he had known in France, with 'the spirits of religion and of freedom almost always marching in opposite directions', he instead found that 'the most free and enlightened people in the world zealously perform all the external duties of religion.' After repeatedly questioning the 'faithful of all communions', Tocqueville found that the Americans themselves attributed religion's 'quiet sway over their country' to 'the complete separation of church and state.'[2] Though accepting this explanation as essentially correct, the French observer nonetheless investigated further; what was it about church-state separation that led to religion's increased vitality in society? 'I wondered', Tocqueville wrote, 'how it could come about that by diminishing the apparent power of religion one increased its real strength...'[3]

In a most trenchant analysis of this question, Tocqueville identified two answers:

1. One of these answers is seen in Tocqueville's discussion of the central role played in egalitarian America by 'public opinion'. In the absence of caste and class distinctions, ascribed authority is problematic and tends, therefore, to be replaced by what 'the people' think. Public opinion thus can reach the status of religion in its power to influence individuals' behaviour, and Churches are conduits of this power. 'There is an innumerable multitude of sects

in the United States', Tocqueville observed. 'They are all different in the worship they offer to the Creator, but all agree concerning the duties of men to one another. Each sect worships God in its own fashion, but all preach the same morality in the name of God.'[4] Americans, he was noting, enjoy religious freedom in a great variety of ways.

2. The second answer Tocqueville gives to the question of how religion's influence can actually be stronger under church-state separation is his observation, made repeatedly, that Churches take care to remain non-partisan and politically unaligned:

When a religion seeks to found its sway only on the longing for immortality equally tormenting every human heart, it can aspire to universality; but when it comes to uniting itself with a government, it must adopt maxims which apply only to certain nations. Therefore, by allying itself with any political power, religion increases its strength over some but forfeits the hope of reigning over all... The American clergy were the first to perceive this truth and to act in conformity with it. They saw that they would have to give up religious influence if they wanted to acquire political power, and they preferred to lose the support of authority rather than to share its vicissitudes.[5]

Churches, in other words, in exchange for their right to promulgate the religion they chose, agreed not to seek favoured status in the eyes of the government.

These two answers, of course, are related: (1) Whatever their sectarian peculiarity, Tocqueville was saying, religious people take care not to deviate from widely perceived opinion and thus largely escape government efforts to regulate them. But (2), by staying out of partisan politics, Churches also are free to cater to whatever religious niche they care to serve. Stated in the usual terms, in the America Tocqueville investigated, there was 'no law respecting an establishment of religion' nor was there any prohibition of the 'free exercise' of religion. There was, as everyone told him, separation of church and state.

The place in the U. S. Constitution containing the church-state doctrine — the First Amendment — permits various interpretations, however, and Tocqueville somehow saw through this ambiguity.

At the time they adopted the First Amendment as part of the Bill of Rights, the Congress was well aware that some of the thirteen newly united states still had established Churches. Their wording, therefore — 'Congress shall make no law respecting an establishment of religion, or prohibiting the free exercise thereof' — clearly could not have been intended to outlaw established religion. At most, its intention may have been to prevent any *federal* or *national* established Church, but certainly also it served to protect established Churches in the individual states from congressional interference. As Tocqueville saw, religion was regarded as a beneficial force, and, in all its sectarian expressions, was to be immune from government regulation (though not denied state sponsorship if a state so desired), and free to appeal to citizens' religious appetites.

Just as Tocqueville's two answers merge dialectically into one, so too, by the above account, do the two religion clauses of the U.S. Constitution. 'No establishment' means to leave religion alone for people to practise it as they wish, and 'free exercise' means to recognize and allow religious behaviour irrespective of the political standing of its practitioners.

In due time, the 'no establishment' clause came to mean both no interference and also no sponsorship. (Massachusetts in 1833 was the last state to rid itself of officially sponsored religion.) And 'free exercise' came to mean that, only if government had a compelling interest on behalf of the general welfare, could it move to restrict religious behaviour. Thus has the U.S. addressed the church-state problem by trying to protect both religious equality and religious liberty; government 'protects' the free exercise of religion by not showing favouritism toward any religion and by allowing considerable diversity of religious expression. This was what Tocqueville perceived — that, generally speaking, the American government looked with favour on religion as long as it did not depart far from mainstream American morality and as long as it remained non-partisan in politics.

Generalizing from Tocqueville

With only a little change of wording, Tocqueville's analysis becomes generalizable to every jurisdiction, since something of a church-state situation is unavoidable and must therefore be addressed somehow by every government and its people. Understandably, perhaps, there is more convergence on the actual 'solution' adopted by various nations than their formal ideologies would suggest. After a careful analysis of this issue in a handful of otherwise divergent societies, Demerath reports:

Despite religion's prominence as a source of political legitimacy and campaign rhetoric, it is rarely a dominant factor in the affairs of state. The United States is less distinctive in this regard than many Americans suppose, and insofar as its own tradition of 'church-state separation' continues, this may owe less to legal and constitutional requirements than to a range of social and political constraints which we share with other nations.[6]

Francis makes a similar observation: 'At this time, virtually every church, at least in Western Europe, has achieved a remarkable measure of autonomy in the determination of its leadership, its size, and the direction of its clergy.'[7] Caplow's assessment of the church-state situation in contemporary Europe would thus seem in need of revision. He writes:

The one element that survives unchanged from the Europe of Tocqueville, Wellington, Garibaldi, and the young Marx, is the inextricable connection of politics and religion which makes it impossible for individuals to take up a political position without reference to their religious affiliations and vice-versa.[8]

Granted, the European situation may not be identical to that of the United States, but liberalism made inroads throughout nineteenth and twentieth century Europe, one effect of which has been the loosening of ties between 'church' and 'state'. And this 'loosening' has resulted, as in America, not in a literal separation, of course, but in changing government responses to the two issues Tocqueville so perceptively noted: What limits, if any, will be placed on religious free expression? And what help and/or recognition will be given to religious organizations? Despite a convergence in the direction of looser ties between church and state, therefore, European societies exhibit differences in how they respond to these two issues.

How might these differences be characterized? Fortunately, a growing literature in the sociology of religion provides answers. Beginning with Stark and Bainbridge's introduction in 1985 of the concept of a 'religious economy', there developed — by Iannacone,[9] by Finke and Stark,[10] and by Chavez and Cann[11] — clear notions of government regulation/sponsorship of religion on the one hand, and religious heterogeneity or pluralism on the other hand. We will soon show that these two dimensions are empirically related (inversely), but that they are analytically distinct, reflecting rather closely the issues addressed in the U.S. Constitution by the terms 'no establishment' and 'free exercise.' Indeed, if Tocqueville had been familiar with this conceptual development, he might have suggested that the unexpected religious vitality he encountered in America could be attributed, first, to a largely unregulated religious economy and, second, to the many religious 'firms' competing in that economy.

In fact, that is exactly what he inadvertently observed, inasmuch as his visit came toward the end of what historians of American religion call the Second Great Awakening. Finke and Stark, for example, calculate that in 1776 only 20 per cent of the American population were adherents of a Church, but 55 per cent of these adherents were connected to the three denominations enjoying some 'establishment' status: Congregational, Episcopal, and Presbyterian. By contrast, only 21 per cent adhered to the Baptist, Methodist, and Catholic denominations. By 1850, however, the percentage adhering had climbed to 34 per cent, but the 'established' share had dropped from 55 to 19 per cent, while the other three denominations climbed to 69 per cent. The Methodists alone went from 2.5 per cent in 1776 to 34 per cent in 1850, chiefly by offering services at times and places and in a variety of ways people found attractive.[12] During the latter decades of this period, too, Mormons, Millerites, and Adventists entered the religious marketplace. Clearly, by the time of Tocqueville's visit, the American religious economy was less regulated than in 1776, and competition in it had increased.

Implications for the New Europe

As we have already remarked, relationships between Churches and states in the modern period have loosened in Europe, though not everywhere to the same degree. We are now in a position to think of this differential loosening as occurring in two ways: as diminished regulation or sponsorship of religion, and as increased religious competition or pluralism. The question to be addressed, therefore, is what effect might such changes have on religious activity in the New Europe. Has religious vitality increased there with church-state separation, as Tocqueville noted about America nearly two centuries ago? In truth, the answer is No, Yes, and It Depends, but the evidence is not as confusing as that answer at first suggests.

Let us look first at the No answer. Religious vitality has not only *not* increased with church-state separation, but the very processes of declining state sponsorship and increasing religious pluralization are seen as evidence of secularization. This generalization is the received wisdom handed down since the Enlightenment, and a lot of data tend to support it *as a generalization*.[13] Thus, rates of Church attendance seem everywhere in Europe to have declined, though it is now recognized that the comparison periods of high rates differ considerably from one society to another, that Catholic countries have experienced such decline differently from Protestant countries, etc. Complicating the generalization further is the fact that the influence of religion in education, giving money to the Church, and observance of religious holidays and rituals, follow yet other patterns. Still, if asked whether Europe today is more religious or less religious than yesterday, most observers will answer 'less', even as they have a multitude of meanings in mind. Thus, as a forthcoming book[14] makes clear, one indicator experienced in every European society surveyed is the low rates of Church involvement among the young as compared with the old.

But if the generalization is in some sense correct — that with declining state regulation and sponsorship of religion and increasing religious pluralism, comes, not *increased*, but *decreased* religious vitality — it is misleadingly correct if it is understood to mean that decreasing regulation and increasing pluralism *causes* that declining vitality. The facts suggest just the reverse, as Chaves and Cann[15] have recently shown. With data on fourteen European societies, plus the U.S. and Canada, Australia and New Zealand, those investigators develop an index of state sponsorship (regulation) based on six attributes such as state recognition of one or more denominations, state approval of Church leaders, state salaries for Church personnel, etc. They also employ the Herfindahl Index, a measure of religious 'concentration', and thus the obverse of pluralism. What are their findings?

First of all, a calculation (not performed by Chaves and Cann but readily done from their graphs) using data from the fourteen European societies shows a significant inverse relationship between sponsorship and pluralism. It is stronger for predominantly Protestant countries (Pearson's $r = -0.82$) than for predominantly Catholic countries ($r = -0.48$), but it is obvious that declining religious regulation and increasing religious pluralism go together.

Secondly, they find that religious vitality, as measured by Church attendance, is negatively related to state sponsorship, and, because sponsorship and religious concentration go together, religious vitality is also positively related to pluralism. Chaves and Cann demonstrate, however, that pluralism's effect is very small *independently* of the sponsorship measure. In other words, we can assume that pluralism enhances religious participation, but it does so only to the degree that it brings about diminution of state sponsorship. Thus it can be said that loosening the church-state relationship — meaning little or no state regulation of religion — does not itself lead to religious vitality, but it permits and encourages religious competition which *does* result in religious vitality.[16] To the negative answer already given to the question of church-state separation and religious vitality in Europe, we add a second, qualified, positive answer. The overall secular trend may serve to decrease religiousness in European societies, just as it tends to loosen church-state ties, but to the degree it does the latter, it retards the former. In this special sense, one can say that, Yes, church-state separation increases religious vitality.

Which leaves the third of the answers — It Depends — to be discussed. I am not being facetious in offering this third option, nor do I mean to trivialize the generalization we have been exploring.

Rather, my intention is to point to what may be the most interesting, contemporary European application of Tocqueville's
insights. With state deregulation of religion comes increased
freedom for religions to compete in the marketplace. More religious
needs can be met in more ways under those circumstances, and —
if everything else is equal — greater religious vitality can be
expected. This is what we observed in the second answer, except
that everything else is not equal, but, instead, embedded in a
secular trend that tends to depress religious vitality. Hence the first
answer is still correct, though also qualified. Now we can add the
third answer — It Depends — by noting that in a highly
competitive religious marketplace, the very notions of religious
needs, religious values, and the religious means of meeting those
needs and expressing those values are made volatile.

Sects, cults, therapies, etc., can enter the marketplace, raising
questions about what religion *is*, and what religious involvement
means. In the New Europe, as in early nineteenth century America,
religious novelty abounds, and, in their ambiguity about what
religion is, people speak instead of spirituality and meditation, of
being holistic or centred. They can be religious without a Church,
and, in carrying to the extreme the cult of individualism, may even
be religious in a manner unlike anyone else. Emerson, in his essay,
'Self Reliance', written almost simultaneously with Tocqueville's
writing of *Democracy in America*, stated, 'Whoso would be a man,
must be a nonconformist.' Do not simply comply with the demands
of some sect, Emerson advised, 'But do your work, and I shall know
you.'[17]

If there is one common theme running through the essays
referred to above, assessing the religious situation of post-War
European generations, it is that, religiously, people are 'doing their
own work'. Religion has become a 'personal collage' rather than
'received', 'subjective' rather than 'objective'. 'Personal spiritual
benefit' is replacing 'institutional demand', even as 'individualism
is affirmed'. A 'diffused religion' increases as the 'monolithic
character' of organized, orthodox religion declines.[18] But does this
heightened religious individualism constitute increased religious
vitality? That is where the answer becomes, It Depends. There
seems no doubt that new religions have sprouted in Europe as in

other parts of the world. Moreover, in keeping with the second answer offered here, the evidence suggests that Stark and Bainbridge[19] are correct in asserting that new religious movements have had greater success in those European societies they judge to be more 'secular' (for which, read, 'religiously deregulated and pluralistic'). But, as Wallis and Bruce, in a critique of several papers by Stark and Bainbridge which preceded the latter's 1985 volume, argue:

... the evidence suggests that the new faiths have made negligible inroads into the mass of the unchurched, who remain indifferent to organized religion of any sort. The scale of decline in the major denominations and that of the growth of the new religious movements are simply not comparable.[20]

Thus they cite figures for Britain between 1970 and 1975, showing that Protestant Churches lost over half a million members while the 'conservative churches that were growing gained about fourteen thousand new members.'[21] In other words, not even 3 per cent of the drop-outs dropped back in somewhere else; the notoriety and consequent visibility of the 'new' movements in religion can lead us to exaggerate their impact on religion's vitality.

A judicious reading of the evidence regarding the impact of loosened church-state ties on religious vitality thus requires not a single answer but a mix of answers. The inexorable nature of secularization means that whatever loosens church-state ties does not restore religious vitality to once higher levels, but, on the other hand, it creates conditions for greater competition among suppliers of religion and thus leads to some greater vitality than would otherwise be the case. At the same time, however, the very nature of religion undergoes redefinition when church-state ties loosen, with the consequence that the boundaries of the religious marketplace broaden to include potentially more persons. In this latter case, the answer to the original question becomes, It Depends — not just on whether vitality has increased but also on whether what has increased is 'religion'.

Tocqueville no doubt would be of help at this point were he around to make fresh observations in the New Europe. Even as it is, however, his powers of discernment in early nineteenth century

America assist us in understanding the present situation. The relationship between Churches and states is undergoing change in today's Europe just as change is taking place in the ways Europeans experience religion. It seems reasonable to assume some connection between these two changes, and Tocqueville helps us explore that connection.

Notes

1. Alexis de Toqueville, *Democracy in America*, trans. George Lawrence, Garden City, N.Y.: Doubleday Anchor, 1969 (first publd 1835), p. 295.
2. *Ibid.*
3. *Op. cit.*, p. 296.
4. *Op. cit.*, p. 290.
5. *Op. cit.*, pp. 297-99.
6. N. J. Demerath III, 'Religious Capital and Capital Religions: Cross-Cultural and Non-Legal Factors in the Separation of Church and State', *Daedalus*, Summer 1991, p. 38.
7. John G. Francis, 'The Evolving Regulatory Structure of European Church-State Relations', *Journal of Church and State*, 34, 1992, pp. 778-79.
8. Theo Caplow, 'Contrasting Trends in European and American Religion', *Sociological Analysis*, 46, 1985, p. 106.
9. Laurence R. Iannacone, 'The Consequences of Religious Market Structure', *Rationality and Society*, 3, 1991, pp. 156-77.
10. Roger Finke and Rodney Stark, *The Churching of America*, New Brunswick, N.J.: Rutgers University Press, 1992.
11. Mark Chaves and David E. Cann, 'Regulation, Pluralism, and Religious Market Structure', *Rationality and Society*, 4, 1992, pp. 272-90.
12. Finke and Stark, *op. cit.*, chapter 3.
13. Bryan Wilson, 'Secularization: The Inherited Model', in P. E. Hammond (ed.), *The Sacred in a Secular Age*, Berkeley and Los Angeles: University of California Press, 1985, pp. 9-20.
14. W. C. Roof, J. Carroll and Roozen (eds), *The Postwar Generation and Religious Establishments*, forthcoming.
15. *Op. cit.*
16. Predominantly Catholic countries are higher on the concentration index than all predominantly Protestant countries except Finland and Denmark. Also, their scores on the regulation index range only from 0 to 3, not 0 to 6 as with Protestant countries. The generalization just stated is therefore more applicable to Protestant Europe, although,

within their limited ranges, Catholic Europe shows the same directional effects.

17. Ralph Waldo Emerson, *Collected Works*, Boston: Houghton Mifflin, 1865, vol. 2, p. 54; 'Self Reliance' was drawn from lectures given in 1836-3. Today, people do their own 'thing'.

18. Roof, Carroll and Roozen, *op. cit.* Even in Russia this is true. In a special report to the *Los Angeles Times* (11 February 1993), Beth Knobel claims that, 'With Russian society in transition and the Russian people frustrated by the unpredictability of their daily lives, thousands of people from Siberia to Estonia have turned for comfort to meditation, vegetarianism, holistic health, crystals and other aspects of spiritual study...'

19. *Op. cit.*, chapter 21.

20. Roy Wallis and Steve Bruce, 'The Stark-Bainbridge Theory of Religion: A Critical Analysis and Counter Proposals', *Sociological Analysis*, 45, 1984, p. 20.

21. *Ibid.*

Index